Financial Contributtions

The IVSC acknowledges the financial contributions towards the development of the eighth edition of the International Valuation Standards received from the following organisations:

- American Appraisal Associates
- American Society of Appraisers
- Appraisal Institute of Canada
- Appraisal Institute, US
- Atisreal Ltd.
- Canadian Institute of Chartered Business Valuators
- China Appraisal Society
- Cushman & Wakefield
- Drivers Jonas
- DTZ Debenham Tie Leung Ltd
- Gerald Eve
- GVA Grimley
- Jones Lang LaSalle
- JSC "International Valuation Center"
- Khong & Jaafar, Malaysia
- King Sturge-Knight Frank
- The National Association of Romanian Valuers
- RICS - Royal Institution of Chartered Surveyors

IVSC Membership as of 12 April 2007 is comprised of the following:

iv

The following are non-member representatives but are Observers to the IVSC

- The Albanian Society of Real Property Valuers
- Barbados Association of Professional Valuers
- Finnish Association for Real Estate Valuation
- Georgian Federation of Professional Assets Valuators
- Expertise Institute for Valuation of Assets of Georgia
- Macedonian Appraisal Society
- Slovak Association of Economic Appraisers
- Ukrainian Society of Appraisers

The following are non-member representatives but are IVSC Correspondents

- Palestinian Auditors and Accountants Association
- Price Control Department, Ministry of Finance, Vietnam

INTERNATIONAL BUREAU
12 Great George Street
London SW1P 3AD
United Kingdom
Tel/Fax: +44 1442 879306
Email: ivsc@ivsc.org
http://www.ivsc.org

31 July 2007

I am pleased to introduce the eighth edition of the International Valuation Standards (IVSs). The Standards Board of the International Valuation Standards Committee (IVSC) keeps the IVSs under constant review to ensure that the IVSC responds to growing market needs for consistent global valuation standards, to changes introduced into related standards such as the International Financial Reporting Standards and the International Public Sector Accounting Standards, and to the recommendations of the Basle Committee for Banking Supervision. There are several important changes in this new edition. IVS 2, *Bases Other Than Market Value,* and IVA 2, *Valuation for Secured Lending Purposes,* have been significantly revised. A new Application, *Valuation of Public Sector Assets for Financial Reporting,* and a new Guidance Note, *Valuation of Historic Property,* have been introduced. While wording may change and new material may be developed, the universal concepts, definitions, and principles underlying the standards are the same. The purpose of the IVSs remains identical to that of previous editions, namely to provide a clear set of internationally recognised and accepted valuation standards.

The IVSC has always been dynamic and in the late 1990s, the Committee vigorously responded to the new round of financial reporting changes and the drive towards the development of a global financial language. The progress of the IVSC since 2000 has been nothing less than dramatic.

But time and the world do not stand still. Change is the law of life and if we look only to the past and present, we will certainly miss the future. Thus, the development and evolution of the IVSC continues. Despite the strengths the Committee has demonstrated, the changing environment, in which it operates, means that structural change is needed to enable the IVSC to meet future challenges.

Restructuring of the IVSC

Three years ago, the Management Board recognised that the IVSC would have to be restructured in order for it to survive technically and financially. In January 2007, the IVSC issued proposals for the restructuring of the Committee. The proposals were sent to a wide audience, and invitation to comment was solicited. Comments were received from valuation institutes and societies, past IVSC Chairmen, consulting firms, academics, government offices, and national and regional standards setters. The overwhelming majority of these were supportive of the proposals.

I am proud to report that at a Special Meeting, held on April 12, 2007, IVSC members voted unanimously to proceed with the restructuring of the Committee. After the restructuring is completed, the key components of the IVSC will include:

- a new Standards Board, which will function as an independent and autonomous decision-making body;
- an Interpretations Committee;
- a Board of Trustees, strictly responsible for the management and financial health of the organisation;
- a place for all stakeholders to have a voice—while the IVSC will remain a membership based organisation, the criteria for membership will be broadened beyond national professional valuation institutes. Valuation companies, users of valuations, academics and others will have the opportunity to be represented and involved in the work of the IVSC;
- a Professional Board to buttress the standards; and
- a structure that is similar to the International Accounting Standards Board model—this means that the Standards Board will become the focal point, or "heart and soul" of the organisation--rather than a body representing an organisation of valuation organisations.

IVSC members will vote on the new By-Laws and Regulations for the restructured organisation at the 2007 Annual General Meeting to be held in London late in 2007. A short transition period is anticipated before the restructured IVSC will become operational during the second quarter of 2008. The IVSC has set a challenging and aggressive timetable as it cannot afford to become preoccupied with a protracted governance transition that would divert resources and focus away from its primary goal of standards setting. The transition to the new structure will be seamless and completed as quickly as is practically possible.

Valuation of Intangible Assets

There are two very significant IVSC projects currently under way. The greater worldwide use of fair value has raised the profile of valuations undertaken for financial reporting. The International Financial Reporting Standards (IFRSs) for business combinations, intangible assets, employee options, and financial instruments highlight the need for more regular valuations of assets and liabilities. As the trend accelerates, the importance of valuation for financial reporting to the capital markets is triggering increased scrutiny from regulators and other parties. The IVSC has been encouraged to extend the International Valuation Standards to cover all aspects of valuation, including the valuation of intangible assets, liabilities, and various equity and debt instruments. The IVSC has begun by bringing together a group of leading experts to develop guidance for the valuation of intangible assets for the purpose of reporting under International Financial Reporting Standards. A discussion paper will be issued for comment during the second quarter of 2007.

Critical Review of the IVSs

The structure of the IVSs has served the Standards document well and was essential to advance it to this current stage. But the IVSC Management Board believed it is the time to pause and consider the fundamentals of what it is that the IVSC is trying to achieve, and how best to do it without being constrained by a perceived need to work within the confines of the structure of the current book. A group was brought together from both members of the valuation and accounting professions for the purpose of:

- agreeing on a format for an ideal set of international valuation standards-- how these standards should be organised, and what they should cover and contain;

- reviewing the current edition of the IVSs against this ideal and considering its strengths, weaknesses, and omissions; and
- developing a "road map" for proceeding with the enhancement of the IVSs.

A discussion paper detailing the group's conclusions will be issued for comment during the second quarter of 2007.

IVSC Achievements

The IVSC has come a long way since its creation over 25 years ago and should be proud of its many successes, including the agreed definition of Market Value, the Committee's evolution into a body of global representation, and perhaps most significantly, the fostering of considerable trust, goodwill, and cooperation amongst key players. The IVSC success in setting international standards and its growing profile amongst world regulators and international agencies are leading to greater recognition of the valuation profession and wider understanding of the importance of valuation, which positively impacts every Valuer. All of these achievements would not have been possible without the tireless work and contributions of the IVSC members, who volunteered their time and skills to carry the IVSC to the position it holds today. I would like to express my sincere gratitude to the members of the IVSC Management Board, Standards Board, Expert Groups, and technical writers, who worked cohesively to make this publication a reality. Thanks must also go to our sponsors, whose generous financial contributions have underpinned the work of the IVSC.

Thank you for your continued support and involvement

Joseph J. Vella, MAI, CRE, FRICS
Chairman, International Valuation Standards Committee

x

Changes Between the Seventh Edition (2005) and Eighth Edition (2007) of the IVSs

This section provides an overview of the principal changes that were introduced into the eighth edition of the International Valuation Standards. Because of the dynamic nature of the valuation profession, printed versions of the Standards, whether in English or in translation, tend to have a brief shelf life. Readers are advised to consult the IVSC website for information on current IVSC projects and instruction on obtaining the most up-to-date copy of the Standards. Principal changes in the eighth edition of the IVSs (2007) include the following: 1) extensive revision of IVS 2, Bases Other Than Market Value, and IVA 2, Valuation for Secured Lending Purposes; 2) the introduction of two new components, following exposure in the IVSC website—these include an Application (IVA 3), The Valuation of Public Sector Assets for Financial Reporting; and a Guidance Note (GN 15), The Valuation of Historic Property; and 3) additional updating throughout the document to ensure consistency with the new and rewritten components. The bold type in section 5 of the GNs, which was introduced in the sixth edition, should assist in drawing the reader's attention to critical points, but all statements in the Standards, Applications and Guidance Notes have equal authority. The IVSC also publishes White Papers and Technical Papers on its website. These supplement the Standards but are not considered integral to the Standards document.

In the **Introduction,** paragraphs in several sections have been reorganised, and other information (the Achievements of the IVSC, Management Board of Directors, and Adoption Dates for components of the IVSs) has been updated. Other sections (Objectives and Scope) have been revised. The chart diagramming the **Structure of the Standards Document** was expanded to include the new components incorporated into the eighth edition; the chart illustrating **Bases Other Than Market Value** has been removed. Paras. 4, 5, 7 and 9 on the organisation of the Standards have been revised. White Papers have been taken out of the 8th edition and posted on the IVSC website. Old para. 9, which dealt with White Papers, was deleted.

Concepts Fundamental to Generally Accepted Valuation Principles (GAVP) has replaced the former section name, **General Valuation Concepts and Principles.**

Paras. 4.6, 4.7, 4.11, 9.1, and 9.2.1.3 have been rewritten. Seventh-edition paras. 7.4, 7.6, 7.7, 7.8 and 9.4 were deleted.

The Code of Conduct

Para. 3.6 on *Independent Valuer* has been revised.

Property Types

In first section on *Real Property,* in para. 2.6.1, the term "Synergistic Value" replaced "Marriage or Assemblage Value"; para. 2.7 and all subsections have been deleted (these dealt with real property valuation approaches);

In the section on *Personal Property,* in para. 3.2.2.1, the clause "which in some States is called Plant and Machinery", was deleted; and para. 3.3.1 has been rewritten to reflect the rewrite of IVS 2 in regard to assumptions as to whether the property is held by a going concern, an entity about to undergo liquidation, or to be sold for salvage;

In the section on *Businesses,* in para. 4.3.2, the term "Trade Related Property" has replaced "Specialised Trading Property"; paras. 4.8.1, 4.8.2 and 4.8.3 have been deleted (these dealt with the business valuation approaches); and

In the *Financial Interests* section, para. 5.1.4.2 has been cross-referenced to the new IVSC White Paper on securitisation.

International Valuation Standards

Introduction to International Valuation Standards

Paras. 3.4 (*basis of value*), 4.2 and subparas. 4.2.1 and 4.2.2 were redeveloped to ensure consistency with the revision of IVS 2. The subparas. under 3.4 and old subpara. 4.1.1 were deleted. The term *non-market value* is no longer used (the heads for paras. 1.0 and 4.0 have been changed). Paras. 3.0, 3.3, 4.0 and 4.1.3 have been fine-tuned.

IVS 1

Except for the deletion of the phrase "as part of a going concern" in para. 2.1 and references to the renamed section (Concepts Fundamental to Generally Accepted Valuation Principles) in paras. 1.2, 4.1.1, and 6.1, IVS 1 underwent no revision.

IVS 2

The Standard has been extensively rewritten. Amongst the principal revisions were the rewrite of sections 1, 2, 4, and 6; and the reorganisation of sections 5 and 7 to eliminate repetition. In section 3, four new definitions have been introduced (*basis of value, fair value, special purchaser,* and *synergistic value,* which has replaced *marriage value*), two definitions have been abridged (*investment value or worth,* and *special value*) and seven other definitions have been deleted (*value in use; going concern value; insurable value; assessed, rateable, or taxable value; salvage value; liquidation or forced sale value;* and *mortgage lending value*). Revised IVS 2 categorises bases other than Market Value into three groups. These include entity-specific value, value specific to the parties to the exchange of an asset, and value in accordance with a definition specified by statute or contract. Application of a basis may be further clarified by identifying assumptions as to the specific situation of the entity holding the property, e.g., a going concern, an entity undergoing liquidation, or an entity whose assets are to be sold for salvage.

IVS 3

The definitions have been alphabatised. Para. 3.5, the second paragraph on *valuation certification* and *certification of value* has been deleted; the references to *valuation brief* in para. 3.4 and to *certification of value* in para. 3.1 were deleted; para. 5.1.3.1 was revised; para. 5.1.10.1 which prescribed specific items to be confirmed in the *compliance statement* was taken out and the reference to it in para. 3.5 was deleted.

International Valuation Applications

IVA 1

IVA 1 underwent minimal change. The definitions have been alphabetised. The definition of *depreciated replacement cost* in para. 3.1 now corresponds to the revised definition of DRC in GN 8; the cross-referencing in paragraphs 5.5, 5.6.1 and 5.6.2 was corrected; and "IFRSs" was inserted before IASs in para. 7.2.

IVA 2

The Application has been extensively rewritten. Amongst the principal revisions were the rewrite of sections 1, 2, 4, and 6 and the reorganisation of sections 5 and 7 to eliminate repetition. Four definitions have been introduced into section 3 (*mortgage, specialised property, trade related property* [which has replaced the term *specialised trading property*], and *mortgage lending value*); paragraphs in section 3 of the seventh edition that discussed the applicability of the Market Value basis of valuation to secured loans have been deleted. New text was introduced in section 5 on assumptions as to anticipated changes in the condition of the property (5.5) and in section 6 on leases between related or connected parties (6.7), on valuation of a specialised property that is part of a going concern (6.8), and on lenders' solvency ratios (6.14). In section 6, the seventh-edition paragraph on leveraged yields of investment properties was taken out.

IVA 3 is new text. Following exposure in 2006 and the updating of IPSAS citations in early 2007, the Application was approved for publication.

Guidance Notes

Portions of the text in section 5 of the Guidance Notes are set in bold type (see above).

GN 1 saw the replacement of the term *Specialised Trading Property* by the term *Trade Related Property* and an updating of the references to the newly named Concepts Fundamental to Generally Accepted Value Principles.

GN 2 underwent minimal revision—definitions have been put into alphabetical order, and a new diagram, "Hierarchy of Property Types," was developed for the GN.

GN 3 was posted for exposure on the IVSC website in 2005. Following review, it was approved for publication on the IVSC website in November 2005. The 8th edition version includes new para. 4.3 on requirements under IPSASs; the definitions have also been put into alphabetical order.

GN 4, the definitions of *going concern value* in paras. 3.12.1 and 3.12.2 were deleted; the word "capital" was inserted before "value" in the definitions of *capitalisation factor* and *capitalisation rate* in paras. 3.4 and 3.5.

GN 5, the reference in para. 2.3 to GN 3 as "currently under review" was deleted; the definition of *intrinsic value* in para. 3.10 saw deletion of the phrase "In some States" and the new definition of *plant and equipment,* appearing in GN 3, replaced the 7th edition definition in para. 3.16.

GN 6, the definition of *going concern value* in paras. 3.20.1 and 3.20.2 were deleted; the definitions in paras. 3.4, 3.5, 3.6, 3.24, 3.25, 3.29, and 3.30 were alphabetised.

GN 7 has not been revised.

GN 8, paras. 1.2 and 2.2 have been fine-tuned; the definitions of *depreciated replacement cost* in para. 3.1, *modern equivalent asset* in para. 3.3, *optimisation* in para. 3.4, and *service potential* in para. 3.6 have been revised; the new definition of *plant and equipment,* appearing in GN 3, was added and the definitions of *adequate profitability* and *impairment loss* have been deleted; the definitions have been put into alphabetical order; para. 4.2 is new text; old para. 5.1 was deleted; except for para. 5.12, section 5.0 has been rewritten; previous references to *economic/external obsolescence* now appear simply as *external obsolescence;* an Addendum, Profitability Test When Reporting DRC, was developed for the GN.

GN 9, the title of the GN was changed to Discounted Cash Flow Analysis for Market Valuations and Investment Analyses. The definitions were put into alphabetical order. Paras. 5.1, 5.1.1, and 5.1.3 have been supplemented with additional guidance. Paras. 3.1, 3.2, 3.6, 5.2.2.1, 5.2.6, 5.6, 5.7, 5.9.2.5, and 5.9.3.5 have been fine-tuned.

GNs 10 and 11, the definitions have been put into alphabetical order.

GN 12, the term *trade related property,* which was redefined, has replaced *specialised trading property.*

GN 13 has not been revised.

GN 14, the reference to GN 9 in para. 2.1 was updated; the phrase "or statutory reporting" (before purposes) was deleted in paras. 3.5 and 3.6.

GN 15 is new text.

The **Glossary** reflects changes made in definitions in the various components of the document and incorporates terms introduced in the new Application and new or revised Guidance Notes. IFRSs/IASs definitions have been updated and several other definitions were deleted.

The **Index** entries have been edited to reflect the new content of the Standards document.

Contents

Introduction

International Valuation Standards Committee

The International Valuation Standards Committee

Introduction

Rapid economic changes taking place in the 1970s served to enhance the recognition given by market participants to the importance of professional property valuations. The quickening pace in the globalisation of investment markets further underscored the need for internationally accepted standards for reporting the value of property. It became obvious that without international valuation standards there was considerable potential for confusion. Differences of viewpoints among national professional valuation bodies might lead to unintentional misunderstandings. In response to this situation, members of a technical committee of the Royal Institution of Chartered Surveyors (RICS) and representatives of the U.S. appraisal profession began a dialogue in the late 1970s, which led to the founding of The International Assets Valuation Standards Committee (TIAVSC) in 1981. The Committee changed its name in 1994 to the International Valuation Standards Committee (IVSC). The objectives of the Committee are twofold:

- To formulate and publish, in the public interest, valuation Standards for property valuation and to promote their worldwide acceptance; and

- To harmonise Standards among the world's States[1] and to identify and make disclosure of differences in statements and/or applications of Standards as they occur.

The IVSC has long recognised the diversity of purposes for which property valuations are required, including use in financial statements, decisions on loans and mortgages secured by property, transactions involving transfers of ownership, and litigation and tax settlements. Beyond Standards, the IVSC began publishing Applications dealing with valuation for financial reporting and secured lending purposes, as well as Guidance Notes regarding specific valuation issues and the application of Standards in more specific business and service-providing situations. In particular, the IVSC has sought that the

---

1. Throughout this document, the word 'State' conveys the same meaning as it is used by the United Nations, which recognises and refers to its members as States, i.e., politically organised communities having their own apparatus of government and occupying sovereign territory.

International Valuation Standards (IVSs) be recognised in accounting and other reporting standards, and that Valuers recognise what is needed from them under standards of other disciplines.

In 2003, the IVSC became an incorporated association, comprising professional valuation associations from around the world, and bound by Articles of Incorporation.

The IVSC has undertaken eight revisions of the International Valuation Standards, which were published in 1985, 1994/97, 2000, 2001, 2003, 2005 and 2007. The evolution of these Standards attests to the recognition by IVSC that change is inevitable and continuous even when gradual and not easily discernable. The ongoing development of Standards reflects the commitment of the IVSC to ensure that fundamental valuation definitions and guidance stay current in a dynamic world.

Membership and Organisation

The International Valuation Standards Committee has become a truly international body in terms of both its membership and mission. The Committee, which was founded with a membership of twenty national associations, has grown by the year 2007 to include associations, with member or observer status, representing 52 countries. Member associations in these states subscribe to IVSC objectives concerning valuation and must have a sufficient number of their members capable of conducting valuations that comply with Standards. Member associations support the Standards and Guidance Notes published by IVSC and endeavor to secure recognition of the Standards where appropriate in their respective States.

Member associations are enjoined to disclose to the IVSC any significant differences between domestic and international Standards so that such differences can be reported to the international community. The IVSC recognises that Valuers must act legally and comply with the laws and regulations of the States in which they practise. Member associations work with controlling and regulatory authorities, both statutory and voluntary, and other professional societies to ensure that valuations comply with the IVSC Standards and Guidance Notes. They also play an educative and consultative role in the area of valuation standards within their respective States.

Achievements of IVSC

The International Valuation Standards Committee is a Non-Government Organisation (NGO) member of the United Nations, having been granted Roster status with the United Nations Economic and Social Council in May 1985. The IVSC works cooperatively with Member States and maintains liaison with international agencies, such as the Organisation for Economic Cooperation and Development (OECD), the World Bank, the International Monetary Fund (IMF), the World Trade Organisation (WTO), the Commission of the European Union, the Bank for International Settlements (BIS), and the International Organisation of Security Commissions (IOSCO). The IVSC also maintains a close relationship with the International Accounting Standards Board (IASB), and the independent standards setting boards of the International Federation of Accountants (IFAC)--the International Public Sector Accounting Standards Board and the International Auditing and Assurance Standards Board.

IVSC provides the accounting profession with advice and counsel relating to valuation, seeks to coordinate its Standards and work programs with those of related professional disciplines in the public interest, and cooperates with international bodies in determining and promulgating new Standards. In order to ensure that the international standards governing valuation practice are consistent with the requirements of Valuers under international financial reporting standards, the IVSC annually reviews each new edition of the International Financial Reporting Standards (IFRSs), promulgated by the International Accounting Standards Board (IASB), and the International Public Sector Accounting Standards (IPSASs), promulgated by the International Public Sector Accounting Standards Board. The IVSs make reference to these accounting standards wherever they apply to the work of Valuers. The IVSC publishes White Papers and Technical Papers at its website. At the time this edition was released, the following papers were available: two White Papers, *Valuation in Emerging Markets* and *The Valuation of Real Estate Serving as Collateral for Securitised Instruments;* and one Technical Paper, *Mass Appraisal for Property Taxation.*

Headquarters

The IVSC's international headquarters are in London.

12 Great George Street
London
United Kingdom SW1P 3AD
Telephone: 44 1442 879306
Facsimile: 44 1442 879306

Financial matters and orders are handled at the Committee's international financial bureau in Chicago, IL, USA. Information about the Committee and ongoing development of the Standards can be obtained through the IVSC web site at *http://www.ivsc.org/*.

IVSC officers, who are appointed representatives of their respective national association(s), are chosen through a peer election of all national representatives. A new chairman is elected every two years. The IVSC is directed by a Management Board, which includes Full and Elected Board Members as well as the Chairman and the two Vice Chairmen. The Management Board delegates responsibility for reviewing current standards and guidance, and producing new drafts, where appropriate, to the IVSC Standards Board. Members of the Standards Board are drawn from a wider constituency than IVSC member institutes. In determining the membership of the Standards Board, the IVSC Management Board seeks to draw together a group of people with the best available combination of technical skills and background experience in relevant international business and property markets, who can contribute to the development of high quality, international valuation standards. The IVSC By-Laws and Articles of Incorporation set forth detailed provisions for the membership, management, and operations of the organisation, and are available to view on the IVSC web site.

Members of the IVSC Management Board of Directors as at 1 January 2007 are:

Joseph Vella, *Chairman*
Elvin Fernandez, *Chairman-Designate*
Gheorghe Badescu, *Vice-Chairman*
Igor Artemenkov
Vern Blair

K K Chiu
Richard Chung
Robert Connolly
Brian Glanville
Aart Hordijk
Jang Dong Kyu
Gray A Nthinda
Liu Ping
Chris Thorne
Leandro S. Escobar-Torres
Raymond Trotz
Brad Wagar

The International Valuation Standards

Objectives and Scope

The development of the International Valuation Standards (IVSs) has been guided by three principal objectives

- To facilitate cross-border transactions and contribute to the viability of international property markets by promoting transparency in financial reporting as well as the reliability of valuations performed to secure loans and mortgages, for transactions involving transfers of ownership, and for settlements in litigation or tax matters;

- To serve as a professional benchmark, or beacon, for Valuers around the world, thereby enabling them to respond to the demands of international property markets for reliable valuations and to meet the financial reporting requirements of the global business community; and

- To provide Standards of valuation and financial reporting that meet the needs of emerging and newly industrialised countries.

Users of valuations under IVSs should be able to rely on such valuations as having been carried out by competent professionals who subscribe to high standards of ethical conduct. As the scope of valuation practice becomes broader, the term *property valuation* has gained currency over the more restrictive term *asset valuation,* a term referring to valuations performed primarily for use in financial reporting. A *Professional Property Valuer* is a person who possesses necessary qualifications, ability, and experience to estimate property value for a diversity of purposes including transactions involving transfers of property ownership, property considered as collateral to secure loans and mortgages, property subject to litigation or pending settlement on taxes, and property treated as fixed assets in financial reporting. A *Professional Property Valuer* may also possess the specific expertise to perform valuations of other categories of property, i.e., personal property, businesses, and financial interests.

The International Valuation Standards represent accepted, or best, practice in the Valuation profession, also known as Generally Accepted Valuation Principles (GAVP). Valuer compliance with the IVSs may be voluntary, mandated by law or regulation, or at the instruction of clients, intended users, and/or national societies or organisations. Having no enforcement power of its own, the IVSC looks to national institutes and financial professionals and authorities to enforce standards. It is intended that the International Valuation Standards and the national standards of respective Member States shall be complementary and mutually supportive. The IVSC advocates that differences between statements and/or applications of national and International Valuation Standards be disclosed.

Detailed examination of methodology and its application to specific property types or markets is the province of specialist education and literature. For this reason, the IVSC encourages all professional Valuers to avail themselves of continuing education programs throughout their careers. The International Valuation Standards prescribe what Valuers do rather than explain how specific procedures or methodologies are applied. The IVSs recognise that every application is tied to a specific valuation problem, the solution of which depends on the Valuer's ability to select relevant techniques and exercise appropriate judgment.

Where the standards of other disciplines, such as accounting, may apply to Valuations, the IVSC advises Valuers to understand the accounting use to which their valuations are put.

Organisation of the International Standards

Various valuation principles and techniques are understood within the valuation profession and are well established throughout the global business community. The abbreviated discussions of such principles and techniques included in the Standards, Applications, and Guidance Notes should not be considered exhaustive. Therefore, it is important to the understanding and use of these Standards that, although the individual Standards, Applications, or Guidance Notes may be published as separate sections, each is a component part of the entirety. **Thus, definitions, preface statements, valuation concepts and principles, and other common elements are to be understood as pertaining to each component.** Although an attempt has been made to develop each part of the Standards document as a self-contained item, the requirements of the IVSC Code of Conduct and IVS 3, Valuation Reporting, apply to all elements. Thus, the reader will benefit most from reading the entire document. Extensive cross-referencing facilitates the task of trac-

International Valuation Standards, Eighth Edition

ing related areas throughout the text. **The Standards, Applications, and Guidance Notes include paragraphs in both plain type and bold type, which have equal authority. Paragraphs in bold type indicate the main principles.** Technical Papers published on the IVSC website supplement the Standards, Applications and Guidance Notes but are not considered as integral to the Standards document.

Structure of Standards, Applications, Guidance Notes, and Commentary

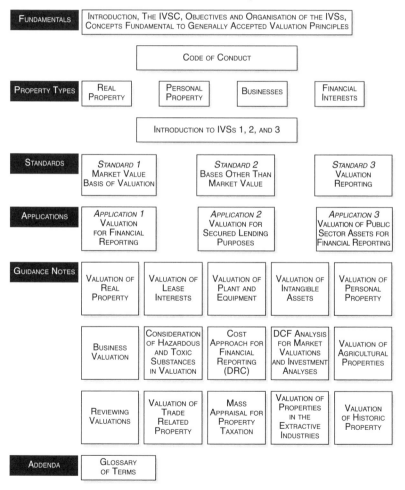

The International Valuation Standards Committee (IVSC) recognises the complexity of professional valuation procedures, the diversity of property situations, the difficulty other professional disciplines may have in interpreting valuation activities, problems in the usage and translation of terminology, and the paramount need of the public for well-founded professional valuations developed in accordance with generally accepted standards. Accordingly, the content and format of these Standards have been designed with these issues in mind and an understanding of the structure of the Standards is, therefore, important to their application. The organisation of the Standards follows.

1. **Introduction** – The introduction offers an overview of the origins of the International Valuation Standards, the work of the International Valuation Standards Committee, and the general context of the Standards. The organisation of the Standards is explained and their intended applicability is discussed.

2. **Concepts Fundamental to Generally Accepted Valuation Principles** – A full discussion of the body of knowledge constituting valuation methods and practices is beyond the scope of these Standards. To foster understanding among professional disciplines and to alleviate difficulties arising from language barriers, this section aims at providing commentary on basic legal, economic, and conceptual frameworks upon which the valuation discipline and its Standards are based. Comprehension of these concepts and principles is crucial to understanding valuation and to the application of these Standards.

3. **Code of Conduct** – A code of conduct addresses the ethical and competency requirements of Valuers in professional practice. Ethical conduct serves the public interest, sustains the trust financial institutions necessarily place in the services of Valuers, and works to the benefit of the valuation profession itself. It ensures that the results of valuations are reliable, consistent, and unbiased.

4. **Property Types** – Real property is distinguished from personal property, businesses, and financial interests. These four property types and the distinctions between them are discussed.

5. **Introduction to the Standards** – This introductory section discusses differences between the Market Value Basis and Bases Other Than Market

Value and the importance of clearly and informatively communicating the valuation. After the valuation is completed, the Valuer has to clearly explain the results and to communicate how those results were obtained.

6. **Standards** – Within the organisation of Standards, Applications, and Guidance Notes, the Standards are considered as most fundamental and permanent. IVSC Standards 1 and 2 deal respectively with Market Value and Bases Other Than Market Value. Standard 3 sets forth the requirements for Valuation Reporting. The Standards also serve as a foundation for the International Valuation Applications (IVAs), which deal with the application of valuation for financial reporting and lending.

7. **Applications** – The application of both private and public sector asset valuation to financial statements or related accounts, and to decisions involving loan or mortgage security is described.

8. **Guidance Notes** – Issues that relate to the application of the Standards frequently arise in valuation practice and from those who use valuation services. The Guidance Notes provide guidance on specific valuation issues and how Standards are to be applied in more specific business and service-providing situations. The Guidance Notes complement and expand on the Standards and Applications, with which they have equal importance. Compliance with the Guidance Notes as with the Standards and Applications is, therefore, mandatory for all Valuers preparing assignments under the International Valuation Standards.

9. **Glossary** – The glossary provides a summary of all terms defined in the Standards, Applications and Guidance Notes.

The three principal elements of the International Valuation Standards, i.e., the Standards, Applications and Guidance Notes, have equal weight, and all valuations prepared in compliance with the IVSs must conform to the principles and procedures elaborated throughout the entire document.

Format of the Standards, Applications and Guidance Notes

Each of the three Standards is written to address a broadly related area of valuation practice. As appropriate, each Standard contains the following nine sections.

1. Introduction
2. Scope
3. Definitions
4. Relationship to Accounting Standards
5. Statement of Standard
6. Discussion
7. Disclosure Requirements
8. Departure Provisions
9. Effective Date

The International Valuation Applications have the following nine sections:

1. Introduction
2. Scope
3. Definitions
4. Relationship to Accounting Standards
5. Statement of Application
6. Discussion
7. Disclosure Requirements
8. Departure Provisions
9. Effective Date

Each of the Guidance Notes deal with issues relating to the application of the Standards that arise in valuation practice or from those who use valuation services. As appropriate, each Guidance Note contains the following six sections:

1. Introduction
2. Scope
3. Definitions
4. Relationship to Accounting Standards
5. Guidance
6. Effective Date

The Guidance Notes (GNs) may be divided into three groups. Four of the GNs address considerations specific to the valuation of different property categories, including Real Property, Lease Interests, Plant and Equipment, and Personal Property. Three of the GNs deal with property or assets that are valued on a cash flow basis, including Intangible Assets, Businesses, and Trade Related Property. Two of the GNs provide guidance in the applica-

Format of the Standards and Applications

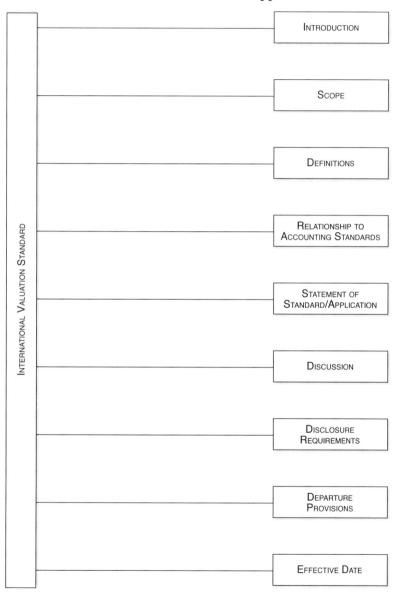

INTRODUCTION

SCOPE

DEFINITIONS

RELATIONSHIP TO ACCOUNTING STANDARDS

STATEMENT OF STANDARD/APPLICATION

DISCUSSION

DISCLOSURE REQUIREMENTS

DEPARTURE PROVISIONS

EFFECTIVE DATE

INTERNATIONAL VALUATION STANDARD

Format of the Guidance Notes

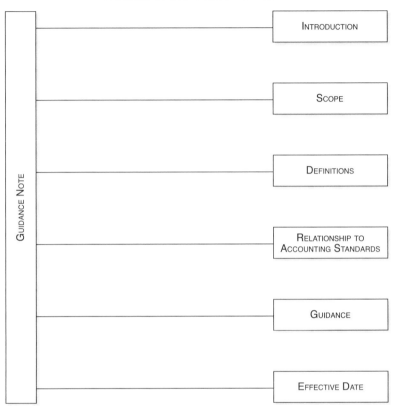

tion of valuation methodologies (The Cost Approach for Financial Reporting-[DRC] and Discounted Cash Flow Analysis for Market Valuations and Investment Analyses). The reader may find it helpful to read these groups of GNs together because of such common basic elements.

Of the remaining six GNs, one addresses environmental issues (Consideration of Hazardous and Toxic Substances), three deal with the valuation of specialised property (agricultural properties, properties in the extractive industries, and historic properties), one provides guidance in an area of professional practice (Reviewing Valuations), and one discusses a cognate area of valuation practice (Mass Appraisal for Property Taxation).

Adoption Dates for Standards Documents

The IVSC Market Value definition and the first two International Valuation Standards were adopted 24 March 1994. Two other Standards adopted at that time (IVS 3 and IVS 4) were revised and became Applications (IVA 1 and IVA 2) 1 July 2000. The third International Valuation Standard, Valuation Reporting, was adopted 30 April 2003, and the third International Valuation Application, Valuation of Public Sector Assets for Financial Reporting, was adopted 31 July 2007. Current IVS 1 and IVA 1; and revised versions of IVS 2, IVS 3 and IVA 2 became effective 31 July 2007.

The Guidance Note on the Consideration of Hazardous and Toxic Substances in Valuation (GN 7) was originally adopted 19 April 1996. In its current form, GN 7 became effective 31 January 2005. The Guidance Note on the Valuation of Plant and Equipment (GN 3) was originally adopted 1 July 1997. An extensive revision of GN 3 was approved 30 November 2005. In its current form, GN 3 became effective 31 July 2007.

The Guidance Notes on Real Property Valuation (GN 1), Valuation of Lease Interests (GN 2), Valuation of Intangible Assets (GN 4) and Business Valuation (GN 6) were adopted 1 July 2000 and the GN on the Valuation of Personal Property (GN 5), 30 April 2003. These five GNs have all been revised, and the current versions became effective 31 July 2007.

The Guidance Notes on Discounted Cash Flow (DCF) Analysis for Market Valuations and Investment Analyses (GN 9), Valuation of Agricultural Properties (GN 10), and Reviewing Valuations (GN 11) were adopted on 30 April 2003. In their current form, GN 9, GN 10, and GN 11 became effective 31 July 2007. The Guidance Note on the Cost Approach for Financial Reporting-DRC (GN 8) was originally adopted 1 July 2000. It has undergone subsequent revision, achieving near current form in the seventh edition. The eighth edition version of GN 8 became effective 31 July 2007. The Guidance Note on the Valuation of Specialised Trading Property (GN 12) was adopted 31 January 2005. It was renamed Valuation of Trade Related Property and further edited in this edition. In its current form, GN 12 became effective 31 July 2007.

The Guidance Notes on Mass Appraisal for Property Taxation (GN 13) and the Valuation of Properties in the Extractive Industries (GN 14) were adopted 31 January 2005. GN 13 underwent no revision since the last edition. GN

14, in its current form, became effective 31 July 2007. New Guidance Note 15, Valuation of Historic Property, was also adopted 31 July 2007.

The Committee will continue to develop Standards, Applications and Guidance Notes as the users of valuations and the market require.

Concepts Fundamental to Generally Accepted Valuation Principles (GAVP)

International Valuation Standards Committee

Concepts Fundamental to Generally Accepted Valuation Principles (GAVP)

1.0 Introduction

1.1 The experience of Valuers and dialogue among nations through the International Valuation Standards Committee (IVSC) have demonstrated that, with few exceptions, there is common worldwide agreement regarding fundamentals that underpin the valuation discipline. Local laws and economic circumstances may, on occasion, require special (and sometimes limited) applications, but fundamentals of valuation methods and techniques are generally similar throughout the world. It is an objective of the International Valuation Standards Committee to avow and promote these fundamentals.

1.2 IVSC's Standards, Applications and Guidance Notes (GNs) are based on these fundamentals, but it is the position of the Committee that it is inappropriate to attempt to articulate all appropriate fundamentals within the body of each Standard. Instead, this section supplements each Standard and provides an overview of fundamentals that are particularly important to understanding the valuation profession and to applying the Standards.

2.0 Land and Property Concepts

2.1 *Land* is essential to our lives and our existence. Its importance brings land into focus for consideration by lawyers, geographers, sociologists, and economists. As each of these disciplines relates to land and to uses of land, the societies and nations of our world are affected.

2.2 Valuation of land as if vacant or of land and improvements to or on the land, is an economic concept. Whether vacant or improved, land is also referred to as *real estate*. Value is created by real estate's utility, or capacity to satisfy the needs and wants of human societies. Contributing to value are real estate's general uniqueness, durability, fixity of location, relatively limited supply, and the specific utility of a given site.

2.3 *Property* is a legal concept encompassing all the interests, rights and benefits related to ownership. Property consists of the rights of ownership, which entitle the owner to a specific interest or interests in what is owned. To distinguish between real estate, which is a physical entity, and its ownership, which is a legal concept, the ownership of real estate is called *real property*. The combination of rights associated with the ownership of real property is, in some States, referred to as the *bundle of rights*. The bundle-of-rights concept likens property ownership to a bundle of sticks with each stick representing a distinct and separate right of the property owner, e.g., the right to use, to sell, to lease, to give away, or to choose to exercise all or none of these rights.

2.4 Ownership of an interest in items other than real estate is referred to as *personal property*. The word *property,* used without further qualification or identification, may refer to real property, personal property, or other types of property such as businesses and financial interests, or a combination thereof. (See Section 3 below and Property Types).

2.5 Property Valuers, Asset Valuers, and Appraisers are those who deal with the special discipline of economics associated with preparing and reporting valuations. As professionals, Valuers must meet rigorous tests of education, training, competence, and demonstrated skills. They must also exhibit and maintain a Code of Conduct (ethics and competency) and Standards of professional practice and follow *Generally Accepted Valuation Principles (GAVP)*.

2.6 Price changes over time result from specific and general effects of economic and social forces. General forces may cause changes in price levels and in the relative purchasing power of money. Operating on their own momentum, specific forces such as technological change may generate shifts in supply and demand, and can create significant price changes.

2.7 Many recognised principles are applied in valuing real estate. They include the principles of supply and demand; competition; substitution; anticipation, or expectation; change; and others. Common to all these principles is their direct or indirect effect on the degree of utility and productivity of a property. Consequently, it may be stated that the utility of real estate reflects the combined influence of all market forces that come to bear upon the value of property.

3.0 Real Estate, Property, and Asset Concepts

3.1 *Real estate* is defined as the physical land and those human-made items, which attach to the land. It is the physical, tangible "thing" which can be seen and touched, together with all additions on, above, or below the ground. Local laws within each State prescribe the basis for distinguishing real estate from personal property. Although these legal concepts may not be recognised in all States, they are adopted here to distinguish important terms and concepts.

3.2 *Real property* includes all the rights, interests, and benefits related to the ownership of real estate. An interest or interests in real property is normally demonstrated by some evidence of ownership (e.g., a title deed) separate from the physical real estate. Real property is a non-physical concept.

3.3 *Personal property* includes interests in tangible and intangible items which are not real estate. Items of tangible personal property are not permanently affixed to real estate and are generally characterised by their moveability.

3.4 In accounting terminology, *assets* are resources controlled by an entity as a result of past events and from which some future economic benefits are expected to flow to the entity. Ownership of an asset is itself an intangible. However, the asset owned may be either tangible or intangible.

3.4.1 The future economic benefits embodied in an asset may flow to the entity in a number of ways. For example, an asset may be: (a) used singly or in combination with other assets in the production of goods or services to be sold by the entity; (b) exchanged for other assets; (c) used to settle a liability; or (d) distributed to the owners of the entity. (International Financial Reporting Standards [IFRSs], Framework, 55)

3.4.2 An asset is recognised in the balance sheet when it is probable that the future economic benefits will flow to the entity and the asset has a cost or value that can be measured reliably. (IFRSs, Framework, 89)

3.5 International Financial Reporting Standards distinguish among tangible and intangible assets. Of particular importance are the following terms and concepts:

3.5.1 *Current assets*. Assets not intended for use on a continuing basis in the activities of an entity. Examples include stocks, obligations owed to the entity, short-term investments, and cash in bank and in hand. In certain circumstances real estate, normally treated as a fixed asset, may be treated as a current asset. Examples include land or improved real estate held in inventory for sale.

3.5.2 *Non-current assets* (*fixed, or long-term, assets*). These are tangible and intangible assets which fall into the following two broad categories:

3.5.2.1 *Property, plant and equipment.* Assets intended for use on a continuing basis in the activities of an entity including land and buildings; plant and equipment; and other categories of assets, suitably identified; less accumulated depreciation. Property, plant and equipment are tangible, or physical assets.

3.5.2.2 *Other non-current assets.* Assets not intended for use on a continuing basis in the activities of an entity, but expected to be held in long-term ownership including long-term investments; long-term receivables; goodwill; expenditures carried forward; and patents, trademarks, and similar assets. This asset category includes both tangible, or physical assets and intangible, or non-physical assets. *Intangible assets* are considered items of intangible personal property, and may include management and marketing skill, credit rating, goodwill, and various legal rights or instruments (patents, trademarks, copyrights, franchises, and contracts).

3.5.3 Where either historic or current cost accounting conventions are upheld, a distinction is drawn between operational and investment assets. Operational assets are considered requisite to the operations of the going concern or corporation. Investment assets that are owned by a corporation are considered extraneous to the operational requirements of the corporate owner.

3.6 Accounting terminology differs somewhat from terms more common to Valuers. Within the classifications discussed in para. 3, Valuers of real property are principally involved with fixed assets. Technically it is the ownership of the asset, or the right of ownership, that is valued rather than the tangible or intangible asset itself. This concept distinguishes the economic concept of valuing an asset objectively based upon its ability to be purchased and sold in a marketplace from some subjective concept such as assuming an intrinsic or other than *Market Value* basis. The objective market concept does, however, have special applications for limited or non-market property valuation as discussed in International Valuation Standard 2.

3.7 The term *depreciation* is used in different contexts in valuation and in financial reporting. In the context of asset valuation, *depreciation,* refers to the adjustments made to the cost of reproducing or replacing the asset to reflect physical deterioration and functional (technical) and external (economic) obsolescence in order to estimate the value of the asset in a hypothetical exchange in the market when there is no direct sales evidence available (see para. 9.2.1.3, Concepts Fundamental to Generally Accepted Valuation Principles). In financial reporting *depreciation* refers to the charge made against income to reflect the systematic allocation of the depreciable amount of an asset over its useful life to the entity. It is specific to the particular entity and its utilisation of the asset, and is not necessarily affected by the market.

4.0 Price, Cost, Market, and Value

4.1 Imprecision of language, particularly in an international community, can and does lead to misinterpretations and misunderstandings. This is particularly a problem where words commonly used in a language also have specific meanings within a given discipline. That is the case with the terms *price, cost, market,* and *value* as they are used in the valuation discipline.

4.2 *Price* is a term used for the amount asked, offered, or paid for a good or service. Sale price is an historical fact, whether it is publicly disclosed or kept confidential. Because of the financial capabilities, motivations, or special interests of a given buyer and/or seller, the price paid for goods or services may or may not have any relation to the value which might be ascribed to the goods or services by others. Price is, however, generally an indication of a relative value placed upon the goods or services by the particular buyer and/or seller under particular circumstances.

4.3 *Cost* is the price paid for goods or services or the amount required to create or produce the good or service. When that good or service has been completed, its cost is an historical fact. The price paid for a good or service becomes its cost to the buyer.

4.4 A *market* is the environment in which goods and services trade between buyers and sellers through a price mechanism. The concept of a market implies that goods and/or services may be traded among buyers and sellers without undue restriction on their activities. Each party will respond to supply-demand relationships and other price-setting factors as well as to the party's own capacities and knowledge, understanding of the relative utility of the goods and/or services, and individual needs and desires. A market can be local, regional, national, or international.

4.5 *Value* is an economic concept referring to the price most likely to be concluded by the buyers and sellers of a good or service that is available for purchase. Value is not a fact, but an estimate of the likely price to be paid for goods and services at a given time in accordance with a particular definition of value. The economic concept of value reflects a market's view of the benefits that accrue to one who owns the goods or receives the services as of the effective date of valuation.

4.6 Value is therefore a hypothetical price, and the hypothesis on which the value is estimated is determined by the valuation basis adopted. A *Basis of Value* is defined in IVS 2 as a statement of the fundamental measurement principles of a valuation on a specified date. A *Basis of Value* defines the nature of the hypothetical transaction, e.g., whether or not there is exposure to a market, and the assumed motivation and behaviour of the parties. A *Basis of Value* is not a description of the method or approach used to produce the estimate, and neither does it describe the state or condition in which the asset is assumed to be transferred. It is of paramount importance to the use and understanding of valuations that the *Basis of Value* be clearly disclosed, and that it is a basis that is appropriate to the particular valuation assignment. A change in the *Basis of Value* can have a material effect on the valuation.

4.7 Professional Valuers, who possess intimate knowledge of a property market; understand the interaction of participants in the market; and are, thereby, able to judge the most likely prices to be concluded between buyers and sellers of property in that market avoid the unqualified term value by preceding the term with some adjective describing the particular type of value involved. *Market Value* is the most common type of value associated with property valuations and is discussed in International Valuation Standard 1.

4.8 The value concept contemplates a monetary sum associated with a transaction. However, sale of the property valued is not a condition requisite to estimating the price for which property should sell if it were sold on the date of valuation under conditions prescribed in the definition of *Market Value*.

4.9 The *Market Value* of real estate is a representation of its market-recognised utility rather than its purely physical status. The utility of assets to a given entity or individual may differ from that which would be recognised by the market or by a particular industry.

4.9.1 Considerations similar to those expressed above are applied to the valuation of property other than real estate. Financial reporting will require application of *Market Value* methods and a clear distinction between such methods and methods used to estimate values other than *Market Value*.

4.10 The total cost of a property includes all direct and indirect costs of its production. If supplemental capital costs are incurred by a purchaser subsequent to acquisition, they will be added to the historical acquisition cost for cost accounting purposes. Depending upon how the utility of such costs is perceived by the market, they may or may not be fully reflected in the property's *Market Value*.

4.11 A cost estimate for a property may be based on either an estimate of reproduction cost or replacement cost. *Reproduction cost* is the cost to create a virtual replica of a property using identical or, if identical materials are not available, similar materials. A *replacement cost* estimate envisions a modern equivalent of comparable utility, employing the design, technology and materials that are currently used in the market.

5.0 Market Value

5.1 The concept of *Market Value* reflects the collective perceptions and actions of a market and is the basis for valuing most resources in market-based economies. Although precise definitions may vary, the *Market Value* concept is commonly understood and applied.

5.2 *Market Value* is defined as:

The estimated amount for which a property should exchange on the date of valuation between a willing buyer and a willing seller in an arm's-length transaction after proper marketing wherein the parties had each acted knowledgeably, prudently, and without compulsion.

5.3 It is important to stress that the professionally derived *Market Value* estimate is an objective valuation of identified ownership rights to specific property as of a given date. Implicit within this definition is the concept of a general market comprising the activity and motivation of many participants rather than the preconceived view or vested interest of a particular individual. *Market Value* is a market-supported estimate developed in accordance with these Standards.

5.4 Real property is distinguished from most goods and services because of the relatively longer period required to market what is a relatively illiquid commodity in order to achieve a price that represents its *Market Value*. This characteristically longer exposure time, the absence of a 'spot market' (a market in which commodities are available for immediate sale), and the nature and diversity of properties and property markets give rise to the need for Professional Valuers and Valuation Standards.

5.5 In some States, the legal term *Fair Market Value* is used synonymously with the term *Market Value*. *Fair Market Value* should not be confused with the accounting term, *Fair Value*. (See para. 8.1 below.) The IVSC position is that the term *Market Value* never requires further qualification and that all States should move toward compliance with this usage.

6.0 Highest and Best Use

6.1 Land is regarded as a permanent asset, but improvements upon or to the land have a finite life. Because of the immobility of land, each real estate parcel possesses a unique location. Land's permanence also means that it will normally be expected to outlast uses and improvements, which have a finite life.

   6.1.1 The unique characteristics of land determine its optimal utility. When improved land is valued separately from improvements to or upon the land, economic principles require that improvements to or on the land be valued as they contribute to or detract from the total value of the property. Thus, the *Market Value* of land based upon the "highest and best use" concept reflects the utility and the permanence of land in the context of a market, with improvements constituting the difference between land value alone and total *Market Value* as improved.

6.2 Most properties are valued as a combination of land and improvements. In such cases, the Valuer will normally estimate *Market Value* by considering the highest and best use of the property as improved.

6.3 *Highest and best use* is defined as:

   The most probable use of a property which is physically possible, appropriately justified, legally permissible, financially feasible, and which results in the highest value of the property being valued.

6.4 A use that is not legally permissible or physically possible cannot be considered a highest and best use. A use that is both legally permissible and physically possible may nevertheless require an explanation by the Valuer justifying why that use is reasonably probable. Once analysis establishes that one or more uses are reasonably probable uses, they are then tested for financial feasibility. The use that results in the highest value, in keeping with the other tests, is the highest and best use.

6.5 Application of this definition permits Valuers to assess the effects of deterioration and obsolescence in buildings, the most appropriate improvements for land, the feasibility of rehabilitation and renovation projects, and many other valuation situations.

6.6 In markets characterised by extreme volatility or severe disequilibrium between supply and demand, the highest and best use of a property may be a holding for future use. In other situations, where several types of potential highest and best use are identifiable, the Valuer should discuss such alternative uses and anticipated future income and expense levels. Where land use and zoning are in a state of change, the immediate highest and best use of a property may be an interim use.

6.7 The concept of highest and best use is a fundamental and integral part of *Market Value* estimates.

7.0 Utility

7.1 The key criterion in the valuation of any real or personal property is its utility. Procedures employed in the valuation process have the common objective of defining and quantifying the degree of utility or usefulness of the property valued. This process calls for interpretation of the utility concept.

7.2 *Utility* is a relative, or comparative term, rather than an absolute condition. For example, the utility of agricultural land is ordinarily measured by its productive capacity. Its value is a function of the quantity and quality of produce, which the land will yield in an agricultural sense, or of the quantity and quality of buildings essential to the agricultural operation. If the land has development potential, however, its productivity is measured by how productively it will support a residential, commercial, industrial, or mixed use. Consequently, land value is established by evaluating its utility in terms of the legal, physical, functional, economic, and environmental factors that govern its productive capacity.

7.3 Fundamentally, property valuation is governed by the way specific property is used and/or how it would ordinarily be traded in the market. For some property, optimum utility is achieved if the property in question is operated on an individual basis. Other property has greater utility if operated as part of a group of properties, e.g., properties owned and managed by a business entity such as a chain of multiple retail outlets, fast food restaurants, or hotels. Therefore, a distinction must be made between a property's utility viewed individually and when considered as a part of a group. A Valuer will regard the property as the market views it, whether as a discrete entity or as part of an aggregate or portfolio. Typically, the Valuer estimates and reports the value of the property as an individual entity. If the value of the property, taken as part of an aggregate or portfolio, is other than its individual value, such value should be considered and reported.

7.4 An individual property may possess an additional, or special, value above its value as a separate entity by reason of its physical or functional association with an adjoining property owned by others or its attractiveness to a purchaser with other special interests. The extent or amount of such additional, or special, value is generally reported separately from *Market Value*.

8.0 Other Important Concepts

8.1 The expression *Market Value* and the term *Fair Value* as it commonly appears in accounting standards are generally compatible, if not in every instance exactly equivalent concepts. *Fair Value,* an accounting concept, is defined in International Financial Reporting Standards and other accounting standards as the amount for which an asset could be exchanged, or a liability settled, between knowledgeable, willing parties in an arm's length transaction. *Fair Value* is generally used for reporting both *Market* and *Non-Market Values* in financial statements. Where the *Market Value* of an asset can be established, this value will equate to *Fair Value*.

8.2 *Specialised property* is property that is rarely, if ever, sold in the market except by way of a sale of the business or entity of which it is part, due to uniqueness arising from its specialised nature and design, its configuration, size, location, or otherwise. Where there is limited or no directly comparable market information for Valuers to consider, the valuation process may become more complex. However, it is the Valuer's responsibility to develop data and reasoning from the market to support and/or explain the value conclusion. Each of the valuation methods may be applied, and all applicable methods should be considered. Where possible, the Valuer develops land value, cost, and accumulated depreciation estimates from market information, and explains the basis for the value estimate.

8.3 Where normal market conditions are disrupted or suspended, or where supply and demand imbalances lead to market prices that do not meet the *Market Value* definition, the Valuer may face a difficult valuation problem. By using the *Market Value* concept and definition, and by applying market data and reasoning to the valuation process, Valuers ensure the relevance and usefulness of asset values reported in financial statements. As availability and/or applicability of market data decrease, the valuation assignment may require a higher degree of professional Valuer vigilance, experience, and judgement.

8.4 A Valuer may be required to apply a particular definition of *Market Value* to meet legal or statutory requirements. If so required, the Valuer must make specific disclosure of the fact and describe the impact of any differences upon the value estimated. Where an assignment is undertaken in accordance with International Valuation Standards, the term *Market Value* will always conform to the IVS definition.

8.5 All valuation reports should make clear the purpose and intended use of the valuation. In addition to other reporting requirements, where financial reporting is involved the report should specifically identify the asset class into which each asset is placed and the basis for such placement. Each asset class should be explicitly explained.

8.6 The estimation and reporting of property and asset values, and related guidance, are the scope of these International Valuation Standards, Applications, and related Guidance Notes. How the results of valuations are to be compiled, conveyed, and incorporated with the findings of other professionals is of crucial importance to Valuers. Proper understanding of terminology is essential for Valuers and those who read their reports. The sound use of experience and expertise and correct application of methodology are also essential. These Standards are intended to serve the common objectives of those who prepare property and asset valuations and those who must rely on their results.

9.0 Valuation Approaches

9.1 In order to estimate the price implied by the appropriate *Basis of Value,* the Valuer will need to apply one or more valuation approaches. A *valuation approach* or *method* refers to generally accepted analytical methodologies that are in common use.

9.2 Market based valuations normally employ one or more of the *valuation approaches* by applying the economic *principle of substitution,* using market-derived data. This principle holds that a prudent person would not pay more for a good or service than the cost of acquiring an equally satisfactory substitute good or service, in the absence of the complicating factors of time, greater risk, or inconvenience. The lowest cost of the best alternative, whether a substitute or the original, tends to establish *Market Value.*

9.2.1 Market based *valuation approaches* include:

9.2.1.1 *Sales Comparison Approach.* This comparative approach considers the sales of similar or substitute properties and related market data, and establishes a value estimate by processes involving comparison. In general, a property being valued (a subject property) is compared with sales of similar properties that have been transacted in the market. Listings and offerings may also be considered.

9.2.1.2 *Income Capitalisation Approach.* This comparative approach considers income and expense data relating to the property being valued and estimates value through a capitalisation process. Capitalisation relates income (usually a net income figure) and a defined value type by converting an income amount into a value estimate. This process may consider direct relationships (known as *capitalisation rates*), yield or *discount rates* (reflecting measures of return on investment), or both. In general, the principle of substitution holds that the income stream which produces the highest return commensurate with a given level of risk leads to the most probable value figure.

9.2.1.3 *Cost Approach.* This comparative approach considers the possibility that, as an alternative to the purchase of a given property, one could acquire a modern equivalent asset that would provide equal utility. In a real estate context, this would involve the cost of acquiring equivalent land and constructing an equivalent new structure.

Unless undue time, inconvenience, and risk are involved, the price that a buyer would pay for the asset being valued would not be more than the cost of the modern equivalent. Often the asset being valued will be less attractive than the cost of the modern equivalent because of age or obsolescence. A depreciation adjustment is required to the replacement cost to reflect this. (See GN 8, The Cost Approach for Financial Reporting-(DRC).)

9.3 Valuations developed for purposes other than establishing *Market Value* may apply similar approaches. For example:

9.3.1 An entity may apply a cost approach to compare the cost of other buildings with the cost of a proposed building to the entity, thereby ascertaining the bargain or premium accruing a particular property at variance with the market at large. This application focuses on a particular property and what may be a non-market cost.

9.3.2 An owner of land may pay a premium price for adjacent property. In applying a sales comparison approach to determine a maximum price that owner is willing to pay for adjacent land, a Valuer arrives at a figure that may well exceed its *Market Value*. Such an estimate is called *Special Value*.

9.3.3 An investor may apply a rate of return that is non-market and particular only to that investor. In applying an income capitalisation approach to determine the price that investor is willing to pay for a particular investment based on the investor's anticipated rate of return, a Valuer arrives at an estimate of *Investment Value* or *Worth* rather than *Market Value*.

9.4 Each valuation approach has alternative methods of application. The Valuer's expertise and training, local standards, market requirements, and available data combine to determine which method or methods are applied. The reason for having alternative approaches and methods is to provide the Valuer with a series of analytical procedures which will ultimately be weighed and reconciled into a final value estimate, depending upon the particular type of value involved.

9.5 Valuation approaches and methods are generally common to virtually all types of valuation, including real property, personal property, businesses, and financial interests. However, valuation of different types of property involves different sources of data that appropriately reflect the market in which the property (and/or service or business) is to be valued. For example, individual buildings are commonly sold and valued in the relevant real estate market whereas the values of the shares of stock in a property company that owns a number of buildings are reflected by pricing in the relevant shares market.

10.0 Summary

10.1 The International Valuation Standards are intended to facilitate cross-border transactions involving property and contribute to the viability of global markets by promoting transparency in financial reporting. Emphasis is placed on the use of factual market information from which informed professional judgements regarding property valuations can be drawn.

Code of Conduct

International Valuation Standards Committee

Code of Conduct

1.0 Introduction

It is fundamental to the operation of International Valuation Standards that valuations performed in compliance therewith should be provided by honest and competent Professional Valuers, free of bias or self-interest, whose reports are clear, will not mislead, and will disclose all matters essential to the proper understanding of the valuation. Valuers should always promote and preserve public trust in the valuation profession.

2.0 Scope

2.1 Valuers comply with these Standards either by choice or by requirement placed upon them by law or regulation or at the instructions of clients, intended users, and/or national societies or organisations. A valuation claiming to be prepared under International Valuation Standards binds the Valuer to follow this Code of Conduct.

2.2 This Code does not have any formal authority in law, neither is it intended to be other than complementary to the rules, by-laws and regulations of national societies or organisations controlling or monitoring the activities of Valuers.

2.3 Valuations prepared under these Standards would only normally be acceptable to end users when prepared by a trained professional member of a recognised national professional body that itself enforces standards of qualification, competence, experience, ethics, and disclosure in valuation. In those countries where the infrastructure does not yet exist for a trained and regulated profession of valuation, primary responsibility lies with the client users to satisfy themselves as to the suitability of Valuers to undertake the task.

3.0 Definitions

3.1 *Assumptions* are suppositions taken to be true. Assumptions involve facts, conditions, or situations affecting the subject of, or approach to, a valuation but which may not be capable or worthy of verification. They are matters that, once declared, are to be accepted in understanding the valuation. All assumptions underlying a valuation should be reasonable.

All valuations are dependent to some degree on the adoption of assumptions. In particular,

the definition of *Market Value* incorporates assumptions to ensure consistency of approach and

the Valuer may need to make further assumptions in respect of facts which cannot be known or facts which could be determined.

3.2 *Limiting Conditions* are constraints imposed on valuations.

Limiting conditions may be imposed:

by clients (e.g., where the Valuer is not permitted to investigate fully one or more of the significant factors likely to affect valuation);

by the Valuer (e.g., where the client may not publish the whole or any part of the Valuation Report or Valuation Certificate without the Valuer's prior written approval of the form and context in which it may appear); or

by local statutory law.

3.3 A *Valuer* is a person who possesses the necessary qualifications, ability, and experience to execute a valuation. In some States, licensing is required before a person can act as a Valuer.

The Valuer shall be a person of good repute who:

- has obtained an appropriate degree at a recognised centre of learning, or an equivalent academic qualification;

- has suitable experience and is competent in valuing in the market and category of the asset;

- is aware of, understands, and can correctly employ those recognised methods and techniques that are necessary to produce a credible valuation;

- is a member of a recognised national professional valuation body;

- pursues a programme of professional learning throughout his or her career; and

- follows all the requirements of this Code of Conduct.

If, in any State, there are no appropriate academic qualifications, as stated above, the Valuer should have a sufficient level of training and experience in the valuation and be either:

a member of a recognised national professional valuation body, or licenced by government or appointed by the Courts or an Authority of an equivalent status.

In some States, to practice as a Valuer a licence or certification by an independent body is required by law.

3.4 An *Internal Valuer* is a Valuer who is in the employ of either the entity that owns the assets or the accounting firm responsible for preparing the entity's financial records and/or reports. An Internal Valuer is generally capable of meeting all the requirements of independence and professional objectivity required under this Code of Conduct, but for reasons of public presentation and regulation may not always be acceptable to fill the role of independent Valuer in certain types of assignments.

3.5 An *External Valuer* is a Valuer who, together with any associates, has no material links with the client, an agent acting on behalf of the client, or the subject of the assignment.

3.6 Since all Valuers undertaking assignments under International Valuation Standards must meet the requirements of impartiality, professional objectivity and disclosure required under this Code of Conduct, such Valuers should meet the requirements for independence which may attach to many assignments. With some clients, and in certain States, additional restraints on who may undertake valuation for a specific purpose may be applied by regulation or law. It is not the purpose of this Code to define different degrees of independence beyond the standard of independence already required under this Code.

4.0 Ethics

Valuers should at all times maintain a high standard of honesty and integrity and conduct their activities in a manner not detrimental to their clients, the public, their profession, or their respective national professional valuation body.

4.1 *Integrity*

4.1.1 A Valuer must not act in a manner that is misleading or fraudulent.

4.1.2 A Valuer must not knowingly develop and communicate a report that contains false, inaccurate, or biased opinions and analysis.

4.1.3 A Valuer must not contribute to, or participate in, a valuation service that other reasonable Valuers would not regard to be justified.

4.1.4 A Valuer must act legally and comply with the laws and regulations of the State in which he or she practices or where an assignment is undertaken.

4.1.5 A Valuer must not claim, or knowingly let pass, erroneous interpretation of professional qualifications that he or she does not possess.

4.1.6 A Valuer should not knowingly use false, misleading or exaggerated claims or advertising in an effort to secure assignments.

4.1.7 A Valuer shall ensure that any staff person or subordinate assisting with the assignment adhere to this Code of Conduct.

4.2 *Conflicts of Interest*

4.2.1 A Valuer must not act for two or more parties in the same matter, except with the written consent of those concerned.

4.2.2 A Valuer must take all reasonable precautions to ensure that no conflicts of duty arise between the interests of his or her clients and those of other clients, the Valuer, his or her firm, relatives, friends, or associates. Potential conflicts should be disclosed in writing before accepting instructions. Any such conflicts of which the Valuer subsequently becomes aware must be disclosed immediately. If such conflicts come to the attention of the Valuer after completion of the valuation, disclosure must be made within a reasonable time.

4.3 *Confidentiality*

4.3.1 A Valuer must at all times deal with client's affairs with proper discretion and confidentiality.

4.3.2 A Valuer must not disclose sensitive factual data obtained from a client, or the results of an assignment prepared for a client, to anyone other than those specifically authorised by the client except when legally required to do so as in situations where a Valuer must comply with certain quasi-judicial proceedings within the recognised national professional valuation body of which the Valuer is a member.

4.4 *Impartiality*

4.4.1 A Valuer must perform an assignment with the strictest independence, objectivity, and impartiality, and without accommodation of personal interests.

4.4.2 A Valuer must not accept an assignment that includes the reporting of predetermined opinions and conclusions.

4.4.3 Fees connected with an assignment must not depend on the predetermined outcome of any valuation or other independent, objective advice contained in the valuation report.

4.4.4 Whether the Valuer's fee is or is not contingent upon any aspect of the report must be disclosed.

4.4.5 A Valuer must not rely upon critical information supplied by a client, or any other party, without appropriate qualification or confirmation from an independent source unless the nature and extent of such reliance is specified as a limiting condition.

4.4.6 A Valuer should not accept an assignment to report on assumed hypothetical conditions that are unlikely to be realised in any reasonable timescale.

4.4.7 Hypothetical conditions that are a reasonable possibility may be reported on provided they are accompanied by some discussion both of the prospects of realising the hypothesis and a consideration of value that reflects the true situation prevailing, e.g., a situation where a client wants to know what the value of land will be pending detoxification.

4.4.8 A Valuer should not use or rely on unsupported conclusions based on prejudice of any kind or report conclusions reflecting an opinion that such prejudice is necessary to maintain or maximise value.

4.4.9 In reviewing another Valuer's report, a Valuer shall exhibit impartial judgment and justify his or her reasons for agreeing or disagreeing with the conclusions of the report.

5.0 Competence

A Valuer must have the knowledge, skill, and experience to complete the assignment efficiently in relation to an acceptable professional standard. Only those Valuers able to conform to the definition of the Valuer set out in Definitions (para. 3.3 above) should undertake work in connection with these Standards.

5.1 *Acceptance of Instructions*

5.1.1 Prior to accepting an assignment or entering into an agreement to perform any assignment, a Valuer must properly identify the problem to be addressed and be certain he or she has the experience and knowledge, or in the event of an assignment overseas, will be able to associate with a professional possessing the experience and knowledge of the market forces, language, and law to complete the assignment competently.

5.2 *Outside Assistance*

5.2.1 When engaging the services of outside assistance necessary to complement a Valuer's own skills, a Valuer should first establish that those assisting have the requisite skills and ethical principles.

5.2.2 The client's consent should be obtained when outside assistance is required, and the identity of the assistants and extent of their role should be disclosed in the Valuer's report.

5.3 *Efficiency and Diligence*

5.3.1 Valuer should act promptly and efficiently in carrying out the client's instructions and should keep the client informed of the Valuer's progress.

5.3.2 Instructions should be declined where circumstances preclude sufficient diligent enquiry, quality of work, and completion within a reasonable time.

5.3.3 Before the valuation is reported, written instructions should be received from the client and/or confirmed in writing by a Valuer in sufficient detail to avoid any misinterpretation.

5.3.4 A Valuer should make diligent enquiries and investigations to ensure that the data for analysis in the valuation are correct and can be relied upon.

5.3.5 A Valuer should prepare a work file for each assignment which, upon completion, should contain a true copy, in paper or electronic form (suitably backed up), of all written reports, correspondence, and memoranda plus adequate file notes which substantiate the Valuer's opinions by way of enquiry, objective comparison, deduction, and calculation.

5.3.6 The work file for each assignment should be retained for a period of at least five years after completion of the assignment.

6.0 Disclosure

It is essential that Valuers develop and communicate their analyses, opinions, and conclusions to users of their services through reports that are meaningful and not misleading and that disclose anything that might be taken to affect objectivity.

6.1 The valuation report should set out a clear and accurate description of the scope of the assignment and its purpose and intended use, disclosing any assumptions, hypothetical scenarios, or limiting conditions that directly affect the valuations and, where appropriate, indicating their effect on the value.

6.2 The valuation report must provide sufficient information to describe the work performed, the conclusions reached, and the context in which they were shaped.

6.3 A Valuer must disclose any direct or indirect personal or corporate relationship with the property or company that is the subject of any assignment and that might lead to a potential conflict of interest.

6.4 Where a Valuer is acting as an Internal Valuer, the relationship with the entity controlling the asset should be disclosed in the valuation report.

6.5 Where a Valuer is acting as an External Valuer but also has worked in a fee-earning capacity for the client, such relationship must be disclosed lest a third party, having to rely on the valuation, deem the Valuer's objectivity compromised.

6.6 Any limitations to quality of the service that a Valuer is able to offer must be disclosed whether this is due to externally imposed constraints or peculiar to the Valuer or the assignment. Where outside assistance has been sought the Valuer must disclose the identity of the assistants, the extent of reliance on, and the nature of, such assistance.

6.7 A Valuer must place a restriction against the publication of a valuation or its conclusions without consent so that the Valuer can keep a measure of control over the form and context in which his or her valuations are publicly disclosed.

6.8 A Valuer should disclose any departures from the International Valuation Standards.

> 6.8.1 Standards are devised for the generality of situations and cannot cater to every eventuality. There will be occasions where departure from Standards is inescapable. When such situations arise, departure would be unlikely to constitute a breach of these Standards, provided such departure is reasonable, complies with the principles of ethics and measures of competence, and a rationale for such departure is provided in the valuation report.

7.0 Reporting of Values

Valuation assignments may deal with one or more properties. The style of the valuation report must be tailored to the nature of the assignment and the needs of the client while meeting certain minimum requirements as to content.

7.1 This paragraph sets out the minimum contents of any report or certificate. The following items must be included. (Also see para, 5.1 of IVS 3, Valuation Reporting.)

- the identity of the Valuer and the date of the report;

- the identity of the client;

- the instructions, date of the value estimate, purpose and intended use of the valuation;

- the basis of the valuation, including type and definition of value;

- the identity, tenure, and location(s) of the interest(s) to be valued;

- the date and extent of inspections;

- the scope and extent of the work used to develop the valuation;

- any assumptions and limiting conditions; and any special, unusual, or extraordinary assumptions;

- a compliance statement that the valuation has been performed in accordance with these Standards and any required disclosures;

- the professional qualification and signature of the Valuer; and

As required in some States, specific certification by the Valuer in the prescribed form.

7.2 The use of the valuation and the complexity of the property determine the level of detail appropriate to the report. Where a single or complex property is being reported, it may be appropriate for the report to go into greater detail on the data upon which the valuation is based and the reasoning behind the conclusions. Where a report is being prepared for a portfolio of properties for use in an audit function, the level of detailed data required for each of the properties within the portfolio may be less extensive.

7.3 This section is not to be taken to represent the enquiries, research and analysis needed to perform a proper valuation, merely the minimum that must be presented in the report.

Property Types

International Valuation Standards Committee

Property Types

1.0 Introduction

Real property represents a considerable portion of the world's wealth, and its valuation is fundamental to the viability of global property and financial markets. Real property has to be distinguished from other categories of property, namely personal property, businesses, and financial interests. Without further qualification or identification, the word *property* may refer to all or any of these categories. Because Valuers often encounter assignments involving property types other than real property or properties whose value includes several property categories, an understanding of each property type and its distinguishing characteristics is essential. While the customary division of property into four discrete categories has long been recognised, new entities and instruments have proliferated over recent decades. The accepted frame of reference has readily accommodated these new classes of property and familiarity with specialised property types and interests is becoming ever more integral to valuation practice. The International Valuation Standards Committee recognises the following four property types: real property, personal property, businesses, and financial interests.

2.0 Real Property

2.1 *Real property* is an interest in real estate. This interest is normally recorded in a formal document, such as a title deed or lease. Therefore, property is a legal concept distinct from real estate, which represents a physical asset. Real property encompasses all the rights, interests, and benefits related to the ownership of real estate. In contrast, real estate encompasses the land itself, all things naturally occurring on the land, and all things attached to the land, such as buildings and site improvements.

> 2.1.1 The term *realty* is sometimes used to distinguish either real property or real estate from items of personal property, which in certain States are legally referred to as *personalty*.

2.2 The combination of all the rights associated with the ownership of real property is sometimes referred to as the *bundle of rights*. These can include the right to use, to occupy, to enter, to sell, to lease, to bequeath, to give away, or to choose to exercise any or none of the above-mentioned. In many situations, specific rights may be separated from the bundle and transferred, leased, or alienated by the State.

2.2.1 Rights or interests in real property derive from *legal estates.* Legal estates are defined by the laws of the State in which they exist. Legal estates are usually subject to outside limitations imposed by the State, such as taxation (assessments/ratings), compulsory acquisition (eminent domain/compulsory purchase/condemnation), regulation (police power/ planning/zoning), or appropriation by government in cases of intestacy (escheat/ bona vacantia).

2.2.2 Absolute ownership subject only to limitations imposed by the State is known as a *fee simple estate,* or *freehold.*

2.2.3 Leases are contractual arrangements, which create other estates in real property. Under a lease, the landlord, or lessor, maintains the ownership interest, known in some States as the leased fee estate, with the right of use and occupancy being conveyed or granted to a tenant. The interest which the tenant, or lessee, acquires under the lease, known in some States as the *leasehold estate,* is the right of use and occupancy for a stated term under certain conditions.

2.2.3.1 *Subleaseholds* are created when the tenant or lessee in a prior lease conveys to a third party, a sublessee, the interest that the tenant, or lessee, enjoys, i.e., the right to use and occupy the property.

2.2.3.2 A Valuer analyses whether any terms or conditions in a lease may affect property value.

2.2.4 Besides restrictions by the State, other lawful limitations may be imposed upon the rights inherent in the ownership of real property.

2.2.4.1 *Deed restrictions* and *restrictive covenants,* which run with the land, may affect the use, development, and conveyance of ownership.

2.2.4.2 *Easements* are nonpossessory (incorporeal) interests in landed property conveying use, but not ownership, of a portion of that property. Rights-of-way are rights or privileges, acquired through use or contract, to pass over a portion or strip of landed property owned by another.

2.2.5 Other important ownership and financial interests may be associated with real property.

2.2.5.1 *Partial or fractional interests* in real property rights are created by legal divisions of the ownership interest. For example, real property is not only owned in sole proprietorships. It may also be held by corporations (shareholders), partnerships, joint tenancies, and tenancies in common.

2.2.5.2 Trusts create another type of interest in real property rights. The interest of a beneficiary under a trust is known as the *equitable* or *equity interest* as opposed to the legal interest of the trustee(s). (A beneficiary is said to hold equitable title while legal title is held by the trustee[s].)

2.2.5.3 Security or *financial interests* are created by mortgage pledges where the property is used as collateral to secure finance or a charge is taken over the property. An owners' equity position in the property is considered a separate financial interest.

2.3 Real property, in the terminology of accounting, usually falls into the category of fixed, or long-term, assets. Sometimes, real property may be considered a current asset, e.g., where land or improved real estate is held in inventory for sale.

2.3.1 The asset is the interest held in the real estate, i.e., the asset is the real property.

2.3.2 It is the ownership of the asset that is valued rather than the real estate as a physical entity.

2.3.3 Where the ownership of an asset is purchased and sold in a marketplace, market participants ascribe specific values to ownership of particular interests in real estate. These values ascribed by market participants form the objective basis for estimating the *Market Value* of real property.

2.4 Valuation of real property is undertaken for a variety of reasons, which include the following categories: financial reporting, transactions involving transfers of ownership, loans and mortgages to be secured by property, litigation, tax matters, and counseling or investment decision making. With the exception of the last category, *Market Value* is the value basis in all the following groupings:

2.4.1 Valuations of fixed assets prepared for financial statements and related accounts to reflect the effect of changing prices or current values;

2.4.2 Valuations to assist a prospective buyer in setting an offering, to assist a prospective seller in establishing an acceptable asking price, or to help both parties in determining the sale price for a proposed transaction; valuations to establish the basis for reorganising or merging the ownership of multiple properties;

2.4.3 Valuations required to estimate the value of collateral property offered for a proposed mortgage loan or to establish a basis for insuring or underwriting a loan on the property;

2.4.4 Valuations performed in compulsory acquisition (eminent domain/ condemnation proceedings), in litigation or arbitration involving disputes over contracts and partial interests, and settlements of damages caused by environmental accidents or violations;

2.4.5 Valuations required to estimate assessed value/rating; to separate assets into depreciable and non-depreciable items and, thereby estimate applicable depreciation; or to determine gift or inheritance taxes;

2.4.6 Valuations and ancillary assignments performed for a broad spectrum of clients, e.g., investors, insurers, claims adjusters, auctioneers or liquidators, and zoning boards (on the probable effects of planning proposals) as well as for a diversity of purposes, e.g., market or feasibility analyses, cost/benefit analyses, determination of book value for new stock issues (or revisions thereof), and the setting of prospective rent schedules and lease provisions.

2.5 In any valuation of real property, the relevant characteristics of the property must be identified. Property characteristics include:

2.5.1 the location, the physical and legal description, and the economic or income-producing attributes;

2.5.2 the real property interest (fee simple/freehold, leased fee, leasehold, subleasehold) to be valued;

2.5.3 any personal property, trade fixtures, or intangible items that are not real property but that are included in the valuation (see Para. 3.2 below);

2.5.4 any known easements, restrictions, encumbrances, leases, covenants, or special assessments/ratings on the property or other items of similar nature; and

2.5.5 whether the subject property is a partial or fractional interest or a physical segment of a larger land parcel.

2.6 The valuation of real property may be influenced by special considerations, such as:

2.6.1 A requirement to analyse the merger of estates *(Synergistic Value)* or the separation of property interests *(Component Value);*

2.6.2 The effects of likely zoning changes and infrastructure development, e.g., the extension of public utility systems or access corridors;

2.6.3 Depressed markets characterised by weak demand, oversupply, and few sale transactions, where estimates of *Market Value* may be difficult to support on the basis of current or historical evidence. In such circumstances, the focus of market participants may shift to other indicators of property value or performance.

3.0 Personal Property

3.1 *Personal property* refers to ownership of an interest in items other than real estate. These items can be tangible, such as a chattel, or intangible, such as a debt or patent. Tangible personal property represents interests in items that are not permanently attached or affixed to real estate and are generally characterised by their moveability. In some States, items of personal property are legally recognised as *personalty* in distinction to *realty* (see Property Types, para. 2.1.1).

3.2 Examples of personal property includes interests in:

3.2.1 Identifiable, portable, and tangible objects considered by the general public to be personal, e.g., furnishings, collectibles, and appliances. Ownership of the current assets of a business, trade inventories, and supplies is considered to be personal property.

3.2.1.2 In some States, the above are referred to as *goods and chattels personal.*

3.2.2 Non-realty fixtures, also called *trade fixtures* or *tenant's fixtures* (*fixtures and fittings*), are attached to the property by the tenant and used in conducting the trade or business. *Leasehold improvements,* or *tenant's improvements,* are fixed improvements or additions to the land or buildings, installed and paid for by the tenant to meet the tenant's needs. Trade or tenant's fixtures are removable by the tenant upon expiration of the lease. Their removal causes no serious damage to the real estate. Leasehold or tenant's improvements are finishings or fittings, such as partitions and outlets constructed on site. The useful life of tenant's improvements may be shorter or longer than the term of the lease. If longer than the lease term, the tenant may be entitled to compensation reflecting the extent to which the leasehold improvements have increased the value of the rented premises.

3.2.2.1 By extension, the above category may include specialised, non-permanent buildings, machinery and equipment.

3.2.2.2 In some States, the term *Furniture, Fixtures, and Equipment* (FF&Es) comprises both of the categories described in para. 3.2.1 and 3.2.2.

3.2.3 Net working capital and securities, or net current assets, are the sum of liquid assets less short-term liabilities. Net working capital may include cash, marketable securities, and liquid supplies less current liabilities such as accounts payable and short-term loans.

3.2.4 *Intangible assets* are interests held in intangible entities. Examples of intangible property interests include the right to recover a debt and the right to profit from an idea. It is the right, i.e., to recover or to profit, as distinct from the intangible entity itself, i.e., the debt or the idea, which is the property and to which value is ascribed.

3.3 A valuation that includes both personal property and real property must identify the personal property and consider its effects on the value estimate given.

3.3.1 Valuations of personal property may be an element of a larger assignment. The definition of value by which the personal property is valued must be consistent with the purpose of the property valuation, whether that purpose is to sell, to renovate, or to demolish the property. Personal property may be valued according to its *Market Value* under various assumptions, e.g., that the personal property is included among the assets of a hotel that was sold as a going concern, or that the personal property was among the assets of a hotel, which went out of business, and consequently were to be liquidated or sold for salvage. (See IVS 2, para. 6.9.)

3.3.2 A Valuer must be able to distinguish personal property from real property and on occasion may be required to exclude it, e.g., in assignments undertaken for government-related functions such as taxation or compulsory acquisition.

3.3.3 In a valuation of business assets, the Valuer must consider whether such assets are to be valued as part of a going concern or as separate assets.

3.4 A Valuer should be familiar with local custom regarding whether an item is considered personal property or real property. In certain circumstances, a securely affixed item, nominally treated as personal property, may revert to real property upon termination of occupancy, especially if its removal and relocation would result in costly damage to the item itself or the building in which it is located.

3.5 The techniques used in the three valuation approaches may be applied to the valuation of personal property. (See GN 5, Valuation of Personal Property.)

3.5.1 If a Valuer finds that personal property included in the property subject to valuation is either superior or inferior to that typically found in comparable properties, the Valuer should make allowance for the differing contributory value of the personal property.

3.5.2 In certain assignments, a Valuer may have to determine the degree of physical deterioration, functional obsolescence, and external obsolescence afflicting items of personal property. Such a determination will also consider the remaining economic life of the building(s) with which the related personal property is associated.

4.0 Businesses

4.1 A *business* is any commercial, industrial, service or investment entity pursuing an economic activity. Businesses are generally profit-making entities operating to provide consumers with products or services. Closely related to the concept of business entity are the terms *operating company,* which is a business that performs an economic activity by making, selling, or trading a product or service, and *going concern,* which is an entity normally viewed as continuing in operation in the foreseeable future with neither the intention nor necessity of liquidation or of curtailing materially the scale of its operations.

4.2 Business entities are constituted as legal entities. A business may be unincorporated or incorporated.

4.2.1 Examples of unincorporated entities include sole proprietorships, joint ventures, and general and limited partnerships.

4.2.2 Examples of incorporated entities include closely-held corporations, or close companies, and publicly-held corporations, or public companies whose stock is available to and held by the public.

4.2.3 Other legal forms of business entities include *trust arrangements* whereby control is vested in either individual trustees or corporate trustees, and *multiple entities* combining parent and associate or subsidiary corporations, partnership interests, and trusteeships.

4.3 Business entities cut across an extremely broad range of economic activities, encompassing both private and public sectors. Business activities include *manufacturing, wholesaling, retailing, lodging, health care,* and *financial, legal, educational and social services,* among others. Business entities established to provide infrastructure services to the public, i.e., public utilities, are in many States set up as corporations controlled but not owned by the government.

4.3.1 *Investment businesses* or *holding companies,* which maintain the controlling interest in subsidiary companies by virtue of ownership of stock in those companies, include property and agricultural businesses, among others.

4.3.2 Properties such as hotels; fuel stations; restaurants; and movie theatres, or cinemas, variously called *properties associated with a business entity, properties with trading potential, trade related properties* or *operational entities,* are valued at *Market Value,* but their *Market Value* includes value components constituting land, buildings, personal property, intangible assets, and the business itself. Because these properties are commonly sold in the market as an operating package, separate identification of land, building, and other values may be difficult, so additional care should be taken to identify the property components included in the valuation. (See GN 12, Valuation of Trade Related Property.)

4.4 Under the terminology of accounting, both tangible and intangible assets are included among the assets of a business entity:

4.4.1 Tangible assets include current assets, and long-term assets such as realty, fixtures, equipment, and tangible personal property.

4.4.2 Intangible assets, which are considered intangible personal property, include management skill, marketing know-how, credit rating, an assembled work force, an operational plant, goodwill, and ownership of various legal rights and instruments (e.g., patents, copyrights, franchises, and contracts).

4.4.2.1 Goodwill may include two distinct components: goodwill that is property-specific, or inherent within the property and transferable to a new owner on sale of the property, and personal goodwill that is associated with the proprietor or manager.

4.5 The valuation of businesses (see the Guidance Note on Business Valuation, GN 6, para. 5.0) is undertaken for a variety of purposes including:

4.5.1 the acquisition and disposition of an individual business, a business merger, or the estimation of the value of the capital stock owned by the shareholders in the business.

4.5.2 Business valuations are often used as a basis for allocating and reflecting the *Value in Use* of the various assets of a business. Business valuations may also provide the basis for estimating the extent of obsolescence of specified fixed assets of a business.

4.6 Business valuations may be based on the *Market Value* of the business entity. The *Market Value* of a business is not necessarily equivalent to the *Value in Use* of the business. Valuations done for financial reporting are generally required to report *Fair Value,* which may or may not be equivalent to *Market Value*. In such situations, a Valuer should indicate whether the value satisfies or does not satisfy both *Market Value* and *Fair Value* definitions (see Concepts Fundamental to Generally Accepted Valuation Principles, para. 8.1). Valuations of going concerns (defined in Property Types, para. 4.1) are generally based on *Value in Use*. For financial reporting purposes, *Value in Use* has a specific meaning under International Accounting Standard 36, Impairment of Assets, which distinguishes the term from its common usage in valuation practice.

4.7 A Valuer must clearly define the business (e.g., operating company, holding company, trading company), business ownership interest, or security (e.g., closely held or publicly held company stock, and investment trust shares) being valued.

4.7.1 An ownership interest may be undivided, divided among shareholders, and/or involve a majority interest and minority interest.

4.7.2 A Valuer must consider the rights, privileges and conditions that attach to the ownership interest, whether held in corporate form, partnership form, or as a proprietorship.

4.8 Business valuations employ three approaches to value. Valuers commonly reconcile the indications derived from two or more of these approaches and associated methods. (See the Guidance Note on Business Valuation, GN 6, para. 5.14.)

5.0 Financial Interests

5.1 Financial interests in property result from the legal division of ownership interests in businesses and real property (e.g., partnerships, syndications, corporations, cotenancies, joint ventures), from the contractual grant of an optional right to buy or sell property (e.g., realty, stocks, or other financial instruments) at a stated price within a specified period, or from the creation of investment instruments secured by pooled real estate assets.

5.1.1 Ownership interests may be legally divided to create partnerships, in which two or more persons jointly own a business or property and share in its profits and losses.

5.1.1.1 A *general partnership* is an ownership arrangement in which all partners share in investment gains and losses and each is fully responsible for all liabilities.

5.1.1.2 A *limited partnership* is an ownership arrangement consisting of general and limited partners; the general partners manage the business and assume full liability for partnership debt while the limited partners are passive and liable only to the extent of their own capital contributions.

5.1.2 Other legal entities related to partnerships are syndications and joint ventures.

5.1.2.1 A *syndication* is often organised by a general partner. Investors in the syndication become limited partners. A syndication pools funds for the acquisition and development of real estate projects or other business ventures.

5.1.2.2 A *joint venture* is a combination of two or more entities that join to undertake a specific project. A joint venture differs from a partnership in that it is limited in duration and project-specific.

5.1.3 An *option* is an agreement to keep open an offer to buy, sell, or lease real property for a specified period and at a stated price. An option creates a contractual right, the exercise of which is generally contingent upon the fulfillment of specified conditions. The holder may or may not ultimately choose to exercise the option. In this respect, an option differs from a contract to buy or sell a property. *Purchase options* may also be written into leases. Purchase options often contain the provision that certain parts of all rents paid may be applied to the purchase price.

5.1.4 Real estate investment through the ownership of *securities*, or instruments securing both debt and equity positions, represents an alternative to the direct ownership of property. Investors are able to own and trade shares of an interest in a property or pool of properties in the same way they would buy and sell shares of corporate stock.

5.1.4.1 The market for such securities includes both a private, or institutional, sector (partnerships, corporations, pension/superannuation funds, and insurance companies) and a public sector (individual investors who trade in a securities market).

5.1.4.2 Securitised investment instruments include real estate investment trusts (REITs) (property investment or unit trusts), collateralised mortgage obligations (CMOs), commercial mortgage-backed securities (CMBSs), real estate operating companies (REOCs), and separate and commingled accounts. (Such instruments are discussed in the IVSC White Paper, Valuation of Real Estate Serving as Collateral for Securitised Instruments.)

5.2 Financial interests are intangible assets and can include:

5.2.1 the rights inherent in the ownership of a business or property, i.e., to use, to occupy, to sell, to lease, or to manage;

5.2.2 the rights inherent within a contract granting an option to buy, or a lease containing a purchase option, i.e., to exercise or not to exercise; or

5.2.3 the rights inherent in ownership of a security issue (i.e., to hold or to dispose thereof).

5.3 Financial interests require valuation for a wide variety of reasons.

5.3.1 A financial interest may be included among the assets of a partner. To establish the total value of assets owned by the partner, the value of the financial interest must be determined. Or a partner may wish to sell his or her interest, or the interest may have passed into an estate subject to inheritance taxes and probate proceedings. A general partner may also purchase interests for the purpose of transferring them to a limited partnership.

5.3.2 Options to buy, which are often obtainable for a small amount of money, create considerable leverage, or gearing, the impact of which must be considered in the final transaction price. Lease purchase options restrict the marketability of the leased property, and may limit the *Market Value* of the leased property and/or leasehold interest.

5.3.3 Valuations of securitised investment instruments are done for purposes of underwriting and rating the securities prior to initial public offerings.

5.4 International Accounting Standard, IAS 32, Financial Instruments: Disclosures and Presentation, para. 11, defines *financial asset, financial liability, financial instrument,* and *equity instrument;* IAS 32, para. 28, defines *compound (financial) instrument.* Under IAS 32, para. 86, an entity shall disclose information about *Fair Value* for each class of financial assets and financial liabilities, in a way that permits comparison with the corresponding carrying amount in the balance sheet. IAS 32, para. 92, summarises the items an entity is required to disclose.

5.4.1 A *financial asset* is any asset that is a) cash; b) an equity instrument of another entity; c) a contractual right: (i) to receive cash or another financial asset from another entity; or (ii) to exchange financial instruments with another entity under conditions that are potentially favorable; or d) a contract that will or may be settled in the entity's own equity instruments and is: (i) a non-derivative for which the entity is or may be obliged to receive a variable number of the entity's own equity instruments; or (ii) a derivative that will or may be settled other than by the exchange of a fixed amount of cash or another financial asset for a fixed number of the entity's own equity instruments.

5.4.1.1 Common examples of financial assets representing a contractual right to receive cash in the future are a) trade accounts receivable and payable; b) notes receivable and payable; c) loans receivable and payable; and d) bonds receivable and payable.

5.4.2 A *financial liability* is any liability that is: (a) a contractual obligation (i) to deliver cash or another financial asset to another entity; or (ii) to exchange financial assets or financial liabilities with another entity under conditions that are potentially unfavourable to the entity; or (b) a contract that will or may be settled in the entity's own equity instruments and is: (i) a non-derivative for which the entity is or may be obliged to deliver a variable number of the entity's own equity instruments; or (ii) a derivative that will or may be settled other than by the exchange of a fixed amount of cash or another financial asset for a fixed number of the entity's own equity instruments. For this purpose the entity's own equity instruments do not include instruments that are themselves contracts for the future receipt or delivery of the entity's own equity instruments. (An entity may have a contractual obligation that it can settle by delivery of cash or another financial asset, exchange of financial assets and liabilities, or by payment in the form of its own equity instruments, either non-derivative or derivative.)

5.4.2.1 Common examples of financial liabilities representing a contractual obligation to deliver cash in the future are a) trade accounts receivable and payable; b) notes receivable and payable; c) loans receivable and payable; and d) bonds receivable and payable.

5.4.3 A *financial instrument* is any contract that gives rise to both a financial asset of one entity and a financial liability or equity instrument of another entity. Financial instruments range from traditional primary instruments such as bonds to various forms of derivative financial instruments:

5.4.3.1 Derivative financial instruments give one party a contractual right to exchange financial assets with another party under conditions that are potentially favorable, or a contractual obligation to exchange financial assets with another party under conditions that are potentially unfavorable. However, they generally do not result in a transfer of the underlying primary financial instrument on inception of the contract, nor does such a transfer necessarily take place on maturity of the contract. (IAS 32, AG 16)

5.4.3.2 Derivative financial instruments create rights and obligations, effectively transferring between the parties to the instrument one or more of the financial risks inherent in an underlying financial instrument. (IAS 32, AG 16)

5.4.3.3 Many other types of derivative financial instruments embody a right or obligation to make a future exchange, including interest rate and currency swaps, interest rate caps, collars and floors, loan commitments, note issuance facilities, and letters of credit. (IAS 32, AG 19)

5.4.3.4 A *finance lease* is regarded as a financial instrument but an operating lease is not regarded as a financial instrument (IAS 32, AG 9).

5.4.4 An *equity instrument* is any contract that evidences a residual interest in the assets of an entity after deducting all its liabilities.

5.4.4.1 Examples of equity instruments include non-puttable ordinary shares, some types of preference shares, and warrants or written call options that allow the holder to subscribe for or purchase a fixed number of non-puttable ordinary shares in the issuing entity in exchange for a fixed amount of cash or another financial asset (IAS 32, AG 13).

5.4.4.2 A purchased call option or other similar contract acquired by an entity that gives it the right to reacquire a fixed number of its own equity instruments in exchange for delivering a fixed amount of cash or another financial asset is not a financial asset of the entity (IAS 32, AG 14).

5.4.5 A *compound (financial) instrument* is a financial instrument that, from the issuer's perspective, contains both a liability and an equity element.

5.5 The value of the assemblage of all the various financial interests in a property may be larger or smaller than simply the sum of the individual interests in that property.

5.5.1 The value of the 100% ownership interest (inclusive of all shareholders or partners) in income-generating properties held by partnerships or syndications will likely exceed the aggregate value of minority interests in the properties. Similarly, the value of a REIT portfolio, representing an assemblage of various properties, is likely to differ from simply the sum of the values of all the properties that make up the portfolio, a consequence attributable to the specific assemblage of properties in the portfolio and/or the management of the portfolio.

5.5.2 A Valuer estimates the value of the entirety or whole interest in the property before dealing with the disaggregated or fragmented ownership interests.

5.5.3 In assignments involving financial interests, a Valuer must clearly identify the exact ownership interest being valued, whether it be a majority or minority ownership interest in a business or property, a contractual right, or a majority or minority ownership interest in securitised real estate investment. The Valuer must examine the contractual arrangements between parties or articles of association (articles of incorporation or articles of partnership) to verify the percentage share or stake that the financial interest in the property represents.

5.6 The valuation of financial interests involves highly specialised considerations. Therefore, a Valuer must adapt the valuation approach or approaches to the nature of the financial interest subject to valuation.

5.6.1 All three approaches may be appropriate to the valuation of property held by general partnerships.

5.6.1.1 When comparable sales are analysed in the *sales comparison approach,* the Valuer determines whether non-realty items were included in the purchase price. If non-realty items were included, they should be identified and their effect on value considered and estimated.

5.6.2 In situations where a general partner has acquired interests in partnership or syndications for sale as limited partnership interests, the Valuer considers the effect of non-realty items on the transaction price. These items may include special financing, guarantees of occupancy or income, and management services.

5.6.3 Options to buy are considered at the cost to the buyer when the option is exercised. Thus, the cost of an option to buy that has been exercised is to be added to the sale price of the realty. A Valuer considers the effect of leverage, or gearing, produced by a purchase option on the final transaction price for a property. When a purchase option in a lease is exercised and past rent payments are credited to the purchase price, such payments are treated as installment payments.

5.6.4 Units or shares in securitised real estate investment are priced in markets where such securities are traded. Valuations of real estate assets held as part of a package of investment instruments may be required for underwriting or rating purposes prior to an initial public offering. In such situations, a Valuer applies those approaches and methods consistent with the income-generating characteristics of the real estate.

Introduction to International Valuation Standards 1, 2, and 3

International Valuation Standards Committee

Introduction to International Valuation Standards 1, 2, and 3

Developing and Communicating the Valuation

Valuations are developed on the basis of the *Market Value* of an asset or on bases other than *Market Value*. Central to all valuations are the concepts of market, price, cost and value. These concepts are relevant both to valuations based on *Market Value* and those based on non-market criteria. Of equal importance to the work of Valuers is clear communication of the results of the valuation and an understanding of how those results have been obtained. A well prepared Valuation Report fulfills these functions. It is only appropriate, therefore, that the International Valuation Standards should address each of these three fundamental aspects of valuation: IVS 1, Market Value Basis of Valuation; IVS 2, Bases Other Than Market Value; and IVS 3, Valuation Reporting.

Bases of Value

1.0 Introduction

At the most fundamental level, value is created and sustained by the inter-relationship of four factors that are associated with any product, service, or commodity. These are *utility, scarcity, desire,* and *purchasing power.*

1.1 The working of the economic principle of supply and demand reflects the complex interaction of the four factors of value. The supply of a good or service is affected by its utility and desirability. The availability of the good or service is limited by its scarcity and effective checks on the purchasing power of likely consumers. The demand for a good or service is, likewise, created by its utility, influenced by its scarcity and desirability and restrained by limits on purchasing power.

1.2 The utility for which a good or service is produced and the scarcity, or limited availability, of the good or service are generally considered *supply-related* factors. Consumer preferences and purchasing power, which reflect desire for the good or service and define the affordability of the item, are generally considered *demand-related* factors.

2.0 Markets

A *market* is an environment in which goods, services, and commodities are traded between buyers and sellers through a price mechanism. The concept of a market implies the ability of buyers and sellers to carry on their activities without restriction.

2.1 The *principle of supply* and demand states that the price of a good, service, or commodity varies inversely with the supply of the item and directly with the demand for the item.

2.2 In property markets, *supply* represents the quantity of property interests that are available for sale or lease at various prices in a given market within a given period of time, assuming labour and production costs remain constant.

2.3 *Demand* constitutes the number of possible buyers or renters seeking specific types of property interests at various prices in a given market within a given period of time, assuming other factors such as population, income, future prices, and consumer preferences remain constant.

Supply and Demand Curve

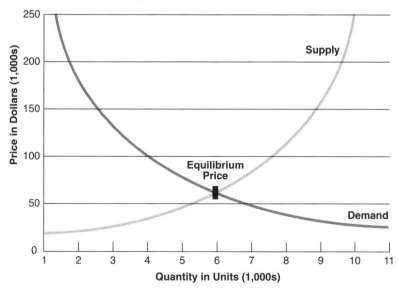

3.0 Price, Cost, and Value

The distinctions between price, cost, and value have previously been discussed. (See section 4.0 of Concepts Fundamental to Generally Accepted Valuation Principles.) These terminological distinctions are important to the operation of markets because of the specific functional relationship each describes, i.e., price pertains to the actual exchange of the good or service; cost reflects the expense of producing the good or service; value represents the price most likely to be concluded by the buyers and sellers of a good or service that is available for purchase.

3.1 *Price* is a concept that relates to the exchange of a commodity, good, or service. Price is the amount that has been asked, offered, or paid for the item. Once the exchange has been transacted, the price, whether disclosed or undisclosed, becomes an historic fact. The price paid represents the intersection of supply and demand.

3.2 *Cost* is a production-related concept, distinct from exchange, which is defined as the amount of money required to create or produce a commodity, good, or service. Once the good is completed or the service is rendered, its cost becomes an historic fact.

3.3 The concept of *Value* addresses the price most likely to be concluded by the buyers and sellers of a good or service available for purchase. Value establishes the hypothetical, or notional, price that typically motivated buyers and sellers are most likely to conclude for the good or service. Thus, value is not a fact, but an estimate of the most likely price that will be paid for a good or service available for purchase at a given time.

3.4 A *Basis of Value* describes the nature of this hypothetical transaction, for example, whether or not it takes place in a public market and what accounts for the motivation and behaviour of the parties. It does not describe the status of the good or service involved in the transaction, for example, whether it is operational or non-operational, or whether or not it is aggregated with other assets. A *Basis of Valuation* will, therefore, usually need to be accompanied by additional assumptions in order to adequately define the valuation hypothesis adopted. Different accompanying assumptions may result in different values for the same asset, and therefore, it is vital that these be clearly understood and expressed.

4.0 Bases of Value

The concept of *Market Value* is tied to the collective perceptions and behaviour of market participants. It recognises diverse factors that may influence transactions in a market, and distinguishes these from other intrinsic or non-market considerations affecting value. *Market Value* is market-based and therefore, all inputs should be developed from market data.

4.1 Market-based valuations of property assume the operation of a market in which transactions occur without restriction by non-market forces.

4.1.1 Market-based valuations must determine the *highest and best use,* or most probable use, of the property asset, which is a significant determinant of its value.

4.1.2 Market-based valuations are developed from data specific to the appropriate market(s) and through methods and procedures that try to reflect the deductive processes of participants in those markets.

4.1.3 Market-based valuations may be performed by application of the *sales comparison, income capitalisation,* and *cost approaches* to value. The data and criteria employed in each of these approaches must be derived from the market.

4.2 Besides the hypothetical exchange value concluded by two typically motivated market participants, valuations of property may also use measurement principles that consider alternative economic utility or function(s) of an asset, value attributable to unusual or atypical motivation on the part of the parties to a transaction, or value specified by statutory or contractual law.

4.2.1 Examples of bases of value other than *Market Value* are Fair Value, Investment Value, Special Value, and Synergistic Value. The additional assumptions required in applying these bases are often more specific than those required for establishing *Market Value* as they may relate to the circumstances of a particular party. For this reason, a valuation reported on one of these bases should ensure that it cannot be construed as *Market Value*.

4.2.2 Valuations performed on bases other than *Market Value* must employ appropriate procedures and analyse sufficient data to produce a reasonable estimate of value.

5.0 Communicating the Results of the Valuation

5.1 The content and presentation of the Valuation Report are of critical importance to

5.1.1 communicating the value conclusion to the client and user(s) of the valuation, and

5.1.2 confirming the basis of the valuation, the purpose of the valuation, and any assumptions or limiting conditions underlying the valuation.

5.2 To help guide the reader through the procedures and evidence used by the Valuer in developing the valuation, the Valuation Report may also provide the analytical processes and empirical data used to arrive at the value conclusion.

5.3 Other essential information contained in the Valuation Report includes

5.3.1 the name of the Valuer and the date as of which the value estimate applies,

5.3.2 the property and property rights or interests subject to the valuation,

5.3.3 the dates of the valuation and the valuation report,

5.3.4 the extent of the inspection,

5.3.5 the applicability of these Standards and any required disclosures.

IVS 1 – Market Value Basis of Valuation

International Valuation Standards Committee

Standard 1
International Valuation Standards

Market Value Basis of Valuation

This Standard should be read in the context of the background material and implementation guidance contained in General Valuation Concepts and Principles.

1.0 Introduction

1.1 The objective of this Standard is to provide a common definition of *Market Value*. This Standard also explains the general criteria relating to this definition and to its application in the valuation of property when the purpose and intended use of the valuation calls for estimation of *Market Value*.

1.2 *Market Value* is a representation of value in exchange, or the amount a property would bring if offered for sale in the (open) market at the date of valuation under circumstances that meet the requirements of the *Market Value* definition. To estimate *Market Value,* a Valuer must first determine highest and best use, or most probable use. (See International Valuation Standards [IVSs], Concepts Fundamental to Generally Accepted Valuation Principles, paras. 6.3, 6.4, 6.5.) That use may be for continuation of a property's existing use or for some alternative use. These determinations are made from market evidence.

1.3 *Market Value* is estimated through application of valuation methods and procedures that reflect the nature of property and the circumstances under which given property would most likely trade in the market. The most common methods used to estimate *Market Value include the sales comparison approach, the income capitalisation approach,* including *discounted cash flow analysis, and the cost approach.*

1.4 All *Market Value* measurement methods, techniques, and procedures will, if applicable and if appropriately and correctly applied, lead to a common expression of *Market Value* when based on market-derived criteria. Sales comparisons or other market comparisons should evolve from market observations.

The *income capitalisation approach,* including *discounted cash flow analysis,* should be based on market-determined cash flows and market-derived rates of return. Construction costs and depreciation should be determined by reference to an analysis of market-based estimates of costs and accumulated depreciation. Although data availability and circumstances relating to the market or the property itself will determine which valuation methods are most relevant and appropriate, the outcome of using any of the foregoing procedures must be *Market Value* if each method is based on market-derived data.

1.5 The manner in which property would ordinarily trade in the market distinguishes the applicability of the various methods or procedures of estimating *Market Value.* When based on market information, each method is a comparative method. In each valuation situation one or more methods are generally most representative of (open) market activities. The Valuer will consider each method in every *Market Value* engagement and will determine which methods are most appropriate.

2.0 Scope

2.1 IVS 1 applies to the *Market Value* of property, normally real estate and related elements. It requires that the property under consideration be viewed as if for sale on the market, in contrast to being evaluated for some other purpose.

3.0 Definitions

3.1 *Market Value* is defined for the purpose of these Standards as follows:

Market Value is the estimated amount for which a property should exchange on the date of valuation between a willing buyer and a willing seller in an arm's-length transaction after proper marketing wherein the parties had each acted knowledgeably, prudently, and without compulsion.

3.2 The term *property* is used because the focus of these Standards is the valuation of property. Because these Standards encompass financial reporting, the term asset may be substituted for general application of the definition. Each element of the definition has its own conceptual framework:

3.2.1 *"The estimated amount..."* refers to a price expressed in terms of money (normally in the local currency), payable for the property in an arm's-length market transaction. *Market Value* is measured as the most probable price reasonably obtainable in the market on the date of valuation in keeping with the *Market Value* definition. It is the best price reasonably obtainable by the seller and the most advantageous price reasonably obtainable by the buyer. This estimate specifically excludes an estimated price inflated or deflated by special terms or circumstances such as atypical financing, sale and leaseback arrangements, special considerations or concessions granted by anyone associated with the sale, or any element of Special Value (defined in IVSC Standard 2, para. 3.5).

3.2.2 *"...a property should exchange..."* refers to the fact that the value of a property is an estimated amount rather than a predetermined amount or actual sale price. It is the price at which the market expects a transaction that meets all other elements of the *Market Value* definition should be completed on the date of valuation.

3.2.3 *"...on the date of valuation..."* requires that the estimated *Market Value* is time-specific as of a given date. Because markets and market conditions may change, the estimated value may be incorrect or inappropriate at another time. The valuation amount will reflect the actual market state and circumstances as of the effective valuation date, not as of either a past or future date. The definition also assumes simultaneous exchange and completion of the contract for sale without any variation in price that might otherwise be made.

3.2.4 *"...between a willing buyer..."* refers to one who is motivated, but not compelled to buy. This buyer is neither over-eager nor determined to buy at any price. This buyer is also one who purchases in accordance with the realities of the current market and with current market expectations, rather than in relation to an imaginary or hypothetical market that cannot be demonstrated or anticipated to exist. The assumed buyer would not pay a higher price than the market requires. The present property owner is included among those who constitute "the market." A Valuer must not make unrealistic assumptions about market conditions nor assume a level of market value above that which is reasonably obtainable.

3.2.5 *"...a willing seller..."* is neither an over-eager nor a forced seller, prepared to sell at any price, nor one prepared to hold out for a price not considered reasonable in the current market. The willing seller is motivated to sell the property at market terms for the best price attainable in the (open) market after proper marketing, whatever that price may be. The factual circumstances of the actual property owner are not a part of this consideration because the 'willing seller' is a hypothetical owner.

3.2.6 *"...in an arm's-length transaction..."* is one between parties who do not have a particular or special relationship (for example, parent and subsidiary companies or landlord and tenant) that may make the price level uncharacteristic of the market or inflated because of an element of Special Value. (See IVS 2, para. 3.8.) The *Market Value* transaction is presumed to be between unrelated parties, each acting independently.

3.2.7 *"...after proper marketing..."* means that the property would be exposed to the market in the most appropriate manner to effect its disposal at the best price reasonably obtainable in accordance with the *Market Value* definition. The length of exposure time may vary with market conditions, but must be sufficient to allow the property to be brought to the attention of an adequate number of potential purchasers. The exposure period occurs prior to the valuation date.

3.2.8 *"...wherein the parties had each acted knowledgeably and prudently..."* presumes that both the willing buyer and the willing seller are reasonably informed about the nature and characteristics of the property, its actual and potential uses, and the state of the market as of the date of valuation. Each is further presumed to act for self-interest with that knowledge, and prudently to seek the best price for their respective positions in the transaction. Prudence is assessed by referring to the state of the market at the date of valuation, not with benefit of hindsight at some later date. It is not necessarily imprudent for a seller to sell property in a market with falling prices at a price that is lower than previous market levels. In such cases, as is true for other purchase and sale situations in markets with changing prices, the prudent buyer or seller will act in accordance with the best market information available at the time.

3.2.9 *"...and without compulsion..."* establishes that each party is motivated to undertake the transaction, but neither is forced or unduly coerced to complete it.

3.3 *Market Value* is understood as the value of an asset estimated without regard to costs of sale or purchase and without offset for any associated taxes.

3.4 *Highest and Best Use* (HABU). The most probable use of a property, which is physically possible, appropriately justified, legally permissible, financially feasible, and which results in the highest value of the property being valued.

4.0 Relationship to Accounting Standards

4.1 Valuation for financial reporting, which is the focus of International Valuation Application 1 (IVA 1), should be read in conjunction with this standard.

4.1.1 IVA 1, Valuation for Financial Reporting, provides guidance to Valuers, Accountants, and the Public regarding valuation standards affecting accountancy. The *Fair Value* of fixed assets is usually their Market Value. (See Concepts Fundamental to Generally Accepted Valuation Principles, para. 8.1.)

4.2 There are numerous examples of terms used interchangeably by Valuers and Accountants. Some lead to misunderstandings and possible Standards abuses. IVS 1 defines *Market Value* and discusses criteria for establishing *Market Value*. Other important terms are defined in IVSs 1 and 2 and contribute to the more specific requirements discussed in IVA 1, Valuation for Financial Reporting.

5.0 Statement of Standard

To perform valuations that comply with these Standards and Generally Accepted Valuation Principles (GAVP), it is mandatory that Valuers adhere to all sections of the Code of Conduct pertaining to Ethics, Competence, Disclosure, and Reporting (sections 4, 5, 6, and 7).

5.1 In performing and reporting a *Market Value* estimate, the Valuer shall

5.1.1 completely and understandably set forth the valuation in a manner that will not be misleading;

5.1.2 ensure that the estimate of *Market Value* is based on market-derived data;

5.1.3 ensure that the estimate of *Market Value* is undertaken using appropriate methods and techniques;

5.1.4 provide sufficient information to permit those who read and rely on the report to fully understand its data, reasoning, analyses, and conclusions; and

5.1.5 comply with the requirements of IVS 3 in reporting the valuation. Accordingly, the Valuer shall

5.1.5.1 define the value being estimated and state the purpose and intended use of the valuation, the effective date of valuation, and the date of the report;

5.1.5.2 clearly identify and describe the property and property rights or interests being valued;

5.1.5.3 describe the scope/extent of the work undertaken and the extent to which the property was inspected;

5.1.5.4 state any assumptions and limiting conditions upon which the valuation is based;

5.1.5.5 fully and completely explain the valuation bases/approaches applied and the reasons for their applications and conclusions; and

5.1.5.6 include a signed Compliance Statement attesting to the Valuer's objectivity, professional contributions, non-bias, non-contingency of professional fees or other compensation, as well as Standards' applicability, and other disclosures.

6.0 Discussion

6.1 The *Market Value* concept and definition are fundamental to all valuation practice. A brief summary of essential economic and procedural foundations is presented in Concepts Fundamental to Generally Accepted Valuaton Principles and Code of Conduct, the documents upon which these Standards are predicated.

6.2 The concept of *Market Value* is not dependent on an actual transaction taking place on the date of valuation. Rather, *Market Value* is an estimate of the price that should be realised in a sale at the valuation date under conditions of the Market Value definition. *Market Value* is a representation of the price to which a buyer and seller would agree at that time under the Market Value definition, each previously having had time for investigation of other market opportunities and alternatives, and notwithstanding the fact that it may take some time to prepare formal contracts and related closing documentation.

6.3 The concept of *Market Value* presumes a price negotiated in an open and competitive market, a circumstance that occasionally gives rise to the use of the adjective *open* before the words *Market Value*. The words *open* and *competitive* have no absolute meaning. The market for one property could be an international market or a local market. The market could consist of numerous buyers and sellers, or could be one characterised by a limited number of participants. The market in which the property is exposed for sale is not a definitionally restrictive or constricted market. Stated conversely, the omission of the word *open* does not indicate that a transaction would be private or closed.

6.4 Market valuations are generally based on information regarding comparable properties. The Valuation Process requires a Valuer to conduct adequate and relevant research, to perform competent analyses, and to draw informed and supportable judgements. In this process, Valuers do not accept data without question but should consider all pertinent market evidence, trends, comparable transactions, and other information. Where market data are limited, or essentially non-existent (as for example with certain specialised properties), the Valuer must make proper disclosure of the situation and must state whether the estimate is in any way limited by the inadequacy of data. All valuations require exercise of a Valuer's judgment, but reports should disclose whether the Valuer bases the *Market Value* estimate on market evidence, or whether the estimate is more heavily based upon the Valuer's judgement because of the nature of the property and lack of comparable market data.

6.5 Because changing conditions are characteristic of markets, Valuers must consider whether available data reflect and meet the criteria for *Market Value*.

6.5.1 Periods of rapid changes in market condition are typified by rapidly changing prices, a condition commonly referred to as *disequilibrium*. A period of disequilibrium may continue over a period of years and can constitute the current and expected future market condition. In other circumstances, rapid economic change may give rise to erratic market data. If some sales are out of line with the market, the Valuer will generally give them less weight. It may still be possible for the Valuer to judge from available data where the realistic level of the market is. Individual transaction prices may not be evidence of *Market Value,* but analysis of such market data should be taken into consideration in the Valuation Process.

6.5.2 In poor or falling markets there may or may not be a large number of "willing sellers." Some, but not necessarily all, transactions may involve elements of financial (or other) duress or conditions that reduce or eliminate the practical willingness of certain owners to sell. Valuers must take into account all pertinent factors in such market conditions and attach such weight to individual transactions that they believe proper to reflect the market. Liquidators and receivers are normally under a duty to obtain the best price in asset disposals. Sales, however, may take place without proper marketing or a reasonable marketing period. The Valuer must judge such transactions to determine the degree to which they meet the requirements of the *Market Value* definition and the weight that such data should be given.

6.5.3 During periods of market transition characterised by rapidly rising or falling prices, there is a risk of over- or under-valuation if undue weight is given to historic information or if unwarranted assumptions are made regarding future markets. In these circumstances Valuers must carefully analyse and reflect the actions and attitudes of the market and take care that they fully disclose the results of their investigations and findings in their reports.

6.6 The concept of *Market Value* also presumes that in a market value transaction a property will be freely and adequately exposed on the (open) market for a reasonable period of time and with reasonable publicity. This exposure is presumed to occur prior to the effective date of value. Markets for fixed assets typically differ from those available for stocks/shares, bonds, and other current assets. Fixed assets tend to be unique. They are usually sold less frequently and in markets which are less formal and more inefficient than, for example, markets for listed securities. Further, fixed assets are less liquid. For these reasons, and because fixed assets do not commonly trade on a public exchange, the application of the concept of *Market Value* requires the use of assumptions such as adequate market exposure over a reasonable time period to allow for proper marketing, and completion of negotiations.

6.7 Revenue producing properties held as long-term investments by a property company, pension (or superannuation fund), property trust, or similar type of owner are typically valued on the basis of individual asset disposal pursuant to an orderly plan. The aggregate value of such assets viewed or treated as a portfolio or as an assembled group of properties could exceed or could be less than the sum of the *Market Value* of each asset individually.

6.8 All valuations should refer to the purpose and intended use of the valuation. In addition to other reporting requirements, the Valuer should make it abundantly clear into which class each asset has been placed if the function of the valuation is related to the preparation of financial statements.

6.9 In exceptional circumstances *Market Value* may be expressed as a negative amount. Situations include certain leasehold properties, some specialised properties, obsolete properties with demolition costs exceeding land value, some properties affected by environmental contamination, and others.

7.0 Disclosure Requirements

7.1 Valuation Reports must not be misleading. Valuations conducted for the purpose of estimating and reporting *Market Value* shall meet the requirements of section 5 above. Reports shall contain a specific reference to the definition of *Market Value* as set forth in this Standard, together with specific reference as to how the property has been viewed in terms of its utility or its *highest and best use* (or most probable use) and a statement of all substantive assumptions.

7.2 In making *Market Value* estimates the Valuer shall clearly identify the effective date of valuation (the date at which the value estimate applies), the purpose and intended use of the valuation, and such other criteria as are relevant and appropriate to ensure adequate and reasonable interpretation of the Valuer's findings, opinions, and conclusions.

7.3 Although the concept, use, and application of alternative expressions of value may be appropriate in certain circumstances, the Valuer shall ensure that if such alternative values are estimated and reported, they should not be construed as representing *Market Value*.

7.4 When valuations are made by an Internal Valuer, i.e., one who is in the employ of either the entity that owns the assets or the accounting firm

responsible for preparing the entity's financial records and/or reports, there shall be a specific disclosure in the Valuation Report or Certificate of the existence and nature of any such relationships.

8.0 Departure Provisions

8.1 In following this Standard any departures must be in accordance with directions provided in IVS 3, Valuation Reporting.

9.0 Effective Date

9.1 This International Valuation Standard became effective 31 July 2007.

IVS 2 –Bases Other Than Market Value.

International Valuation Standards Committee

Standard 2
International Valuation Standards

Bases Other Than Market Value (Revised 2007)

This Standard should be read in the context of the background material and implementation guidance contained in General Accepted Valuation Principles.

1.0 Introduction

1.1 The objectives of International Valuation Standard 2 (IVS 2) are to identify, explain and distinguish bases of value other than *Market Value* and to establish standards for their application.

1.2 *Market Value* is the most appropriate basis of value for a wide range of applications. However, alternative valuation bases may be appropriate in specific circumstances. It is essential that both the Valuer and users of valuations clearly understand the distinction between *Market Value* and these other bases of valuation and the effects (if any) that differences between bases may have on the applicability of the valuation.

1.3 The concept of *Market Value* is based on specific, identified assumptions that are set out in IVS 1. Other bases of valuation require the application of different assumptions, which if not clearly identified, may result in misinterpretation of the valuation.

2.0 Scope

2.1 This Standard defines and discusses the application of valuation bases other than *Market Value* for purposes other than financial reporting.

3.0 Definitions

International Valuation Standards Definitions

3.1 *Basis of Value*. A statement of the fundamental measurement principles of a valuation on a specified date.

3.2 *Fair Value.* The amount for which an asset could be exchanged between knowledgeable, willing parties in an arm's-length transaction.

3.3 *Investment Value, or Worth.* The value of property to a particular investor, or a class of investors, for identified investment or operational objectives. This subjective concept relates specific property to a specific investor, group of investors, or entity with identifiable investment objectives and/or criteria.

3.4 *Special Purchaser.* A purchaser to whom a particular asset has *Special Value* because of advantages arising from its ownership that would not be available to general purchasers in the market.

3.5 *Special Value.* An amount above the *Market Value* that reflects particular attributes of an asset that are only of value to a *Special Purchaser*

3.6 *Synergistic Value.*[1] An additional element of value created by the combination of two or more interests where the value of the combined interest is worth more than the sum of the original interests.

4.0 Relationship to Accounting Standards

4.1 For most purposes, valuations under International Financial Reporting Standards require the use of fair value. This is a specific application of *Fair Value* that may require more restrictive assumptions than are required in general use. International Valuation Application 1, Valuation for Financial Reporting, discusses the specific valuation requirements under accounting standards.

5.0 Statement of Standard

To perform valuations that comply with these Standards and Generally Accepted Valuation Principles (GAVP), it is mandatory that Valuers adhere to all sections of the Code of Conduct pertaining to Ethics, Competence, Disclosure and Reporting (sections 4, 5, 6, and 7).

5.1 When carrying out a valuation under this standard the Valuer shall ensure that

---

1. *Synergistic Value* may also be known as *Marriage Value.*

5.1.1 the estimate of value is based on data and circumstances appropriate to the valuation;

5.1.2 the estimate of value is undertaken using appropriate methods and techniques;

5.1.3 the valuation is developed on the basis of sufficient information to support the analyses and conclusions therein.

5.2 In reporting an estimate of value under this standard the Valuer shall

5.2.1 comply with all the requirements of International Valuation Standard 3, Valuation Reporting. In particular, the Valuer shall report the valuation in a manner that will not be misleading (IVS 3, 5.1.1)

5.2.2 define the basis or bases of value used and state the purpose and intended use of the valuation, the effective date of valuation, and the date of the report (IVS 3, 5.1.2 and 5.1.3);

5.2.3 clearly identify and describe the property and property rights and interests valued and the scope of work undertaken to develop the valuation conclusion (IVS 3, 5.1.4 and 5.1.5);

5.2.4 specify all assumptions and limiting conditions upon which the valuation is based (IVS 3, 5.1.6 and 5.1.7);

5.2.5 clearly distinguish the assumptions that are different from or additional to those underlying an estimate of *Market Value;*

5.2.6 fully explain the valuation approaches and procedures that have been applied and the reasoning that supports the analyses, opinions and conclusions in the report (IVS 3, 5.1.8);

5.2.7 include a statement that the valuation has been performed in accordance with IVSs, disclose any departure from the specific requirements of the IVSs and provide an explanation for such departure. (IVS 3, 5.1.10)

6.0 Discussion

6.1 A *Basis of Valuation* describes the fundamental measurement principles of a valuation. These principles may vary depending on the purpose of the valuation. A *Basis of Valuation* is not a statement of the method used, nor a description of the state of an asset or assets when exchanged. *Market Value* is the most commonly required basis and is defined and discussed in IVS 1. This Standard defines and discusses other valuation bases. These fall into three principal categories:

6.1.1 The first category reflects the benefits that an entity enjoys from ownership of an asset. The value is specific to that entity. Although under some circumstances, it may be the same as the amount that could be realised from sale of the asset, this value essentially reflects the benefits received by holding the asset, and therefore does not necessarily involve a hypothetical exchange. *Investment Value,* or *Worth,* fall into this category. Differences between the value of an asset to a particular entity and the Market Value provide the motivation for buyers or sellers to enter the market place.

6.1.2 The second category represents the price that would be reasonably agreed between two specific parties for the exchange of an asset. Although the parties may be unconnected and negotiating at arm's length, the asset is not necessarily exposed in the wider market and the price agreed may be one that reflects the specific advantages (or disadvantages) of ownership to the parties involved rather than the market at large. This category includes *Fair Value, Special Value and Synergistic Value.*

6.1.3 The third category is value determined in accordance with a definition set out in a statute or a contract.

6.2 The application of *Fair Value* under accounting standards is discussed in IVA 1. In accounting standards, *Fair Value* is normally equated to *Market Value.*

6.3 For other purposes, *Fair Value* can be distinguished from *Market Value. Fair Value* requires the assessment of the price that is fair between two specific parties taking into account the respective advantages or disadvantages that each will gain from the transaction.

6.4 *Fair Value* is a broader concept than *Market Value.* Although in many cases the price that is fair between two parties will equate to that obtainable in the general market, there will be cases where the assessment of *Fair Value* will involve taking into account matters that have to be disregarded in the assessment of *Market Value*.

6.5 A common application of *Fair Value* is for assessing the price that is fair for the shareholding in a business, where particular synergies between two specific parties may mean that the price that is fair between them is different from the price that might be obtainable in the wider market. In contrast, *Market Value* requires any element of *Special Value,* of which *Synergistic Value* is an example, to be disregarded.

6.6 *Special Value* can arise where an asset has attributes that make it more attractive to a particular buyer, or to a limited category of buyers, than to the general body of buyers in a market. These attributes can include the physical, geographic, economic or legal characteristics of an asset. *Market Value* requires the disregard of any element of *Special Value* because at any given date it is only assumed that there is a willing buyer, not a particular willing buyer.

6.7 *Synergistic Value* can be a type of *Special Value* that specifically arises from the combination of two or more assets to create a new asset that has a higher value than the sum of the individual assets.

6.8 When *Special Value* is reported, it should always be clearly distinguished from *Market Value*.

6.9 A *Basis of Valuation* should not be confused with assumptions that may also be required to clarify the application of the basis to a specific situation. Some terms that are often used to describe a valuation are not distinct bases of value as they describe the state of the asset or the circumstances under which it is assumed to be exchanged, rather than the underlying measurement objective. The value may be measured on one of the bases defined in section 3, or on the basis of Market Value, see IVS 1. Examples of such terms that are in common use include:

6.9.1 *Going Concern Value:* This describes a situation where an entire business is transferred as an operational entity. Alternative valuation scenarios to a going concern could include a transfer of all the assets as a whole but following the closure of the business, or a transfer of specific assets currently used in the business as individual items.

6.9.2 *Liquidation Value:* This describes a situation where a group of assets employed together in a business are offered for sale separately, usually following a closure of the business. Although often associated with a forced sale (see 6.11 below), these terms have distinct meanings. There is no reason why assets cannot be liquidated by an orderly sale following proper marketing.

6.9.3 *Salvage Value:* This describes the value of an asset that has reached the end of its economic life for the purpose it was made. The asset may still have value for an alternative use or for recycling.

6.10 Terms such as those in 6.9 should not be used without further qualification. Used alone, they are insufficient as a reporting basis. By way of illustration, a business that is a going concern may have one value to a specific party *(Investment Value),* another value between two specific parties reflecting business synergies *(Fair Value),* and yet another value in the market *(Market Value).* It is therefore necessary to state the underlying valuation basis by the use of expressions such as *"Market Value* as a going concern", *"Market Value* for the liquidation of the assets" or *"Fair Value* as a going concern."

6.11 The term "forced sale" is often used in circumstances where a seller is under compulsion to sell and/or a proper marketing period is not available. The price obtainable in these circumstances will not meet the definition of *Market Value.* The price that could be obtained in these circumstances will depend upon the nature of the pressure on the seller or the reasons why proper marketing cannot be undertaken. It may also reflect the consequences for the seller of failing to sell within a specified period. Unless the nature of, and reason for, the constraints on the vendor are known, the price obtainable in a forced sale cannot realistically be predicted. The price that a seller will accept in a forced sale will reflect its particular circumstances rather than those of the hypothetical willing seller in the *Market Value* definition. The price obtainable in a forced sale will bear only a coincidental relationship to *Market Value,* or any of the other bases defined in this standard. It is not a *Basis of Valuation* as the forced sale is a description of the situation under which the transfer takes place, not a distinct measurement objective.

6.12 The third category of valuation bases comprises those set by statute, regulation or contract. Statutory bases are often prescribed for taxation purposes. Examples of private contracts, prescribing valuation definitions and assumptions, include criteria for setting the price payable under an option or for reviewing the payments made under a lease. The detailed interpretation of both statutory and contract provisions are often subject to precedent, established by court decisions. Although many of the bases defined by statute and contract may appear similar to bases defined in these standards, unless unequivocal reference is made to these standards, their detailed application may require an approach different from that required by these Standards. Further discussion of statutory or contractual valuation bases is outside the scope of International Standards.

6.13 All valuations will involve different assumptions, which must be clearly identified by the Valuer and reported with the valuation. In some situations, it may be appropriate to provide alternative valuations based on alternative assumptions to illustrate the effect of these assumptions.

7.0 Disclosure Requirements

7.1 Valuation Reports must not be misleading. All valuations shall meet the requirements of section 5 above. The Code of Conduct requires that the purpose and intended use of any valuation be clearly reported, and that full disclosure be made of the basis for the valuation estimate, its applicability, and its limitations.

7.2 If a valuation by an Internal Valuer is made, there shall be a specific disclosure in the Valuation Report of the existence and nature of any such relationship. (IVS 3, 7.1).

7.3 If a Valuer is involved in a valuation assignment in a capacity other than as a Valuer, for example, as an independent or impartial agent, as a consultant or advisor to a business entity, or as a mediator, the Valuer should disclose the specific role taken in each assignment. (IVS 3, 7.2)

7.4 The Valuer shall disclose the regulatory framework and any departure required from these Standards to comply with local legislation, regulation (including accounting rules), or custom. (IVS 3, 7.3)

8.0 Departure Provisions

8.1 In following this Standard any departures must be in accordance with directions provided in IVS 3, Valuation Reporting.

9.0 Effective Date

9.1 This International Valuation Standard became effective 31 July 2007.

IVS 3 -Valuation Reporting

International Valuation Standards Committee

Standard 3
International Valuation Standards

Valuation Reporting (Revised 2007)

1.0 Introduction

1.1 The critical importance of a Valuation Report, the final step in the valuation process, lies in communicating the value conclusion and confirming the basis of the valuation, the purpose of the valuation, and any assumptions or limiting conditions underlying the valuation. The analytical processes and empirical data used to arrive at the value conclusion may also be included in the Valuation Report to guide the reader through the procedures and evidence that the Valuer used to develop the valuation.

1.2 The Valuation Report indicates the value conclusion. It contains the name of the Valuer and the date of the valuation. It identifies the property and property rights subject to the valuation, the basis of the valuation, and the intended use of the valuation. It discloses all underlying assumptions and limiting conditions, specifies the dates of valuation and reporting, describes the extent of the inspection, refers to the applicability of these Standards and any required disclosures, and includes the Valuer's signature.

1.3 Because of the key role of the Valuation Report in communicating the conclusion of a valuation to users and third-party readers, this Standard sets forth the following as its principal objectives:

1.3.1 To discuss reporting requirements consistent with professional best practice

1.3.2 To identify essential elements to be included in Valuation Reports

2.0 Scope

2.1 The reporting requirements addressed in this Standard apply to all types of Valuation Reports.

2.2 Compliance with these reporting requirements is incumbent upon both Internal and External Valuers.

2.3 Some instructions involving valuations undertaken for specific purposes and property types, e.g., financial reporting, and lending, may differ from those given for other assignments. The reader is advised to consult those sections of the International Valuation Standards (IVSs) that address these situations, i.e., International Valuation Applications 1 and 2 (IVA 1 and IVA 2).

3.0 Definitions

3.1 *Compliance Statement.* An affirmative statement attesting to the fact that the Valuer has followed the ethical and professional requirements of the IVSC Code of Conduct in performing the assignment.

3.2 *Oral Report.* The results of a valuation, verbally communicated to a client or presented before a court either as expert testimony or by means of deposition. A report communicated orally to a client must be supported by a work file and at a minimum followed up by a written summary of the valuation.

3.3 *Special, unusual, or extraordinary assumptions.* Before completing the acquisition of a property, a prudent purchaser in the market typically exercises due diligence by making customary enquiries about the property. It is normal for a Valuer to make assumptions as to the most likely outcome of this due diligence process and to rely on actual information regarding such matters as provided by the client. *Special, unusual, or extraordinary assumptions* may be any additional assumptions relating to matters covered in the due diligence process, or may relate to other issues, such as the identity of the purchaser, the physical state of the property, the presence of environmental pollutants (e.g., ground water contamination), or the ability to redevelop the property. (See para. 5.1.7 below.)

3.4 *Specifications for the Valuation Assignment.* The first step in the Valuation Process, which establishes the context and scope/extent of the assignment and resolves any ambiguity involving the valuation issue or problem. A Valuer ensures that the analyses, information and conclusions presented in the report fit the specifications for the assignment. The *specifications for the valuation assignment* include the following seven elements:

3.4.1 An identification of the real, personal (plant and machinery; furniture, fixtures, and equipment), business or other property subject to the valuation and other classes of property included in the valuation besides the primary property category;

3.4.2 An identification of the property rights (sole proprietorship, partnership, or partial interest) to be valued;

3.4.3 The intended use of the valuation and any related limitation; and the identification of any subcontractors or agents and their contribution;

3.4.4 A definition of the basis or type of value sought;

3.4.5 The date as of which the value estimate applies and the date of the intended report;

3.4.6 An identification of the scope/extent of the valuation and of the report; and

3.4.7 An identification of any contingent and limiting conditions upon which the valuation is based

3.5 *Valuation Report.* A document that records the instructions for the assignment, the basis and purpose of the valuation, and the results of the analysis that led to the opinion of value. A Valuation Report may also explain the analytical processes undertaken in carrying out the valuation, and present meaningful information used in the analysis. Valuation Reports can be either oral or written. The type, content and length of a report vary according to the intended user, legal requirements, the property type, and the nature and complexity of the assignment.

3.6 *Written Report.* The results of a valuation communicated to a client in writing, which includes electronic communication. Written reports may be detailed narrative documents containing all pertinent materials examined and analyses performed to arrive at a value conclusion or abbreviated pertinent narrative documents, including periodic updates of value, forms used by governmental and other agencies, or letters to clients.

4.0 Relationship to Accounting Standards

4.1 Where applicable, the Valuation Report shall meet or exceed the requirements of the International Financial Reporting Standards (IFRSs)/International Accounting Standards (IASs) and International Public Sector Accounting Standards (IPSASs).

4.2 Valuation for Financial Reporting, which is the focus of IVA 1, should be read in conjunction with this Standard.

5.0 Statement of Standard

To perform valuations that comply with these Standards and Generally Accepted Valuation Principles (GAAP), it is mandatory that Valuers adhere to all sections of the IVSC Code of Conduct pertaining to Ethics, Competence, Disclosure, and Reporting (sections 4, 5, 6, and 7).

5.1 Each Valuation Report shall

5.1.1 clearly and accurately set forth the conclusions of the valuation in a manner that is not misleading;

5.1.2 identify the client, the intended use of the valuation, and relevant dates:

5.1.2.1 the date as of which the value estimate applies,

5.1.2.2 the date of the report, and

5.1.2.3 the date of the inspection;

5.1.3 specify the basis of the valuation, including type and definition of value;

5.1.3.1 When any component of the valuation is valued on more than one basis of value, a clear distinction must be made between the bases.

5.1.4 identify and describe the

5.1.4.1 property rights or interests to be valued,

5.1.4.2 physical and legal characteristics of the property, and

5.1.4.3 classes of property included in the valuation other than the primary property category;

5.1.5 describe the scope/extent of the work used to develop the valuation;

5.1.6 specify all assumptions and limiting conditions upon which the value conclusion is contingent;

5.1.7 identify special, unusual, or extraordinary assumptions and address the probability that such conditions will occur;

5.1.8 include a description of the information and data examined, the market analysis performed, the valuation approaches and procedures followed, and the reasoning that supports the analyses, opinions, and conclusions in the report;

5.1.9 contain a clause specifically prohibiting the publication of the report in whole or in part, or any reference thereto, or to the valuation figures contained therein, or to the names and professional affiliation of the Valuers, without the written approval of the Valuer;

5.1.10 include a Compliance Statement that the valuation has been performed in accordance with IVSs, disclose any departure from the specific requirements of the IVSs and provide an explanation for such departure in accordance with the IVSC Code of Conduct;

5.1.11 include the name, professional qualifications, and signature of the Valuer.

5.2 When Valuation Reports are transmitted electronically, a Valuer shall take reasonable steps to protect the integrity of the data/text in the report and to ensure that no errors occur in transmission. Software should provide for security of transmission.

5.2.1 The origin, date and time of the sending as well as the destination, date and time of receipt should be identified. Software should allow confirmation that the quantity of data/text transmitted corresponds to that received and should render the report as 'read-only' to all except the author.

5.2.2 The Valuer should ensure that the digital signature(s) is/are protected and fully under the Valuer's control by means of passwords (PIN numbers), hardware devices (secure cards), or other means. A signature affixed to a report electronically is considered as authentic and carries the same level of responsibility as a written signature on a paper copy report.

5.2.3 A true electronic and/or paper copy of an electronically transmitted report must be retained by the Valuer for the period required by law in his or her jurisdiction, in any event not less than five years. Files of the records of electronically transmitted reports may be kept on electronic, magnetic, or other media.

5.3 The presentation of a Valuation Report is decided by the Valuer and the client based on the instructions or specifications for the assignment.

5.4 The type, content, and length of a report depend on the intended user of the report, legal requirements, property type, and the nature and complexity of the valuation issue or problem.

5.5 For all Valuation Reports, sufficient documentation must be retained in the work file to support the results and conclusions of the valuation and must be held for a period of at least five years after completion.

6.0 Discussion

6.1 The context in which a valuation figure is reported is as important as the basis and accuracy of the figure itself. The value conclusion should make reference to the market evidence, and procedures and reasoning that support that conclusion.

6.2 Communicating the answer to the valuation question in a consistent and logical manner demands a methodical approach that enables the user to understand the processes followed and their relevance to the conclusion.

6.3 The report should convey to the reader a clear understanding of the opinions being expressed by the Valuer and also be readable and intelligible to someone with no prior knowledge of the property.

6.4 The report should demonstrate clarity, transparency, and consistency of approach.

6.5 The Valuer should exercise caution before permitting the valuation to be used other than for the originally agreed purpose.

7.0 Disclosure Requirements

7.1 When valuations are made by an Internal Valuer, specific disclosure shall be made in the Valuation Report of the existence and nature of the relationship between the Valuer and entity controlling the asset.

7.2 If a Valuer is involved in a valuation assignment in a capacity other than as a Valuer, for example, as an independent or impartial agent, as a consultant or advisor to a business entity, or as a mediator, the Valuer should disclose the specific role taken in each assignment.

7.3 The Valuer shall disclose the regulatory framework and any departure required from these Standards to comply with local legislation, regulation (including accounting rules), or custom.

8.0 Departure Provisions

8.1 No departure is permissible from the requirements that each Valuation Report clearly and accurately set forth the conclusions of the valuation, and clearly disclose any assumptions and limiting conditions, which affect the valuation and value conclusion.

8.2 If a Valuer is asked to perform an assignment that departs from these requirements or calls for something less than, or different from, the work normally performed in compliance with the IVSs and the IVSC Code of Conduct, the Valuer should accept and perform such services only when the following conditions can be met:

8.2.1 The Valuer determines that the instructions will not tend to mislead the intended users.

8.2.2 The Valuer determines that the valuation is not so limited that the results are no longer reliable and credible for the intended purpose and use of the valuation.

8.2.3 The Valuer advises the client that the instructions for the assignment involve a departure from the Standards that must be disclosed in full in the Valuation Report.

8.3 In any circumstances involving a departure from the reporting of *Market Value*, the Valuer should clearly identify that the valuation reported is other than *Market Value*.

9.0 Effective Date

9.1 This International Valuation Standard became effective 31 July 2007.

International Valuation Application 1
Valuation for Financial Reporting

International Valuation Standards Committee

International Valuation Application 1
Valuation for Financial Reporting

Material for this Application is drawn from International Financial Reporting Standards (IFRSs) published by the International Accounting Standards Board (IASB). IFRSs comprise individually numbered standards. Those originally published before 2004 are denoted IASs (International Accounting Standards) 1-41. Those published subsequently are prefixed as IFRSs. Extracts from IFRSs are reproduced in this publication of the International Valuation Standards (IVSs) with the permission of IASB.

The approved text of the IFRSs is that published by IASB in the English language, and copies may be obtained directly from IASB, 30 Cannon Street, London EC4M 6HX, United Kingdom, E-mail: *publications@iasb.org.uk*

IFRSs, Exposure Drafts and other publications of the IASB are protected by the copyright of the IASB.

"IFRS", "IAS", "IASC", "IASB" and "International Accounting Standards" are Trade Marks of the IASB and should not be used without the approval of the International Accounting Standards Board.

1.0 Introduction

1.1 The objective of this Application is to explain the principles that apply to valuations prepared for use in financial statements and related accounts of business entities. Valuers undertaking work of this nature should have an understanding of the accounting concepts and principles underlying the relevant International Accounting Standards.

1.2 The Valuer's adherence to market-based definitions, objectivity, and full disclosure of relevant matters within a pertinent and user-friendly format are fundamental to the requirements of valuation for financial reporting.

2.0 Scope

2.1 This Application applies to all valuations of asset classes included in any financial statement, which fall within the skills and expertise of Valuers.

2.2 IVSs facilitate cross-border transactions and the viability of global markets through harmonisation and transparency in financial reporting. As such this Application is developed in the context of International Financial Reporting Standards (IFRSs) as at 31 March 2004.

2.3 IFRSs adopt two models for the recognition of property assets in the balance sheet: a cost model, and a fair value model. Where the fair value model is applied, a current revaluation of the asset is required, and this Application focuses on these particular circumstances where Market Values are to be reported.

2.4 Legislative, regulatory, accounting, or jurisprudence requirements may oblige modification of this Application in some countries or under certain conditions. Any departure due to such circumstances must be referred to and clearly explained in the Valuation Report.

3.0 Definitions

International Valuation Standards Definitions

3.1 *Depreciated Replacement Cost.* The current cost of replacing an asset with its modern equivalent asset less deductions for physical deterioration and all relevant forms of obsolescence and optimisation.

3.2 *Improvements.* Buildings, structures or modifications to land, of a permanent nature, involving expenditures of labour and capital, and intended to enhance the value or utility of the property. Improvements have differing patterns of use and economic lives.

3.3 *Market Value.* The estimated amount for which a property should exchange on the date of valuation between a willing buyer and willing seller in an arm's-length transaction after proper marketing wherein the parties had each acted knowledgeably, prudently, and without compulsion (IVS 1, para. 3.1).

3.4 *Specialised Property.* A property that is rarely if ever sold in the market, except by way of sale of the business or entity of which it is part, due to uniqueness arising from its specialised nature and design, its configuration, size, location, or otherwise.

International Financial Reporting Standards Definitions

3.5 *Carrying Amount.* The amount at which an asset is recognised after deducting any accumulated depreciation (amortisation) and accumulated impairment losses thereon (IAS 36, para. 6).

3.6 *Cash-Generating Unit.* The smallest identifiable group of assets that generates cash inflows that are largely independent of the cash inflows from other assets or group of assets (IAS 36, para. 6)

3.7 *Depreciable Amount.* The cost of an asset, or other amount substituted for cost (in the financial statements), less its residual value (IAS 16, para. 6).

3.8 *Depreciation.* The systematic allocation of the depreciable amount of an asset over its useful life (IAS 16, para. 6; IAS 36, para. 6)

3.9 *Economic Life.* Either

  a) the period over which an asset is expected to be economically usable by one or more users; or

  b) the number of production or similar units expected to be obtained from the asset by one or more users (IAS 17, para. 4).

3.10 *Fair Value.* The amount for which an asset could be exchanged or a liability settled between knowledgeable willing parties in an arm's length transaction (IAS 16, para. 6).

3.11 *Fair Value Less Costs to Sell.* The amount obtainable from the sale of an asset or cash-generating unit in an arm's length transaction between knowledgeable, willing parties, less the costs of disposal (IAS 36, para. 6).

3.12 *Impairment Loss.* The amount by which the carrying amount of an asset or a cash-generating unit exceeds its recoverable amount (IAS 36, para. 6).

3.13 *Investment Property.* Property (land or building, or part of a building, or both) held (by the owner or by the lessee under a finance lease) to earn rentals or for capital appreciation, or both, rather than for:

  a) use in the production or supply of goods or services or for administrative purposes, or

b) sale in the ordinary course of business (IAS 40, para. 5).

3.14 *Net Realisable Value.* The estimated selling price in the ordinary course of business, less the estimated costs of completion and the estimated costs necessary to make the sale (IAS 2, para. 6). Net realisable value refers to the net amount that an entity expects to realise from the sale of inventory in the ordinary course of business. Fair value reflects the amount for which the same inventory could be exchanged between knowledgeable and willing buyers and sellers in the market place. The former is an entity-specific value; the latter is not. Net realisable value for inventories may not equal fair value less costs to sell (IAS 2, para. 7).

3.15 *Owner-Occupied Property.* Property held (by the owner or by the lessee under a finance lease) for use in the production or supply of goods or services or for administrative purposes (IAS 40, para. 5).

3.16 *Property, Plant and Equipment.* Tangible items that

a) are held for use in the production or supply of goods or services, for rental to others, or for administrative purposes; and

b) are expected to be used during more than one period. (IAS 16, para 6)

3.17 *Recoverable Amount.* The recoverable amount of an asset or cash-generating unit is the higher of its fair value less costs to sell and its value in use. (IAS 36, para. 6)

3.18 *Residual Value.* The estimated amount that an entity would currently obtain from disposal of an asset, after deducting the estimated costs of disposal, if the asset were already of the age and in the condition expected at the end of its useful life (IAS 16, para. 6)

3.19 *Revalued amount.* The fair value of an asset at the date of the revaluation less any subsequent accumulated depreciation and subsequent accumulated impairment losses (IAS 16, para. 31).

3.20 *Useful Life.* Either

a) the period over which an asset is expected to be available for use by an entity; or

b) the number of production or similar units expected to be obtained from the asset by an entity (IAS 16, para. 6; IAS 36, para. 6; IAS 38, para. 8).

In regard to leases, useful life is defined as:

The estimated remaining period, from the commencement of the lease term, without limitation by the lease term, over which the economic benefits embodied in the asset are expected to be consumed by the entity (IAS 17, para. 4).

3.21 *Value in Use*. The present value of the future cash flows expected to be derived from an asset or cash-generating unit (IAS 36, para. 6).

4.0 Relationship to Accounting Standards

4.1 This Application applies the principles developed in IVS 1, IVS 2, and IVS 3 to the requirements of IASs/IFRSs.

4.2 This Application focuses on valuation requirements under IAS 16, *Property Plant and Equipment;* IAS 17, *Leases;* and IAS 40, *Investment Property.* Reference is also made to valuation requirements under IAS 36, Impairment of Assets; IAS 2, Inventories; and IFRS 5, *Non-current Assets Held for Sale and Discontinued Operations.*

4.3 IASB is currently undertaking fundamental reviews of both the measurement of assets and liabilities in financial statements and of lease accounting. Although this Application has been updated to reflect the revisions made to various standards in 2003 as part of the IASB "Improvements Project", further changes may be necessary as a result of these continuing review projects.

5.0 Application

To perform valuations that comply with this Application and Generally Accepted Valuation Principles (GAVP), it is essential that Valuers adhere to all sections of the IVS Code of Conduct pertaining to Ethics, Competence, Disclosure, and Reporting (sections 4, 5, 6, and 7)

5.1 *Classification of Assets.* **Valuers shall obtain from the directors of the owning entity a list of assets to be valued, designating them as operational assets, i.e., assets requisite to the operations of the entity, or non-operational assets, being properties held for future development, investment, or assets surplus to the operations of the entity.**

5.2 *Applicable Standards.* **The classification of assets determines which IAS or IFRS applies. IAS 16 requires non-current property and plant assets held for the production or supply of goods or services to be recognised initially in the balance sheet at cost and thereafter carried in accordance with either the cost model or fair value model described in 5.3. Other accounting standards that require or permit the valuation of tangible assets include:**

- **Investment Property – IAS 40**

- **Leases – IAS 17**

- **Impairment of Assets – IAS 36**

- **Inventories – IAS 2**

- **Business Combinations – IFRS 3**

- **Non current Assets Held for Sale and Discontinued Operations – IFRS 5**

5.3 IAS 16, *Cost and Fair Value*

5.3.1 IAS 16 deals with the cost model in paragraph 30 as follows:

"After recognition as an asset, an item of property, plant and equipment shall be carried at its cost less any accumulated depreciation and any accumulated impairment losses."

5.3.2 The fair value model, which requires regular revaluations, is explained in paragraph 31 as follows:

"After recognition as an asset, an item of property, plant and equipment whose fair value can be measured reliably shall be carried at a revalued amount, being its fair value at the date of the revaluation less any subsequent accumulated depreciation and

subsequent accumulated impairment losses. Revaluations shall be made with sufficient regularity to ensure that the carrying amount does not differ materially from that which would be determined using fair value at the balance sheet date."

5.3.3 Fair value is not necessarily synonymous with *Market Value*. It is used throughout IFRSs in differing contexts.

5.3.4 Financial statements are produced on the assumption that the entity is a going concern unless management either intends to liquidate the entity or cease trading, or has no realistic alternative but to do so. (IAS 1, para 23). This assumption therefore underlies the application of fair value to property plant and equipment, except in cases where it is clear that there is either an intention to dispose of a particular asset or that option of disposal has to be considered, e.g. when undertaking an impairment review.

5.4 *Valuations under IAS 16*.

Where an entity adopts the fair value revaluation option under IAS 16, the assets are included in the balance sheet at their fair value as follows:

a) "The fair value of land and buildings is usually determined from market-based evidence by appraisal that is normally undertaken by professionally qualified valuers. The fair value of items of plant and equipment is usually their market value determined by appraisal" (IAS 16, para. 32).

b) "If there is no market-based evidence of fair value because of the specialised nature of the item of property, plant and equipment and the item is rarely sold, except as a part of a continuing business, an entity may need to estimate fair value using an income or a depreciated replacement cost approach" (IAS 16, para. 33).

5.4.1 IVSC considers that a professional Valuer undertaking an appraisal for this purpose should report the *Market Value* of the asset. Any assumptions or qualifications made in applying *Market Value* should be discussed with the entity and disclosed in the report.

5.4.2 The valuation conclusion shall be reported in accordance with IVS 3, Valuation Reporting. Valuers shall ensure that reports include sufficient information for the entity to meet the requirements of IAS 16, para. 77, when preparing financial statements:

a) the effective date of the revaluation;

b) whether an Independent Valuer was involved (Note, IVSC interprets this as an *External Valuer*);

c) the methods and significant assumptions applied;

d) the extent to which the values were determined directly by reference to observable prices in an active market or recent market transactions on arm's length terms, or were estimated using other valuation techniques

5.5 *Valuations under IAS 40 - Investment Property.*

Where an entity opts to account for investment property using the fair value model, IVSC considers that the requirements of this model are met by the Valuer adopting *Market Value*. Further guidance on Investment Property is provided at para. 6.7.

5.5.1 IAS 40, para. 75, requires amongst others the following disclosures, which the Valuer should include in the Report in addition to the requirements of IVS 3

a) the methods and significant assumptions applied in determining the fair value of investment property, including a statement whether the determination of fair value was supported by market evidence or was more heavily based on other factors (which the entity should disclose) because of the nature of the property and lack of comparable market data; and

b) the extent to which the fair value of investment property (as measured or disclosed in the financial statements) is based on a valuation by an Independent Valuer (IVSC interprets this as an *External Valuer*), who holds a recognised and relevant professional qualification and who has recent experience in the location and category of the investment property being valued.

5.6 *Valuation Requirements for Leased Assets – IAS 17*

5.6.1 Leased assets are classified under IAS 17 as either finance leases or operating leases (see para. 6.6.1 below and Addendum A). If a lease is classified as a finance lease, the fair value of the asset is required to establish the amount of the asset and liability recorded by the entity on its balance sheet, IAS 17, para 20.

5.6.2 For leases of land and buildings special rules apply, which are described in para. 6.6.3. For all property, other than investment property, land and buildings have to be considered separately for classification as either a finance lease or an operating lease.

5.6.3 IAS 40 allows Investment Property held by a lessee to be accounted for as a finance lease under IAS 17, subject to further special rules. Firstly, no allocation is made between the land and buildings. Secondly, the fair value is recognized as the value subject to the lessee's future liabilities under the lease.

5.6.4 IVSC considers that in each case the requirement to establish the fair value of the leased asset under IAS 17, para 20, is met by the Valuer reporting the *Market Value*. For leases of real estate, this is the *Market Value* of the lease interest held by the lessee. For leases of other assets, it is normally the *Market Value* of the asset unencumbered by the lease, as the liability is recorded separately.

5.7 *Valuation of Impaired Assets – IAS 36*

5.7.1 Impairment arises where there is a permanent decrease in the value of an asset below its carrying amount. The entity is required to write down the carrying amount of an impaired assert to the higher of its *value in use* or *fair value less costs to sell*. The requirements are discussed further at para. 6.8.2.

5.8 *Valuations after Business Combinations – IFRS 3*

5.8.1 Where a business acquires or is merged with another, the acquirer has to account for the assets and liabilities of the acquiree at their fair value as of the acquisition date. For identifiable assets and liabilities, IVSC considers that the Valuer should report the Market Value as they existed at the date of acquisition.

5.9 *Surplus Assets – IFRS 5*

5.9.1 Under **IFRS 5,** *Non-Current Assets Held for Sale and Discontinued Operations,* surplus assets are to be separately identified. Such assets may be accounted for individually or as a "disposal group", i.e., a group of assets to be disposed of together, by sale or otherwise, and the liabilities directly associated with those assets that will also be transferred in the transaction. Surplus assets are to be initially accounted for at the lower of the carrying amount and the fair value less costs to sell, and subsequently at fair value less cost to sell. Valuers should therefore ascertain whether surplus assets are to be valued as individual items, or as a group or portfolio of assets that will be disposed of in a single transaction, and report the *Market Value* with the appropriate assumptions.

5.10 *Properties Held for Sale in the Ordinary Course of Business – IAS 2*

5.10.1 Valuations of properties held for sale in the ordinary course of business should comply with the requirements of IAS 2, Inventories. These properties are measured at the lower of cost and *net realisable value.* Net realisable value is the *Market Value* less the costs of sale.

5.11 *Selling Costs*

5.11.1 When instructed to value impaired or surplus assets, or assets that are held for sale in the course of business, the Valuer must report their *Market Value* without deducting selling costs. If the client requests the Valuer to advise on the costs to sell the assets, such costs are to be reported separately.

5.12 *Biological Assets – IAS 41*

5.12.1 These include Agricultural and Forestry assets. The Valuer should value these assets in accordance with the guidance in GN 10.

5.13 *Co-operation with Auditors.* Subject to first obtaining the consent of their client, Valuers shall discuss and explain their valuations openly with the entity's auditors.

6.0 Discussion

6.1 Identification of Asset Class

Separate disclosures are required for each class of property, plant and equipment. IAS 16, para. 73, requires that financial statements shall disclose for each class the measurement basis used for determining the gross carrying amount, the depreciation method used, and the useful lives or the depreciation rates used. A class of property, plant or equipment is a grouping of assets of a similar nature and use. The following are examples of separate classes (IAS 16, para. 37):

a) land;

b) land and buildings;

c) machinery;

d) ships;

e) aircraft;

f) motor vehicles;

g) furniture and fixtures;

h) office equipment

When an item is revalued, the entire class to which it belongs should be revalued in order to avoid both selective revaluations and the reporting of a mix of costs and fair values as at different dates. An asset class for this purpose is a grouping of assets of a similar nature and use in an entity's operation

6.2 Depreciation – IAS 16

6.2.1 IAS 16, paras. 43–62, sets out the requirements for an entity to account for the depreciation of property, plant and machinery assets. Valuers may be requested to allocate value between different elements of an asset, to advise on the residual value or to advise on the future life of an asset.

6.2.2 *Elements of cost.* Any part of an item, which has a cost that is significant in relation to the total cost of the item, has to be depreciated separately. Where parts have a similar useful life and will depreciate at a similar rate, they may be grouped in determining the depreciation charge. Valuers may be consequently requested to allocate a valuation they have provided to the different component parts of an asset in order to enable the entity to depreciate them separately.

6.2.3 *Residual Value.* The residual value is deducted from the carrying amount of the asset to determine the amount the entity has to depreciate. If the management policy of the entity involves disposal after a specific time, the useful life of an asset may be less than its economic life. IAS 16, para. 58, recognises that land normally has an unlimited useful life and therefore should be accounted for separately. It also provides that an increase in the value of land should not affect the determination of the depreciable amount of the building.

6.2.4 *Future life.* A Valuer can advise on the remaining economic life of the asset. When reporting the economic life of buildings, improvements, plant and equipment, it should be stated that this is not necessarily the same as the useful life to the entity, which is subject to any policy of the entity on future disposal or renewal.

6.2.5 *Reporting requirements:* When providing allocations, or estimating the residual value of an element of an asset based on an apportionment of the value of the complete asset, the Valuer should state that the figures provided are hypothetical allocations of the value of the whole item prepared solely for calculating the appropriate rate of depreciation in the entity's financial statements, and that these figures should not be relied upon for any other purpose.

6.3 *Alternative Use Value*

If an owner-occupied property has potential for an alternative use, which would result in its value in isolation from the business being higher than its *value* as part of the *cash-generating unit* to which it belongs, the Valuer shall report the *Market Value* for that alternative use. A statement should also be made that the *value* for the alternative use takes no account of issues such as business closure or disruption and the associated costs that would be incurred in achieving the alternative use, and that these should be considered by the entity when deciding the appropriate amount to adopt as fair value.

6.4 *Specialised Property*

Both IVSs and IAS 16 recognise that there are categories of assets for which market-based evidence may be unavailable because of their specialised nature. It endorses the application of either an income or depreciated replacement cost approach to the valuation of these assets. The choice of approach is not dictated by the type of asset but by the presence or absence of market evidence. For further discussion and guidance on the use of these approaches see paras. 5.12 and 5.13 of GN 1 and section 5 of GN 8.

6.5 *Frequency of Revaluation*

Paragraph 31 of IAS 16 states:

"Revaluations shall be made with sufficient regularity to ensure that the carrying amount does not differ materially from that which would be determined using fair value at the balance sheet date"

6.6 IAS 17 – *Leased Property, Plant and Equipment*

6.6.1 IAS 17 deals with the accounting for assets that are held under a lease. All leases require classification as either operating leases or finance leases (see para. 5.6.1 above and Addendum A). Different accounting treatments apply to each type of lease. A finance lease is recorded in a lessee's balance sheet as both an asset and a liability at amounts equal to the fair value of the asset or, if lower, the present value of the minimum lease payments, each determined as at the inception of the lease. Any initial direct costs incurred by the lessee are added to the amount recognized as an asset.

6.6.2 Valuers may be required to advise on the fair value of the asset at the inception of the lease to enable a lessee to account for the asset correctly in accordance with IAS 17.

6.6.3 Special provisions apply to leases of land and buildings. IAS 17, para. 14, states that "because a characteristic of land is that it normally has an indefinite economic life … a lease of land will be an operating lease". Where a lease is of land and buildings, these elements have to be considered separately for the purposes of lease classification (IAS 17, para. 15). Most leases of real property will grant the lessee rights to occupy both the land and buildings, following which the interest in both elements reverts to the lessor. If the lessee also has to maintain the building and hand it back to the lessor in good repair, it is probable that both elements will correctly be classified as operating leases (see Addendum A). If both elements are not considered to share the same classification, the minimum lease payments (including any initial capital payment) are allocated between the land and buildings elements in proportion to the relative fair values of the leasehold interests in the two elements at the inception of the lease. If the lease payments cannot be reliably allocated the entire lease is treated as a finance lease, unless it is clear that both elements are operating leases (IAS 17, para. 16). This allocation is not required in the case of a lessee's interest accounted for as investment property (IAS 17, para. 18).

6.6.4 For further guidance on Leasehold interests, see Addendum A.

6.7 IAS 40 — *Investment Property*

6.7.1 IAS 40 defines an *investment property* as a property (land or a building--or part of a building--or both) held by the owner, or by a lessee under a finance lease, to earn rentals, or for capital appreciation or both. It excludes owner-occupied property used for the production or supply of goods or services, or for administrative purposes, and also property held for sale in the ordinary course of business.

6.7.1.1 If part of a property is held as an investment property and part is owner-occupied, or if the parts could be sold or leased separately, the parts are accounted for separately. If the parts could not be sold separately, the property is an investment property only if an insignificant proportion is held for the production or supply of goods or services or for administrative purposes (IAS 40, para. 10).

6.7.1.2 Property leased to a subsidiary or parent under an inter-company leasing arrangement does not qualify as investment property in the consolidated financial statements of the group, but may be treated as such in the individual financial statements of the lessor entity (IAS 40, para. 15).

6.7.2 Investment property is measured initially at cost. After initial recognition an entity may choose to adopt either:

a) *The Fair Value Model. Investment property* should be measured at fair value and changes recognised in the profit and loss statement; or

b) *The Cost Model.* The "historic" cost model is in accordance with the model described in IAS 16. An entity that chooses the (historic) cost model should nonetheless disclose the fair value of its investment property.

6.7.2.1 The fair value model is described in detail in IAS 40, paras. 33 - 55. The *Market Value* of the entity's interest in the investment property derived in accordance with IVS 1 accords with these detailed requirements. The *Market Value* will reflect any current leases, current cash flows and any reasonable assumptions about future rental income or outgoings.

6.7.3 *Leasehold investment property.* A property held under a lease, rather than owned outright, and that otherwise meets the definition of an investment property, may be accounted for using the fair value model. If this option is taken for one such property held under a lease, all property classified as investment property shall be accounted for using the fair value model (IAS 40, para. 6).

6.7.3.1 IAS 40, para. 50(d), recognizes that the fair value of an investment property held under a lease will reflect the net income after deduction of future lease liabilities. Although the entity is required to add to the reported fair value any recognised lease liability to arrive at the carrying amount for accounting purposes, this does not affect the requirement for the Valuer to report *Market Value*.

6.7.3.2 At initial recognition an investment property held under a lease shall be accounted for as though it were a finance lease under IAS 17, para. 20, i.e., at the fair value of the property, or if lower, at the present value of the minimum lease payments. Any capital sum paid to acquire the property interest is treated as part of the minimum lease payments and is therefore included in the cost of the asset (IAS 40, para. 25).

6.7.3.3 Subsequent measurement of an investment property held under an operating lease requires the fair value model to be adopted (see para. 6.6.3.1 above).

6.7.4 *External Valuations.* Entities are encouraged, but not required, to determine the fair value of investment property on the basis of a valuation by an Independent (External) Valuer who holds a recognised and relevant professional qualification and who has recent experience in the location and category of the investment property being valued (IAS 40, para. 26).

6.8 Other Requirements under IASs

6.8.1 *Portfolios:* A collection or aggregation of properties held by a single ownership and jointly managed is referred to as a portfolio. The Market Value of such assets viewed or treated as a portfolio or as an assembled group of properties could exceed or could be less than the sum of the Market Value of each asset individually. Where this is the case, it should be reported separately to the directors or trustees.

6.8.2 *Impairment:* An entity is required, under IAS 36, *Impairment of Assets,* to review, at each balance sheet date, whether there is any indication that a tangible asset may be impaired. Impairment might be indicated by, for example, a reduction in the value of the asset because of market or technological changes, obsolescence of the asset, asset underperformance in comparison to the expected return, or an intention to discontinue or restructure operations. If impairment is considered to have arisen, the *carrying amount* of the asset, derived from either its historic cost or an earlier valuation should be written down to the *recoverable amount,* which is the higher of the asset's *value in use* or its *fair value less costs to sell. Value in use* reflects the value that the entity will obtain from the asset throughout its remaining useful life to the business and its eventual disposal. Although entity-specific, the valuation inputs for the *value in use* of an asset should be market determined wherever possible. However, if the value an entity can obtain from the continued use of an asset is less than the net proceeds that could be obtained from its immediate retirement and disposal, the *carrying amount* should reflect this latter figure. The *fair value* less *costs to sell* of an asset is its Market Value less the reasonably anticipated selling costs.

6.8.3 *Disrupted Markets:* When markets are disrupted or suspended, Valuers must be vigilant in their analyses as explained in IVS 1, paragraph 6.5. Under IAS 29, *Financial Reporting in Hyperinflationary Economies,* Valuers may be required to assess balance sheet value.

7.0 Disclosure Requirements

7.1 **The Valuer shall make all disclosures required under IVS 3, Valuation Reporting.**

7.2 **For disclosures required under IFRSs/IASs, see paragraphs 5.4.2, 5.5.1 and 6.1 above.**

7.3 **The Valuer shall disclose the regulatory framework and any departure required from these Standards to comply with local legislation, regulation (including accounting rules), or custom.**

8.0 Departure Provisions

8.1 **In following this Application any departures must be in accordance with directions made in IVS 3, Valuation Reporting.**

9.0 Effective Date

9.1 This International Valuation Application became effective 31 July 2007.

Addendum A
Further Guidance on Lease Accounting

International Valuation Standards Committee

Lease Classification

Under IAS 17, leases have to be classified for inclusion in financial statements as either operating leases or finance leases:

A *finance lease* is a lease that transfers substantially all the risks and rewards incidental to ownership of an asset. Title may or may not be eventually transferred.

An *operating lease* is a lease other than a finance lease.

The following examples are listed in IAS 17, paras 10-11, as situations that could be indicative of a finance lease, either individually or in combination. These are not absolute tests but illustrations, i.e., one or more of these circumstances may arise, but the lease would still not be classified as a finance lease if it is clear from the overall context that substantially all the risks and rewards of ownership have not been transferred from the lessor to the lessee.

(a)   the lease transfers ownership of the asset to the lessee by the end of the lease term;

(b)   the lessee has the option to purchase the asset on advantageous terms;

(c)   the lease term is for the major part of the economic life of the asset even if title is not transferred;

(d)   at the inception of the lease the present value of the minimum lease payments amounts to at least substantially all of the fair value of the leased asset;

(e)   the leased assets are of such a specialised nature that only the lessee can use them without major modifications;

(f)   if the lessee can cancel the lease, the lessor's losses associated with the cancellation are borne by the lessee;

(g)   gains or losses from the fluctuation in the fair value of the residual accrue to the lessee;

(h)   the lessee has the ability to continue the lease for a secondary period at a rent that is substantially lower than market rent.

If it is concluded that substantially all the risks and rewards of ownership are not transferred to the lessee, then the lease is an operating lease.

As classification does involve an assessment of the degree to which economic benefits are transferred by a lease, Valuers are likely to be requested to provide advice to assist classification by lessor and lessees. IVSC considers that in the majority of cases, a qualitative assessment of the lease terms will quickly indicate the correct classification without the need for detailed calculation of the value of the different lease interests. The relative values of the lessor's and lessee's interests are not a key factor in classification; the key test is whether the lessor has transferred substantially all the risks and rewards of ownership.

Land and Building Allocation

Where a lease is of land and buildings together, IAS 17, para. 15, requires that the two elements be considered separately for the purposes of classification. If it appears that the buildings element could be a finance lease, it will be necessary to make an allocation of the initial rent based on the relative fair values of the leasehold interests in each element at the inception of the lease (IAS 17, para. 16).

In most leases of real property, the interest in the land and buildings is not distinguishable, and in any event the interest in both normally reverts to the lessor at the end of the lease. There are often provisions for the rent to be reviewed periodically to reflect changes in the *Market Value* of the property and also an obligation on the lessee to hand the buildings back to the lessor in good repair. These are all clear indicators that the lessor has not transferred substantially all the risks and rewards of ownership of either the buildings or the land to the lessee.

Consequently, finance leases of real property will generally arise only where the lease is clearly designed as a way of funding the eventual purchase of the land, buildings, or both by the lessee, often by means of an option to acquire the lessor's interest for a nominal sum after the rental payments have been made. Occasionally leases that are not clearly structured as finance agreements may meet some of the criteria of a finance lease, for example, where the rental payments do not reflect the underlying value of the property. In those cases a more detailed analysis of the value of the risks and benefits transferred may be required in order to confirm or rebut their classification.

Under IAS 17, para. 17, allocation between the land and buildings elements of an investment property held under a lease is not required. Under IAS 40, even though the investor may hold the investment property under an operating lease, the whole is accounted for as though it were a finance lease.

Where a lease is of a self-contained plot of land and the building upon it, allocating the rent to each element is a task that could be undertaken reliably where there is an active market for land for similar development in the locality. In other situations, for example where the lease is of part of a multi-let building with no identifiable land attributable to any particular lease, reliable allocation may be impossible. IAS 17, para. 16, recognises that such cases can arise and makes the proviso that where a reliable allocation cannot be made, the whole lease should be treated as a finance lease, unless it is clear that both elements are operating leases. If it were clear that both elements were operating leases from the outset, the allocation exercise would not be necessary.

In practice, leases of part of a multi-let building will normally be operating leases and the whole property will be classified as investment property by the lessor. In such cases allocation will be unnecessary. In cases where the buildings element is clearly a finance lease, the land element is likely to be identifiable. It will be comparatively rare for the buildings element to meet the criteria for classification as a finance lease and for the land element not to be clearly identifiable. In such cases, the Valuer should not attempt an allocation based on unreliable criteria, but should advise that the allocation cannot be reliably made. The entity will then have to treat the whole as a finance lease.

International Valuation Application 2
Valuation for Secured Lending Purposes

International Valuation Standards Committee

International Valuation Application 2 Valuation for Secured Lending Purposes (Revised 2007)

1.0 Introduction

1.1 The objective of International Valuation Application 2 (IVA 2) is to provide a framework for valuations of assets that are to be offered or taken as loan security.

1.2 It is important that Valuers consistently apply accepted valuation principles within the scope of these standards, providing clear, independent and objective opinions that are relevant to the needs of valuation users.

2.0 Scope

2.1 This Application applies in all circumstances where valuations are required of assets that are, or are proposed to be, held as security for lending. The lending may be done by different means, including mortgage or other forms of fixed or floating charge.

3.0 Definitions

International Valuation Standards Definitions

3.1 *Market Value.* The estimated amount for which a property should exchange on the date of valuation between a willing buyer and willing seller in an arm's-length transaction after proper marketing wherein the parties had each acted knowledgeably, prudently, and without compulsion (IVS 1, para. 3.1).

3.2 *Mortgage.* A pledge of an interest in property as security or collateral for repayment of a loan with provision for redemption on repayment. In the event the borrower (mortgagor) defaults, the lender (mortgagee) has the power to recover the property pledged.

3.3 *Specialised Property.* A property that is rarely if ever sold in the market, except by way of sale of the business or entity of which it is part, due to uniqueness arising from its specialised nature and design, its configuration, size, location, or otherwise.

3.4 *Trade Related Property.* Certain classes of real property, which are designed for a specific type of business and that are normally bought and sold in the market, having regard to their trading potential.

European Union Legislation Definition

3.5 *Mortgage Lending Value.* The value of the property as determined by a prudent assessment of the future marketability of the property taking into account long term sustainable aspects of the property, the normal and local market conditions, and the current use and alternative appropriate uses of the property. Speculative elements shall not be taken into account in the assessment of the mortgage lending value. The mortgage lending value shall be documented in a clear and transparent manner. (This definition is from Directive 2006/48/EC of the European Parliament.)

4.0 Relationship to Accounting Standards

4.1 A valuation prepared for lending purposes will not necessarily be the same as one made for accounting purposes, particularly one made for financial reporting purposes. Although a similar base such as *Market Value* may be applicable, the assumptions on which the valuation is based may be different.

4.2 By way of example, the underlying principle of many valuations for financial reporting is the presumption that the entity will continue as a going concern. However, this would not usually be appropriate for valuations undertaken for lending purposes. Such a presumption has particular implications for specialised assets where the value and marketability of the secured property, separate from the business of which it forms part, may be limited.

5.0 Application

To perform valuations that comply with this Application and Generally Accepted Valuation Principles (GAVP), Valuers shall adhere to all

sections of the IVS Code of Conduct pertaining to Ethics, Competence, Disclosure, and Reporting (sections 4, 5, 6, and 7).

5.1 In performing valuations of property for lending purposes, Valuers will normally provide the *Market Value* of such property in accordance with these International Valuation Standards.

5.2 If the circumstances are such that a departure from the *Market Value* basis is justified, the departure shall be clearly set out and explained in the Valuation Report along with the identification and definition of the alternative basis used and an explanation of the reasons for the departure. If there is a material difference between the *Market Value* of the property and the alternative value, this should be reported.

5.3 The valuation opinion shall be reported in accordance with IVS 3, Valuation Reporting.

5.4 In addition to fulfilling the requirements of IVS 3, Valuation Reports for secured lending of real property will normally include comment, where relevant, on the following items:

5.4.1 current activity and trends in the relevant market:

5.4.2 historic, current and anticipated future demand for the category of property in the locality;

5.4.3 the potential and likely demand for alternative uses;

5.4.4 both the current marketability of the property and if requested, the likelihood of its sustainability;

5.4.5 any impact of foreseeable events (at the date of valuation) on the value of the security;

5.4.6 the valuation approach adopted, and the extent of market-based evidence in support of the valuation.

5.5 Valuations for lending purposes may be required on an assumption there has been a change in the state or condition of the property, for example, the assumed development of a new building, or upgrade of a building. Such a valuation will normally be provided on the assumption that the change has occurred at the valuation date. It is not a projection of the value at the date in the future when the change will have actually occurred. The report must make it clear that the valuation is based on the assumption that the change specified had already been made at the valuation date. Use of the term *Market Value* without a modifier in these circumstances can be misleading. The term *"Market Value* as if complete"* is an example of a suitable modification of *Market Value* that may be used in these circumstances.

5.6 A valuation of a property may also be required on the assumption that an estimated occupancy level had been achieved. This should also reflect the realistic expectations and perceptions of market participants as at the date of the report.

5.7 Corporate and individual loans from banks and other financial institutions are often secured by specific property assets. Valuers need to have a general understanding of the requirements of such institutions, and possibly the structure of loan terms and agreements. Lenders will usually require that the terms of a loan be kept confidential, but this does not relieve the Valuer of the obligation to have a general understanding of the lending process.

6.0 Discussion

6.1 At the outset of an assignment, the Valuer needs to clearly identify the property that is to serve as the security. Particular care is required to distinguish between property types where real property and personal property are combined.

6.2 The manner in which property would ordinarily trade in the market will determine the applicability of the various approaches to assessing *Market Value*. Based upon market information, each approach is a comparative method, and the use of more than one method may be required.

6.3 Each relevant valuation method will, if appropriately and correctly applied, lead to a similar result. All valuation methods should be based on market observations. Construction costs and depreciation, where they apply, should be determined by reference to an analysis of market-based estimates of costs and accumulated depreciation. The use of an income method, particularly discounted cash flow techniques, will also be based on market-determined cash flows and market-derived rates of return.

6.4 Occasionally a lender may request a valuation on a basis other than *Market Value*. IVS 2 addresses the types, use and reporting of some common alternative bases of valuation. The Valuer should ensure that an alternative basis is not confused with *Market Value*. Although there may be circumstances where an alternative basis is appropriate for secured lending, users of such valuations should be made aware that such value may not be realisable if the alternative assumptions made are no longer applicable.

6.5 *Investment Properties*

6.5.1 Income-producing properties are usually valued as individual properties. Lending institutions may also wish to have a property assessed as part of a portfolio of properties. In such instances, the distinction between the value of the individual property, assuming it is sold individually, and its value as part of the portfolio should be clearly expressed.

6.5.2 Although the Valuer should comment on the expected demand and marketability of the property over the life of the loan (see para. 5.4 above), it is normally outside the scope of the valuation exercise to advise on the ability of a tenant to meet future lease obligations beyond comment on the market's current perception of the tenant's quality.

6.6 *Owner-Occupied Properties*

6.6.1 Owner-occupied properties valued for lending purposes will normally be valued on the assumption that the property is transferred unencumbered by the owner's occupancy, i.e., that the buyer is entitled to full legal control and possession. This does not preclude consideration of the existing owner as part of the market, but it does require that any special advantage attributable to the owner's occupancy, which may be reflected in a valuation of the business, be excluded from the valuation.

6.7 *Leases Between Related or Connected Parties*

6.7.1 Caution is required where property offered as security is subject to a lease to a party connected to the borrower. If the valuer considers that the lease creates a more favourable income stream than would be obtainable on a letting to an unconnected third party in an arm's-length transaction, the lender should be alerted and it may be appropriate to disregard the existence of the lease in a valuation of the property as security.

6.8 Sales Incentives

6.8.1 It is not uncommon for a seller of property, especially developers of real property, to offer incentives to buyers. Examples of such incentives include rental income guarantees, contributions to the buyer's removal or fitting out costs, or the supply of personal property such as furnishings or equipment. *Market Value* ignores any price inflated by special considerations or concessions (IVS 1, para 3.2.1). It may also be appropriate to alert the lender as to the effect that any incentives being offered have on the actual selling prices achieved.

6.9 Specialised Properties

6.9.1 Specialised properties by definition may have limited marketability and significant value only as part of a business (see Concepts Fundamental to Generally Accepted Valuation Principles, para. 8.2). For loan security purposes, such properties will normally be valued on a vacant possession basis (see para. 6.6.1 above) and a valuation based on the highest and best alternative use is usually applicable. This will involve consideration of the costs and risks that would be involved in achieving that use. Lenders may not consider specialised property to be suitable as a security for lending purposes.

6.9.2 A valuation may be required of a specialised property where the property is part of a going-concern business. The lender should be alerted to the valuation being dependent on the continuing profitability (or otherwise) of the going concern. If the value on a vacant possession basis is potentially lower, this should be drawn to the attention of the lender.

6.10 Trade Related Properties

6.10.1 Certain classes of property, including but not limited to hotels and other trading businesses, where the property is approved and purpose-designed for only that use, are usually valued based on profitability but excluding *Personal Goodwill* (see GN 12, para. 3.3.2). In such cases, the lender should be made aware of the significant difference in value that may exist between an operating concern and a non-operating concern where the business is closed, the inventory is removed, licences (and other intangible assets such as certificates, franchise agreements, or permits) are removed or are in jeopardy, and any other circumstances exist that may impair future profitability and value.

6.10.2 If the income from a property is critically dependent on a tenant or tenants from a single sector or industry or some other factor, which could cause future income instability, the Valuer should address these factors in the Valuation Report. In certain cases, an assessment of the value of the property based on an alternative use, assuming vacant possession, may be appropriate.

6.11 *Development Properties*

6.11.1 Properties held for redevelopment or sites intended for development of buildings should be valued taking into account existing and potential development entitlements and controls. Any assumptions as to planning issues and other material factors must be reasonable, validated by market behaviour and explicitly stated in the Valuation Report.

6.11.2 The approach to the valuation of development properties will depend on the state of development of the property at the date of valuation and may take into account the degree to which the development is pre-sold or pre-leased. The valuation approach may need to be discussed with the lender prior to undertaking the valuation. Care should be taken by the Valuer to:

6.11.2.1 make a reasoned estimate of the development period from the date of valuation. The effect of additional development requirements on costs and revenues, using present value discounting where appropriate, will be reflected in this analysis;

6.11.2.2 evaluate as far as is possible at the date of valuation, market behaviour during the period of the development;

6.11.2.3 consider and outline the risks associated with the development; and

6.11.2.4 consider and disclose any known special relationships between the parties involved in the development.

6.12 *Wasting Assets*

6.12.1 Specific lending issues arise in relation to the valuation of wasting assets such as mines or quarries. The lender's attention needs to be drawn to the risk associated with this type of a wasting asset and the planned program for its extraction or use.

6.12.2 Property rental that exceeds the current market or economic rent may constitute a wasting asset because any value attributable to this factor diminishes as the term of the lease decreases.

6.13 *The Valuer*

6.13.1 The nature and scope of the Valuer's engagement should be clear to the Valuer and the user of the valuation. Valuers should be aware of the risk associated with valuations for lending purposes where miscommunication, misunderstanding or error may lead to a dispute or litigation between the lender and the Valuer.

6.13.2 In some jurisdictions financial services legislation requires licencing or registration of advisers when advice is related not only to the value of property, but also to securities issues such as equity, participatory interests, collective investment schemes, or syndicated loans. Valuers may be restricted in the advice they can provide in these jurisdictions.

6.13.3 In undertaking valuations for lending purposes, it is particularly important that the Valuer be independent of the borrower.

6.13.4 It is important that the Valuer possess appropriate experience in relation to the particular property type and locale for the property involved, or if not, seek expert assistance.

6.14 *Forced Sales and Limited Marketing or Disposal Periods*

6.14.1 Lending institutions may request valuations on a forced, or liquidation, sale basis or impose a time limit for disposal of the security. Because the impact of a constraint on the price obtainable will depend upon the specific circumstances under which the sale takes place, it is not realistic for the Valuer to speculate on a price that could be obtained without either knowledge of the reasons for the constraint, or the circumstances under which the property might be offered for sale. An alternative valuation may be provided based on defined assumptions, but the Valuer should draw the lender's attention to the fact that this opinion is valid only at the valuation date, and may not be relied upon in the event of a future default, when both market conditions and the sale circumstances may be different.

6.15 *Lenders' Solvency Ratios*

6.15.1 Major banks and other lenders are normally subject to regulations that limit the total amount they can lend as a proportion of the lenders' assets, known as the *solvency ratio*. In the international context, the Basle II Accord sets out rules for the minimum solvency ratios to be maintained by lending institutions and how those ratios are to be calculated. The value of assets over which the lender holds security is used in calculating the solvency ratio.

6.15.2 In exceptional circumstances for well-developed and long-established markets, the Basle II Accord requires the estimation of the *Market Value* and *Mortgage Lending Value* of a security backed by commercial real estate. A preferential risk weight of 50% is assigned to the tranche of a secured loan that does not exceed the lower of 50% of the *Market Value* or 60% of the *Mortgage Lending Value*.

6.15.3 *Mortgage Lending Value* is a long-term, risk assessment technique. As such, it is not a basis of value. MLV is a technique that is primarily used by banks in a number of European countries. Further information on *Mortgage Lending Value* is available on the IVSC website.

7.0 Disclosure Requirements

7.1 In reporting *Market Value* for lending security purposes, the Valuer shall make all disclosures required under IVS 3, *Valuation Reporting*.

7.2 The basis of the Valuer's engagement is to be clearly set out in any reports to be used by third parties. All reports should be presented in a way that would not be considered by a reasonable person to be misleading.

7.3 The Valuer shall disclose the regulatory framework and any departure required from these Standards to comply with local legislation, regulation, or custom.

8.0 Departure Provisions

8.1 In following this Application any departures must be in accordance with directions provided in IVS 3, Valuation Reporting.

9.0 Effective Date

9.1 This International Valuation Application became effective 31 July 2007.

International Valuation Application 3

Valuation of Public Sector Assets for Financial Reporting

International Valuation Standards Committee

International Valuation Application 3 Valuation of Public Sector Assets for Financial Reporting (Adopted 2007)

1.0 Introduction

1.1 Public sector assets are those assets owned and/or controlled by governmental or quasi-governmental entities to provide goods or services to the general public. The principles that apply to the valuation of public sector assets are essentially the same as for any other assets.

1.2 The valuation of public sector assets may be undertaken for a range of purposes including financial reporting, privatisation planning, loan origination, bond issuance, and cost-benefit or economic analyses performed by governments and quasi-government entities either to determine whether a public sector asset is being used and managed efficiently or to set pricing for monopoly services.

1.3 The International Federation of Accountants' International Public Sector Accounting Standards Board (IPSASB) develops accounting standards for public sector entities, referred to as International Public Sector Accounting Standards (IPSASs). IPSASs, which apply to accrual accounting, are based on the International Financial Reporting Standards (IFRSs), issued by the International Accounting Standards Board (IASB). IPSASs cover public sector specific financial reporting issues, some of which are not addressed by IFRSs.

1.4 IVA 1 generally addresses the application of valuation bases to accounting principles in the context of IFRSs. Because of parallels between IPSASs and IFRSs, this Application necessarily repeats some of the content of IVA 1 while also addressing the specific requirements for the valuation of public sector assets and their treatment in financial reporting.

1.5 Property in the public sector comprises conventional cash-generating and non-cash-generating property assets as well as specialised property assets, including *heritage and conservation assets, infrastructure assets, public buildings, public utility plants, and recreational assets.* As with private sector assets, public sector assets fall into *operational* and *non-operational* categories. Non-operational assets include investment and surplus assets.

2.0 Scope

2.1 This Application applies to all valuations of public sector asset classes, included in any financial statement, which fall within the skills and expertise of Valuers (with the exception of valuations of Government Business Enterprises or GBEs that are performed according to IVA 1).

2.2 IVSs facilitate cross-border transactions and the viability of global markets through harmonisation and transparency in financial reporting. As such, this Application is developed in the context of International Public Sector Accounting Standards (IPSASs). In September 2005, the IPSAS Board issued an Exposure Draft of eleven IPSASs that had been updated to converge with the amended International Accounting Standards issued by IASB in December 2003 as part of its General Improvements Project. This Application is developed in the context of the proposed revisions to IPSASs contained within this Exposure Draft.

2.3 IPSASs and IFRSs adopt two models for the recognition of property assets in the balance sheet: a cost model, and a fair value model. Where the fair value model is applied, a current revaluation of the asset is required, and this Application focuses on these particular circumstances where Market Values are to be reported.

2.4 Legislative, regulatory, accounting, or jurisprudence requirements may require the modification of this Application in some countries or under certain conditions. Any departure due to such circumstances must be referred to and clearly explained in the Valuation Report.

3.0 Definitions

International Valuation Standards Definitions

3.1 *Depreciated Replacement Cost.* The current cost of replacing an asset with its modern equivalent asset less deductions for physical deterioration and all relevant forms of obsolescence and optimisation.

3.2 *Market Value.* The estimated amount for which a property should exchange on the date of valuation between a willing buyer and willing seller in an arm's-length transaction after proper marketing wherein the parties had each acted knowledgeably, prudently, and without compulsion (IVS 1, para. 3.1).

3.3 *Obsolescence.* A loss in value due to a decrease in the usefulness of property caused by decay, changes in technology, people's behavioural patterns and tastes, or environmental changes. Obsolescence is sometimes classified according to items of outmoded design and functionality, items with structural design unable to meet current code requirements, and factors arising outside the asset, such as changes in user demand.

3.4 *Optimisation.* The process by which a least cost replacement option is determined for the remaining service potential of an asset. It is a process of adjusting the replacement cost to reflect that an asset may be technically obsolete or over-engineered, or the asset may have a greater capacity than that required. Hence optimisation minimises, rather than maximises, a resulting valuation where alternative lower cost replacement options are available.

3.5 *Public building.* A building that serves some community or social function and is held in public ownership. Examples include courthouses, municipal centres, schools, prisons, police stations, military facilities, libraries, hospitals, clinics, and social or public housing.

3.6 *Public sector asset.* An asset, owned and/or controlled by a governmental or quasi-governmental entity, for the provision of some public service or good. Public sector assets comprise different asset types, including conventional assets as well as heritage and conservation assets, infrastructure assets, public utility plants, recreational assets, and public buildings (e.g., military facilities), each category of which constitutes property, plant and equipment within the meaning of IPSASs and IFRSs.

Public sector assets typically include:

a) assets, which have atypical tenure, are irreplaceable, are non-cash-generating, or provide goods or services in the absence of any market competition;

b) land with restrictions on its sale or leasing; and

c) land, which is designated for a specialised use that is not necessarily its highest and best use.

See also *Heritage assets, Infrastructure assets, Public building, Public utility,* and *Recreational assets.*

3.7 *Public utility.* A property that:

a) produces a service or good for general public consumption; and

b) is usually a monopoly or quasi-monopoly provider subject to some form of governmental control.

3.8 *Recreational assets.* Properties held in public ownership that:

a) are managed by or on behalf of national, municipal, or local governmental authorities; and

b) provide for recreational use by the general public.

Examples include parks; playgrounds; greenbelts; walks and trails; swimming pools; playing courts, fields and courses; and other properties equipped with recreational and athletic facilities.

3.9 *Service potential.* The capacity of an asset to continue to provide goods and services in accordance with the entity's objectives.

3.10 *Value of improvements.* The value added to the land by improvements such as buildings, structures or modifications to the land, of a permanent nature, involving expenditures of labour and capital, and intended to enhance the value or utility of the property. Improvements have differing patterns of use and economic lives.

International Public Sector Accounting Standards Definitions

3.11 *Cash Generating Assets.* Assets held to generate a commercial return. (IPSAS 21.14)

3.12 *Depreciable Amount.* The cost of an asset, or other amount substituted for cost, less its residual value (IPSAS 17.13).

3.13 *Depreciation.* The systematic allocation of the depreciable amount of an asset over its useful life (IPSAS 17.13, IPSAS 21.14).

3.14 *Government business enterprise* (GBE). An entity that has all of the following characteristics:

a) is an entity with the power to contract in its own name;

b) has been assigned the financial and operational authority to carry on a business;

c) sells goods and services, in the normal course of its business, to other entities at a profit or full cost recovery;

d) is not reliant on continuing government funding to be a going concern (other than purchases of outputs at arm's length); and

e) is controlled by a public service entity. (IPSAS 21.14)

3.15 *Heritage assets.* Assets having some cultural, environmental or historical significance. Heritage assets may include historical buildings and monuments, archaeological sites, conservation areas and nature reserves, and works of art. Heritage assets often display the following characteristics (although these characteristics are not necessarily limited to heritage assets):

a) their economic benefit in cultural, environmental, educational and historic terms is unlikely to be fully reflected in a financial value based purely on market price;

b) legal and/or statutory obligations may impose prohibitions or severe restrictions on disposal by sale;

c) they are often irreplaceable and their economic benefit may increase over time even if their physical condition deteriorates; and

d) it may be difficult to estimate their useful lives, which in some cases could be hundreds of years.

The above definition is consistent with the description of heritage assets in IPSAS 17.9

3.16 *Impairment*. A loss in the future economic benefits, or service potential of an asset, over and above the systematic recognition of the loss of the asset's future economic benefits or service potential through depreciation (IPSAS 21.14).

3.17 *Infrastructure assets*. Assets that usually display some or all of the following general characteristics:

a) they are part of a system or network;

b) they are specialised in nature and do not have alternative uses;

c) they are immovable; and

d) they may be subject to constraints on disposal.

The above definition is consistent with the description of infrastructure assets in IPSAS 17.21

3.18 *Non-cash-generating assets*. Assets other than cash-generating assets (IPSAS 21.14).

3.19 *Recoverable service amount*. The higher of a non-cash-generating asset's fair value less costs to sell and its value in use (IPSAS 21.14).

3.20 *Useful life (of property, plant and equipment)*. Either

a) the period over which an asset is expected to be available for use by an entity; or

b) the number of production or similar units expected to be obtained from the asset by an entity. (IPSAS 17.13, IPSAS 21.14)

3.21 *Value in use of a non-cash-generating asset*. The present value of the asset's remaining service potential. (IPSAS 21.14)

4.0 Relationship to Accounting Standards

4.1 This Application applies the principles developed in IVS 1, IVS 2, IVS 3 and IVA 1 to the requirements of IPSASs.

4.2 This Application focuses on valuation requirements under IPSAS 17 (Exposure Draft, September 2005), Property, Plant and Equipment; and IPSAS 21, Impairment of Non-Cash-Generating Assets. Further requirements may become mandatory, pending publication of revised IPSAS 17.

5.0 Application

To perform valuations that comply with this Application and Generally Accepted Valuation Principles (GAVP), it is essential that Valuers adhere to all sections of the IVS Code of Conduct pertaining to Ethics, Competence, Disclosure, and Reporting (sections 4, 5, 6, and 7)

5.1 *Classification of Assets.* Valuers shall obtain from the directors of the owning entity a list of assets to be valued, designating them as operational assets, i.e., assets requisite to the operations of the entity, or non-operational assets, being properties held for future development, investment, or assets surplus to the operations of the entity.

5.2 *Applicable Standards.* The classification of assets determines which IPSAS applies. IPSAS 17, paras. 26 and 27, requires non-current property, plant and equipment assets held for the production or supply of goods or services to be measured upon recognition at cost, or where an item is acquired through a non-exchange transaction, its cost shall be measured at its fair value at the date of acquisition. IPSAS 17, para. 42 requires that after recognition, such assets be carried in accordance with either the cost model or revaluation (fair value) model described in 5.3. Other accounting standards that require or permit the valuation of tangible assets include:

- Leases – IPSAS 13

- Investment Property – IPSAS 16

- Impairment of Non-Cash Generating Assets – IPSAS 21

5.3 IPSAS 17, *Cost and Fair Value*

5.3.1 IPSAS 17 deals with the cost model in paragraph 43 as follows:

"After recognition as an asset, an item of property, plant and equipment shall be carried at its cost less any accumulated depreciation and any accumulated impairment losses."

5.3.2 The fair value model, which requires regular revaluations, is explained in paragraph 44 as follows:

"After recognition as an asset, an item of property, plant and equipment whose fair value can be measured reliably shall be carried at a revalued amount, being its fair value at the date of the revaluation less any subsequent accumulated depreciation and subsequent accumulated impairment losses. Revaluations shall be made with sufficient regularity to ensure that the carrying amount does not differ materially from that which would be determined using fair value at the reporting date."

5.3.3 Fair value is not necessarily synonymous with *Market Value*. It is used throughout IPSASs in differing contexts.

5.3.4 Financial statements are produced on the assumption that the entity is a going concern unless management either intends to liquidate the entity or cease operation, or has no realistic alternative but to do so. This assumption therefore underlies the application of fair value to property plant and equipment, except in cases where it is clear that there is either an intention to dispose of a particular asset or that option of disposal has to be considered, e.g. when undertaking an impairment review.

5.4 *Valuations under IPSAS 17*

Where an entity adopts the fair value revaluation option under IPSAS 17, the assets are included in the balance sheet at their fair value as follows:

a) "The fair value of items of property is usually determined from market-based evidence by appraisal. The fair value of items of plant and equipment is usually their market value determined by appraisal" (IPSAS 17, para. 45).

b) "If no market evidence is available to determine the market value in an active and liquid market of an item of property, the fair value of the item may be established by reference to other items with similar characteristics, in similar circumstances and location…" (IPSAS 17, para. 47).

c) "If there is no market-based evidence of fair value because of the specialized nature of the item of plant and equipment, an entity may need to estimate fair value using ... depreciated replacement cost, or the restoration cost or service units approaches..."(IPSAS 17, para. 48). (See paras. 6.5, 6.6 and 6.7 below.)

5.4.1 IVSC considers that a professional Valuer undertaking an appraisal under 5.4 (a) to (c) above should report the *Market Value* of the asset. Any assumptions or qualifications made in applying *Market Value* should be discussed with the entity and disclosed in the report.

Where a reliable assessment of *Market Value* is not possible, the Valuer must disclose the basis for this conclusion to the reporting entity.

5.4.2 The valuation conclusion shall be reported in accordance with IVS 3, Valuation Reporting. Valuers shall ensure that reports include sufficient information for the entity to meet the requirements of IPSAS 17, para. 92, when preparing financial statements:

a) the effective date of the revaluation;

b) whether an Independent Valuer was involved (Note, IVSC interprets this as an *External Valuer*);

c) the methods applied and significant assumptions made ...; and

d) the extent to which the asset's fair values were determined directly by reference to observable prices in an active market or recent market transactions on arm's length terms, or were estimated using other valuation techniques.

5.5 Valuations under IPSAS 16 - Investment Property

All public sector investment property is valued in accordance with IVA 1.

5.6 Valuation Requirements for Leased Assets – IPSAS 13

5.6.1 Leased assets are classified under IPSAS 13 as either finance leases or operating leases. (For further explanation, see IVA 1, para. 6.6.1 and Addendum A.) If a lease is classified as a finance lease, the fair value of the asset is required to establish the amount of the asset and liability recorded by the entity on its balance sheet (IPSAS 13, para 20).

5.6.2 For leases of land and buildings special rules apply. (See IVA 1, para. 6.6.3.) For all property, other than investment property, land and buildings have to be considered separately for classification as either a finance lease or an operating lease.

5.6.3 IVSC considers that in each case the requirement to establish the fair value of the leased asset under IPSAS 13, para. 28, is met by the Valuer reporting the *Market Value*. For leases of real estate, this is the *Market Value* of the lease interest held by the lessee. For leases of other assets, it is normally the *Market Value* of the asset unencumbered by the lease, as the liability is recorded separately.

5.7 *Valuation of Impaired Non-Cash Generating Assets – IPSAS 21*

5.7.1 Impairment arises where there is a permanent decrease in the recoverable service amount of an asset below its carrying amount. IPSAS 21, para. 48, requires that if, and only if, the recoverable service amount of an asset is less than its carrying amount, the carrying amount of the asset shall be reduced to its recoverable service amount. That reduction is an impairment loss. IPSAS 21, para. 51, further states that when the amount estimated for an impairment loss is greater than the carrying amount of the asset to which it relates, an entity shall recognize a liability if, and only if, that is required by another IPSAS.

5.7.2 The entity is required to write down the carrying amount of impaired cash-generating assets to the higher of their *value in use* or *fair value less costs to sell.* The requirements for cash-generating assets are discussed further in IVA 1, para. 6.8.2.

5.8 *Valuations after Business Combinations*

5.8.1 Where a governmental or quasi-governmental entity acquires or is merged with another, the acquirer has to account for the assets and liabilities of the acquiree at their fair value as of the acquisition date. For identifiable assets and liabilities, IVSC considers that the Valuer should report their Market Value as they existed at the date of acquisition.

5.9 *Surplus Assets*

5.9.1 Surplus assets are to be separately identified. Such assets may be accounted for individually or as a "disposal group", i.e., a group of assets to be disposed of together, by sale or otherwise, and the liabilities directly associated with those assets that will also be transferred in the transaction. Surplus assets are to be initially accounted for at the lower of the carrying amount and the fair value less costs to sell, and subsequently at fair value less cost to sell. Valuers should therefore ascertain whether surplus assets are to be valued as individual items, or as a group or portfolio of assets that will be disposed of in a single transaction, and report the *Market Value* with the appropriate assumptions.

5.10 *Properties Held for Sale in the Ordinary Course of Business – IPSAS 12 Inventories*

5.10.1 Valuations of properties held for sale in the ordinary course of business should comply with the requirements of IPSAS 12, *Inventories*. These properties are measured at the lower of cost and *net realisable value*. Net realisable value is the estimated selling price in the ordinary course of operations less the estimated costs of completion and the estimated costs necessary to make the sale, exchange or distribution.

5.11 *Selling Costs*

5.11.1 When instructed to value impaired or surplus assets, or assets that are held for sale in the ordinary course of business, the Valuer must report their *Market Value* without deducting selling costs. If the client requests the Valuer to advise on the costs to sell the assets, such costs are to be reported separately.

5.12 *Non-Agricultural Biological Assets*

5.12.1 These include naturally occurring flora and fauna. The Valuer should value these assets in accordance with the guidance in GN 10.

5.13 *Co-operation with Auditors*. Subject to first obtaining the consent of their client, Valuers shall discuss and explain their valuations openly with the entity's auditors.

6.0 Discussion

IPSAS 17 and 21 provide the following clarification, which is useful in understanding the correct application for public sector accounting.

6.1 *Absence of Market Evidence - IPSAS 17*

"For some public sector assets, it may be difficult to establish their market value because of the absence of market transactions for these assets. Some public sector entities may have significant holdings of these assets". (IPSAS 17, para. 46)

6.1.1 "If no market evidence is available to determine the market value in an active and liquid market of an item of property, the fair value of the item may be established by reference to other items with similar characteristics, in similar circumstances and location. For example, the fair value of vacant government land that has been held for a long period during which time there have been few transactions may be estimated by reference to the market value of land with similar features and topography in a similar location for which market evidence is available. In the case of specialized buildings and other man-made structures, fair value may be estimated by using depreciated replacement cost, or the restoration cost or the service units approach (see IPSAS 21). In many cases, the depreciated replacement cost of an asset can be established by reference to the buying price of a similar asset with similar remaining service potential in an active and liquid market. In some cases, an asset's reproduction cost will be the best indicator of its replacement cost. For example, in the event of loss, a parliament building may be reproduced rather than replaced with alternative accommodation because of its significance to the community". (IPSAS 17, para. 47)

6.1.2 "If there is no market-based evidence of fair value because of the specialized nature of the item of plant and equipment, an entity may need to estimate fair value using depreciated replacement cost, or the restoration cost or service units approaches (see IPSAS 21). The depreciated replacement cost of an item of plant or equipment may be established by reference to the market buying price of components used to produce the assets or indexed price for the same or similar asset based on a price for a previous period. When an indexed price method is used, judgement is required to determine whether technology has changed significantly over the period, and whether the capacity of the reference asset is the same as the asset being valued". (IPSAS 17, para. 48)

6.2 *Government Business Enterprises* (GBEs) – *IPSAS 21*

"GBEs include both trading enterprises, such as utilities, and financial enterprises, such as financial institutions. GBEs are, in substance, no different from entities conducting similar activities in the private sector. GBEs generally operate to make a profit, although some may have limited community service obligations under which they are required to provide some individuals and organizations in the community with goods and services at either no charge or a significantly reduced charge". (IPSAS 21, para. 15)

6.3 *Cash-Generating Assets – IPSAS 21*

"Cash-generating assets are those that are held to generate a commercial return. An asset generates a commercial return when it is deployed in a manner consistent with that adopted by a profit-oriented entity. Holding an asset to generate a 'commercial return' indicates that an entity intends to generate positive cash inflows from the asset (or of the unit of which the asset is a part) and earn a return that reflects the risk involved in holding the asset". (IPSAS 21, para. 16)

"Assets held by GBEs are cash-generating assets. Public sector entities other than GBEs may hold assets to generate a commercial return. For the purposes of this Standard [IPSAS 21], an asset held by a non-GBE public sector entity is classified as a cash-generating asset if the asset (or unit of which the asset is a part) is operated with the objective of generating a commercial return through the provision of goods and or services to external parties". (IPSAS 21, para. 17)

6.4 *Value in Use* – *IPSAS 21*

"The value in use of a non-cash-generating asset is the present value of the asset's remaining service potential. 'Value in use' in this Standard [IPSAS 21] refers to 'value in use of a non-cash-generating asset' unless otherwise specified. The present value of the remaining service potential of the asset is determined using any one of the approaches identified in paragraphs 41 to 45, as appropriate". (IPSAS 21, para. 40)

6.5 Depreciated Replacement Cost Approach – IPSAS 21

"Under this approach, the present value of the remaining service potential of an asset is determined as the depreciated replacement cost of the asset. The replacement cost of an asset is the cost to replace the asset's gross service potential. This cost is depreciated to reflect the asset in its used condition. An asset may be replaced either through reproduction (replication) of the existing asset or through replacement of its gross service potential. The depreciated replacement cost is measured as the reproduction or replacement cost of the asset, whichever is lower, less accumulated depreciation calculated on the basis of such cost, to reflect the already consumed or expired service potential of the asset". (IPSAS 21, para. 41)

"The replacement cost and reproduction cost of an asset are determined on an 'optimized' basis. The rationale is that the entity would not replace or reproduce the asset with a like asset if the asset to be replaced or reproduced is an overdesigned or overcapacity asset. Overdesigned assets contain features which are unnecessary for the goods or services the asset provides. Overcapacity assets are assets that have a greater capacity than is necessary to meet the demand for goods or services the asset provides. The determination of the replacement cost or reproduction cost of an asset on an optimized basis thus reflects the service potential required of the asset". (IPSAS 21, para. 42).

"In certain cases, standby or surplus capacity is held for safety or other reasons. This arises from the need to ensure that adequate service capacity is available in the particular circumstances of the entity. For example, the fire department needs to have fire engines on standby to deliver services in emergencies. Such surplus or standby capacity is part of the required service potential of the asset". (IPSAS 21, para. 43)

6.6 Restoration Cost Approach – IPSAS 21

"Restoration cost is the cost of restoring the service potential of an asset to its pre-impaired level. Under this approach, the present value of the remaining service potential of the asset is determined by subtracting the estimated restoration cost of the asset from the current cost of replacing the remaining service potential of the asset before impairment. The latter cost is usually determined as the depreciated reproduction or replacement cost of the asset whichever is lower". (IPSAS 21, para. 44)

6.7 *Service Units Approach – IPSAS 21*

"Under this approach, the present value of the remaining service potential of the asset is determined by reducing the current cost of the remaining service potential of the asset before impairment to conform with the reduced number of service units expected from the asset in its impaired state. As in the restoration cost approach, the current cost of replacing the remaining service potential of the asset before impairment is usually determined as the depreciated reproduction or replacement cost of the asset before impairment, whichever is lower". (IPSAS 21, para. 45)

6.8 *Other Considerations*

6.8.1 *Heritage Assets.* "Some heritage assets have service potential other than their heritage value, for example, an historic building being used for office accommodation. In these cases, they may be recognized and measured on the same basis as other items of property plant and equipment. For other heritage assets, their service potential is limited to their heritage characteristics, for example, monuments and ruins. The existence of alternative service potential can affect the choice of measurement base". (IPSAS 17, para. 10)

6.8.2 *Non-Agricultural Biological Assets.* Naturally occurring flora and fauna include special conservation assets, which may or may not be protected. Some are so significant that they have international recognition while others may reflect the environment in its natural state.

6.8.3 *Absence of Free Cash Flows to Monopolies.* Some public sector entities can be classed as monopolies. While monopoly service providers often generate cash flows, these cash flows cannot be considered reflective of market levels since there is no market evidence against which to check the characteristic circularity of cash flow, yield, and value. Thus, a critical feature that differentiates certain classes of public sector assets from private sector assets is the absence of "free" cash flows to such public sector entities. In some cases it may be appropriate to use the cost approach either as the primary valuation method or as a cross check to establish that the rate of return being earned from the assets being valued is reasonable. This application does not apply to government business enterprises (GBEs), which are valued according to IVA 1.

6.8.4 *Test of Adequate Service Potential.* As non-cash generating assets have no free cash flows to test the adequate profitability of a public sector asset, the concept of *service potential* becomes the test of an asset's performance. Service Potential is a measure of the suitability of the asset to continue meeting the objectives of the entity. This suitability may be assessed by reference to financial, social or political considerations. The measurement may be tangible, for example the number of visitors to a museum or users of a public library, or intangible, e.g., the social benefits of maintaining an otherwise uneconomic facility in a particular location.

Where a non-cash-generating asset is measured by reference to depreciated replacement cost, it is subject to the test of adequate service potential in order to determine whether the asset is impaired. (Also see GN 8, para. 5.11.)

6.8.5 *Frequency of Revaluations.* "Revaluations shall be made with sufficient regularity to ensure that the carrying amount does not differ materially from that which would be determined using fair value at the reporting date...." (IPSAS 17, para. 44)

In volatile markets the entity may be required to revalue annually whereas in more stable markets revaluations may be required every three to five years.

7.0 Disclosure Requirements

7.1 The Valuer shall make all disclosures required under IVS 3, Valuation Reporting.

7.2 For disclosures required under International Public Sector Accounting Standards (IPSASs), see paragraph 5.4.2 above.

7.3 The Valuer shall disclose the regulatory framework, and any departure required from these Standards to comply with local legislation, regulation (including accounting rules), or custom.

7.3 When no reliable measurement is possible, disclosure must be made to the reporting entity. (See para. 5.4.1 above.)

8.0 Departure Provisions

8.1 In following this Application any departures must be in accordance with directions given in IVS 3, Valuation Reporting.

9.0 Effective Date

9.1 This International Valuation Application became effective 31 July 2007.

Guidance Notes

International Valuation Standards Committee

International Valuation Guidance Note No. 1

Real Property Valuation (Revised 2007)

1.0 Introduction

1.1 The International Valuation Standards Committee's (IVSC) Concepts Fundamental to Generally Accepted Valuation Principles set forth terms and concepts that are fundamental to all valuations. The purpose of Guidance Note No.1 (GN 1) is to amplify those fundamentals so they may be better understood in valuations of real property.

1.2 *Real property* constitutes a substantial portion of the world's wealth. If the operations of property markets are to be established on dependable valuations, there must be generally agreed upon Standards by which *Market Value* and other value types are determined and reported by Valuers. Correct understanding and proper application of these Standards will inevitably promote the viability of international and domestic transactions in real property, improve the relative position of real property among other investment alternatives, and reduce the instances of fraud and abuse.

1.3 The term *property* in a legal sense may be defined as ownership rather than the physical entity of land, buildings, and tangible personal items. In this context, the IVSC identifies four general property types:

    1.3.1 Real Property (GN 1)

    1.3.2 Personal Property (GNs 3, 4, and 5)

    1.3.3 Businesses (GN 6)

    1.3.4 Financial Interests

1.4 As with other property types, there are commonly agreed upon and generally accepted methods for valuing real property. It is important to the Valuer and the users of valuation services that proper methods be thoroughly understood, competently applied, and satisfactorily explained. By meeting this objective, Valuers contribute to the soundness and reliability of *Market Value* estimates and, thereby, the well-being of the markets in which they practice.

1.5 Promotion of understanding and avoidance of abuses in the market require that the Valuer and user of valuation services carefully distinguish between the types of property. Failure to do so can result in improper or ill-advised market decisions and misrepresentations of reported values. Over- or under-reporting of value is a common result where property types are confused or mixed. The same is true when terminology is indistinct or inadequate.

1.6 Real Property Valuers recognise the complexities of markets and the real estate bought and sold therein. Differences in real estate markets and between individual properties are reflected accurately and reliably where Generally Accepted Valuation Principles (GAVP) are followed.

1.7 In all IVSC Member States, it is recognised that the valuation of real property requires special education, training, and experience. Just as the emergence of professional valuation societies at the national level attests to a market need for competent and highly ethical Valuers within each country, the globalisation of property markets and the establishment of IVSC reflect the market need for Valuers to adopt consistent methods throughout the world. GN 1, Real Property, provides an international framework for the application of generally accepted methods used for real property valuation.

1.8 The relationship between GNs 6 and 12, pertaining to business and trade related property (TRP) valuation, and GN 1, pertaining to real property valuation, must be clearly understood. Real property is valued as a distinct "entity," i.e., as physical assets to which particular ownership rights apply. For example, an office building, a residence, a factory, or other property types generally incorporate an underlying land component. Business or TRP valuation, however, values a business entity or TRP asset of which real property may be a component. The *Market Value* of real property is always valued in accordance with International Valuation Standard 1 (IVS 1). When a real property value estimate is incorporated as an element of a business valuation, it is a *Market Value* estimate of the real property. As discussed in GN 1, this convention is distinct from the unacceptable practice of purportedly developing a *Market Value* estimate for real property as an allocation of the value of a going concern.

1.9 It is not the objective of GN 1 to provide specific Guidance as to how a given valuation should be performed or to supercede the qualifications for and procedures applied by Valuers. These are addressed within the training programs of each State. It is the IVSC's intent to establish a framework and requirements for real property valuation that will serve to harmonise worldwide valuation practices.

2.0 Scope

2.1 This GN is provided to assist in the course of rendering or using real property valuations.

2.2 Principal elements of GN 1 include

2.2.1 an identification of key terms and definitions;

2.2.2 a summary of the Valuation Process and its rationale;

2.2.3 an elaboration on the importance of principles and concepts;

2.2.4 a discussion of proper disclosure and reporting requirements;

2.2.5 examples of abuses and misunderstandings; and

2.2.6 a presentation of real property Guidance.

2.3 The specific application of quantitative and qualitative valuation procedures is beyond the scope of GN 1. It is important to stress, however, that Valuers are trained in such procedures, and that the procedures are included in generally accepted practices. In application, Valuers commonly apply several procedures in each valuation and then reconcile the results into a final indication of *Market Value* or other specified value.

3.0 Definitions

3.1 Concepts Fundamental to Generally Accepted Valuation Principles defines the concepts of *land* and *property; real estate, property, and asset; price, cost,* and *value; Market Value, highest and best use,* and *utility.* The Glossary of Terms further defines many of the concepts and technical terms used throughout the Standards and Guidance Notes. The following definitions are specific to GN 1 and are included here for reader convenience.

3.2 *Comparable Data.* Data generally used in a valuation analysis to develop value estimates. *Comparable Data* relate to properties that have characteristics similar to those of the property being valued (the subject property). Such data include sale prices, rents, income and expenses, and market-derived capitalisation and yield/discount rates.

3.3 *Elements of Comparison.* Specific characteristics of properties and transactions that cause the prices paid for real estate to vary. *Elements of comparison* include, but are not limited to, the following: property rights conveyed, financing terms, conditions of sale, market conditions, location, and physical and economic characteristics. (See para. 5.22 of this document for a full presentation of *Elements of Comparison.*)

3.4 *Highest and Best Use.* The most probable use of a property which is physically possible, appropriately justified, legally permissible, financially feasible, and which results in the highest value of the property being valued. (See Concepts Fundamental to Generally Accepted Valuation Principles, section 6.)

3.5 A *Market.* The environment in which goods, services and commodities trade between buyers and sellers through a price mechanism.

3.6 *Market Value.* Definitions are included in Concepts Fundamental to Generally Accepted Valuation Principles and International Valuation Standard 1, section 3.

3.7 *Property Rights.* The rights that are related to the ownership of real estate. These include the right to develop or not develop the land, to lease it to others, to sell it, to give it away, to farm it, to mine it, to alter its topography, to subdivide it, to assemble it, to use it for waste disposal, or to choose to exercise none of these rights. The combination of these property rights is sometimes referred to as the *bundle of rights* inherent in the ownership of real estate. *Property rights* are typically subject to public or private restrictions such as easements, rights-of-ways, specified development density, zoning, and other restrictions that may encumber the property.

3.8 *Real Estate.* Land and all things that are a natural part of the land, e.g., trees and minerals, as well as all things that are attached by people, e.g., buildings and site improvements. All permanent building attachments such as plumbing, heating and cooling systems; electrical wiring; and built-in items like elevators, or lifts, are also part of the *real estate. Real estate* includes all attachments, both below and above the ground. (See also Concepts Fundamental to Generally Accepted Valuation Principles as well as in the Glossary of Terms.)

3.9 *Real Property.* All the rights, interests, and benefits related to the ownership of *real estate. Real property* is a legal concept distinct from *real estate,* which is a physical asset. There may also be potential limitations upon ownership rights to real property. (See Property Types, paras. 2.2.1 and 2.2.4.)

3.10 *Units of Comparison.* Typically a factor produced by two components, which reflects precise differences between properties and facilitates analysis in the three approaches to value, e.g., price per square metre or square foot, or the ratio of a property's sale price to its net income (net income multiplier/years' purchase).

3.11 The *Cost Approach.* One of the approaches to value commonly applied in *Market Value* estimates and many other valuation situations.

Depreciated replacement cost is an application of the cost approach used in assessing the value of specialised assets for financial reporting purposes, where direct market evidence is limited. (See GN 8, The Cost Approach for Financial Reporting-(DRC).)

4.0 Relationship to Accounting Standards

4.1 For a general discussion of the accounting requirements for real property valuations, and the utility of *Market Value* in promoting the objectivity and comparability of real property valuations, see International Valuation Application 1.

5.0 Guidance

5.1 Value, in its broadest sense, is defined as the relationship between something owned and an individual or individuals who wish(es) to own it. To distinguish between the broad subjective relationships that may occur among people, Valuers must identify a particular type of value as the basis of any valuation. *Market Value* **is the most common value type, but valuation bases other than** *Market Value* **also exist.** (See Introduction to Standards 1, 2 and 3; and IVSs 1 and 2.)

5.1.1 *Market Value* has evolved in concept and definition under the influence of market forces and in response to various principles of real estate economics. **By applying a definition of value such as *Market Value* in valuations, Valuers and the users of their services are afforded an objective plan of analysis.**

5.1.2 When *Market Value* is the purpose of a valuation, the Valuer shall apply definitions, processes, and methods consistent with IVS 1.

5.2 Where a type of value other than *Market Value* is the purpose of a valuation, the Valuer shall apply the appropriate definition of value and shall follow IVS 2 and applicable GNs. It is the responsibility of the Valuer to avoid potential misunderstandings or misapplications of the valuation estimate in situations where a value other than *Market Value* is the purpose of the assignment. Proper disclosures, identification and definition of terms, and stated limitations on the applicability of the valuation and the Valuation Report normally ensure compliance.

5.3 GN Figure 1-1 illustrates the Valuation Process as it is applied in many States. The process reflects Generally Accepted Valuation Principles (GAVP) and is approximated in virtually all States, whether or not the particular steps are explicitly followed. The principles from which this process derives are common to all States. Although the process may be used for either *Market Value* or applications founded on other bases of value, *Market Value* applications require the development of valuations solely on the basis of market data.

5.4 A valuation must be distinguished from a Valuation Report. Valuation includes all of the research, data, reasoning, analysis, and conclusions necessary to arrive at a value estimate. A Valuation Report communicates those processes and conclusions. Although requirements differ among States, it is a requisite under these Standards that adequate records be kept to demonstrate that a Valuation Process was followed and that the conclusions are credible and reliable. These records must be available in case reasonable enquiry is subsequently made. (See IVS Code of Conduct, para. 5.3.5 and 5.3.6.) In practice, some forms of reporting may incompletely represent the entire basis for the valuation. **If the report is in any way limited, the Valuer will generally identify and distinguish between the scope of the valuation and that of the Valuation Report.**

Guidance Note Figure 1-1
The Valuation Process

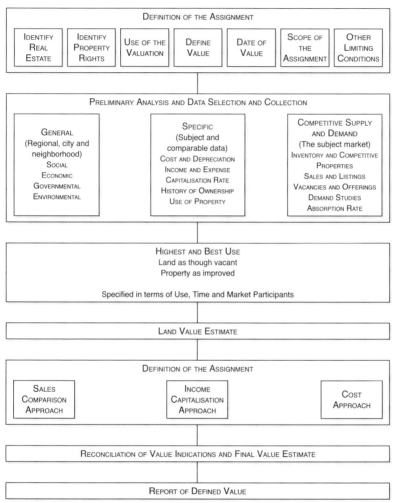

5.5 It is appropriate and customary that a *client's instruction* **(para. 5.6 below) be stated in writing in a** *letter* **or** *contract for services.* In *Market Value* situations it is also common for the independence, or external status, of the Valuer to be established in an affirmative statement. The agreement also sets forth the business relationship between the Valuer and the client, fee and payment terms, special directives and limitations, an identification of the Standards to be applied, and other pertinent matters.

5.6 As GN Figure 1-1 indicates, **a Valuer and the valuation client must agree on the context and scope of the valuation. The** *definition of the assignment* **includes**

5.6.1 an identification of the real estate involved in the valuation;

5.6.2 an identification of the property rights to be valued;

5.6.3 the intended use of the valuation, and any related limitations;

5.6.4 the identification of any subcontractors or agents and their contribution;

5.6.5 a definition of or the basis of the value sought;

5.6.6 the date as of which the value estimate will apply; and the date of the intended report;

5.6.7 an identification of the scope/extent of the valuation and of the report; and

5.6.8 an identification of any contingent and limiting conditions upon which the valuation is based.

5.7 In performing the steps of a *preliminary analysis,* **and** *data selection and collection,* **suggested in the Valuation Process, the Valuer becomes familiar with the general market and subject property, thereby proceeding to a position from which more specific analyses can be made.**

5.7.1 *General economic data* are collected at the neighbourhood, city, regional, and even national and international levels, depending on the property involved. Social, economic, governmental, and environmental factors that may have bearing on *Market Value* (or other defined value type) are examined to better understand the particular property. Any other specific forces that must be considered are investigated in detail.

5.7.2 *Property-specific data,* or data more directly relevant to the property being valued and to comparable properties are also gathered and examined. These include site and improvement data, cost and depreciation data, income and expense data, capitalisation and yield rate data, ownership and utilisation histories, and other information determined to be significant and generally considered by buyers and sellers in their negotiations and transactions.

5.7.3 *Supply and demand data* characteristic of the most probable market for the property are analysed to develop an inventory of properties that compete with the subject property for market share as well as an inventory of existing properties to be adapted or new properties to be built, which will increase the competitive supply. Markets are analysed to determine market trends, relationships between supply and demand, absorption rates, and other market-specific information.

5.8 Once the above data are gathered and analysed, the Valuer will be able to determine possible land uses for the subject property. Because different real estate parcels may have different use potentials, **the first requisite step toward selecting sales and other comparable data is to determine the *highest and best use* (HABU) of the subject property. The Valuer considers both the *highest and best use of the land as though vacant* and the *highest and best use of the property as improved*.** (See the discussion of HABU in Concepts Fundamental to Generally Accepted Valuation Principles, para. 6.0 et seq.)

5.8.1 The concept of HABU is based on the notion that although two or more parcels of real estate may have physical similarities and closely resemble one another, there may be significant differences in how they can be used. How a property can be optimally utilised is a foundation for determining its *Market Value*.

5.8.2 Basic determinants of HABU include the answers to the following questions:

- Is the suggested use a reasonable and likely one?

- Is the use legal, or is there a reasonable likelihood that a legal entitlement for the use can be obtained?

- Is the property physically suited to the use or can it be adapted to the use?

- Is the suggested use financially feasible? and

- Of those uses that meet the first four tests, is the selected HABU the most productive use of the land?

5.9 Several methods are used for land valuation. Their applicability differs according to the type of value estimated and availability of data. **For *Market Value* estimates, any method chosen must be supported by market data.** (See para. 5.25 et seq.)

5.10 In many, but not all, States **three *valuation approaches* are recognised in the Valuation Process: *sales comparison*, *income capitalisation*, and *cost*.** While a well-evidenced market may make the *cost approach* less relevant, a lack of comparable data may cause the *cost approach* to be predominant. The laws of some States preclude or limit the application of one or more of the three approaches. Unless there are such restrictions, or unless there are other compelling reasons for a particular omission, **it is reasonable for the Valuer to consider each approach.** In some States, the use of each approach is mandated unless the Valuer can demonstrate a lack of supporting data or other valid reason for omission of a particular approach. **Each approach is based, in part, on the Principle of Substitution,** which holds that when several similar or commensurate commodities, goods, or services are available, the one with the lowest price attracts the greatest demand and widest distribution. In simple terms, the price of a property established by a given market is limited by the prices commonly paid for properties that compete with it for market share, the financial alternatives of investing money elsewhere, and the cost of building a new property or adapting an old property to a use similar to that of the subject property (property being valued).

5.11 The *sales comparison approach* recognizes that property prices are determined by the market. ***Market Value* can, therefore, be calculated from a study of market prices for properties that compete with one another for market share.** The comparative processes applied are fundamental to the Valuation Process.

5.11.1 When data are available, the *sales comparison approach* is the most direct and systematic approach to estimating value.

5.11.2 When data are insufficient, the applicability of the *sales comparison approach* may be limited. Insufficient research by the Valuer, however, is not an excuse for omission of this approach where data are available or could reasonably be developed. (See section 5.23 et seq. for discussion of market research, data verification, adjustment procedure, and reconciliation of indications.)

5.11.3 After sales data are gathered and verified, one or more *units of comparison* are selected and analysed. Units of comparison use two components to produce a factor (e.g., the price per measurement unit or a ratio such as that produced by dividing a property's sale price by its net income, i.e., net income multiplier, or years' purchase) that reflects precise differences between properties. The units of comparison that buyers and sellers in a given market use in making their purchase and sale decisions take on special relevance and may be afforded greater weight.

5.11.4 *Elements of comparison* are the specific characteristics of properties and transactions that cause the prices paid for real estate to vary. They are crucial considerations in the *sales comparison approach.*

5.11.5 To make direct comparisons between a comparable sale property and the subject property, a Valuer shall consider possible adjustments based on differences in the elements of comparison. Adjustments can narrow the differences between each comparable and the subject. **Valuers apply quantitative and/or qualitative methods to analyse differences and estimate adjustments.**

5.12 The *income capitalisation approach* can be applied in both *Market Value* assignments and other types of valuations. However, for *Market Value* applications, it is necessary to develop and analyse relevant market information. This focus differs distinctly from the development of subjective information for a specific owner or the reflection or viewpoint of a particular analyst or investor.

**5.12.1 The *income capitalisation approach* is based on the same principles that apply to other valuation approaches. In particular, it perceives value as created by the expectation of future benefits (income streams). *Income capitalisation* employs processes that consider the present value of anticipated future income benefits.

5.12.2 As with other approaches, **the** *income capitalisation approach* **can be used reliably only when relevant comparative data are available.** When such information is not available, the approach may be used for general analysis but not for the purpose of direct market comparison. **The** *income capitalisation approach* **is particularly important for properties that are purchased and sold on the basis of their earnings capabilities and characteristics and in situations where there is market evidence to support the various elements incorporated into the analysis.** Nonetheless, the mathematical precision of the procedures used in the approach must not be mistaken as an indication of the precise accuracy of the results.

5.12.3 Market research is important to the *income capitalisation approach* in a number of ways. In addition to **providing specific data that will be processed, market research also furnishes qualitative information to determine comparability and to assist in weighing the applicability of the results of the analysis.** Thus, the approach is not merely quantitative, or mathematical, but requires qualitative assessments as well.

5.12.4 Once appropriate market research is completed and comparable data are collected and verified, **Valuers analyse the income and expense statement provided for the subject property. This step involves a study of the historical incomes and expenses of the property under consideration and of other competing properties for which data are available.** Subsequently, **a cash flow (based upon a** *reconstructed operating statement***) is developed that reflects market expectations, eliminates the special experiences of a particular owner, and provides a format that assists further analysis.** The purpose of this step is to estimate the income that can be earned by the property, which will be capitalised into an indication of value. **This estimate may reflect income and expenses for only a single year or a series of years.**

5.12.5 Following the development of a cash flow (based on a *reconstructed operating statement*), the Valuer must choose a means of capitalisation. **Direct capitalisation applies an** *overall rate,* **or** *all risks yield,* **which, when divided into a single year's or stabilized net operating income, produces a value indication.** *Direct capitalisation* is used in particularly well-evidenced markets. **Yield capitalisation considers the time value of money, and is applied to a series of net operating incomes for a period of years. A method called** *discounted cash flow* *analysis* (DCF) is a prominent example of *yield capitalisation.* (See Guidance Note 9). Either *direct capitalisation* or *yield capitalisation* (or both) can be applied to estimate *Market Value* if the capitalisation and yield rates are appropriately supported by the market. If applied correctly, both procedures should result in the same value estimate.

15.12.6 Reconstructed operating statements specify that the income projection is subject to the assumption that the property is run by a reasonably efficient operator or average competent management.

5.13 The *cost approach,* also known as the contractor's method, is recognised in most States. In any application, **the** *cost approach* **establishes value by estimating the costs of acquiring land and building a new property with equal utility or adapting an old property to the same use with no undue expense resulting from delay.** The cost of land is added to the total cost of construction. (Where applicable, an estimate of entrepreneurial incentive, or developer's profit/loss, is commonly added to construction costs.) The *cost approach* establishes the upper limit of what the market would normally pay for a given property when it is new. **For an older property, some allowance for various forms of accrued depreciation (physical deterioration; functional, or technical, obsolescence; and economic, or external obsolescence) is deducted to estimate a price that approximates** *Market Value.* Depending upon the extent of market data available for the calculations, the cost approach may produce a direct indication of *Market Value.* The *cost approach* is very useful in estimating the *Market Value* of proposed construction, special-purpose properties, and other properties that are not frequently exchanged in the market. (See also GN 8, The Cost Approach for Financial Reporting-(DRC).)

5.14 The three approaches to value are independent of one another even though each approach is based on the same economic principles. All three approaches are intended to develop an indication of value, but **the final value conclusion depends on consideration of all data and processes employed and the reconciliation of the value indications derived from different approaches into a final estimate of value.** As shown in GN Figure 1-1, the reconciliation process is followed by a report of defined value.

5.15 The requirements for valuation reports are addressed in the IVSC Code of Conduct, and IVS 3, Valuation Reporting.

5.16 Where there is sufficient market data to support the valuation, *Market Value* **is derived.** In other circumstances, where there is insufficient market data or special instructions have been given, the result will be a value other than *Market Value.*

5.17 The existence of different types of value must not confuse Valuers or the users of valuation services. *Market Value,* **the value type most commonly sought in the market, is distinct from all other value types. Each of the other value types has its own rationale and application and shall be investigated only in an appropriate context.** By proper reporting, adequate disclosure and discussion, and the assurance that the value type identified in the valuation report suits the intended purpose and use of the valuation, the Valuer assists the market in its reliance on valuations.

5.18 The terms *market* **and** *markets* **imply properties, buyers, sellers, and some degree of competition.** If a property chosen for comparison does not, or cannot, compete in the same market as the property being valued, it is likely that the comparison property belongs to a different market.

5.19 The totality of private ownership rights associated with a particular property is referred to as a *freehold interest,* a *fee simple interest,* or by other appropriate terms depending on the State.

5.20 In any analysis of comparable data, it is essential that the properties from which the comparable data are collected have characteristics similar to the property being valued. These include legal, physical, locational, and use characteristics that are consistent with those of the subject property and reflect conditions in the market where the subject property competes. Differences shall be noted and analysed to develop adjustments in all three valuation approaches.

> **5.20.1 In the** *sales comparison approach,* **comparable sales data** are adjusted to reflect the differences between each comparable property and the subject property. **Elements of comparison** include real property rights conveyed, financing terms, conditions of sale, expenditures made immediately after purchase, market conditions, location, physical characteristics, economic characteristics, use, and non-realty components of a sale.

5.20.2 In the *income capitalisation approach,* **comparable data** include rental, income, expense, and capitalisation and yield rate data. **The categories of** comparable income and expense **data** used in projections of future income and expenses and in the development of capitalisation and yield rates **must be identical.**

5.20.3 In the *cost approach,* **comparable data** refer to the costs of building or development, and adjustments are made to account for differences in quantities, qualities, and utility. In addition, analysis of comparable land data and comparable depreciation estimates is undertaken.

5.21 Suitable *units of comparison* are selected to conduct proper analyses. Different units of comparison may be used, depending on the property type and focus of the analyses. Office buildings and warehouse properties can be compared using price per square metre or square foot of leaseable or lettable area. In some markets, comparison of warehouse properties may use price per cubic metre or cubic foot; apartments can be compared using price per apartment unit or flat; and agricultural properties can be compared, using crop yield per hectare or per acre or supportable Animal Units (AU) per hectare or per acre. **Units of comparison are only useful when they are consistently selected and applied to the subject property and the comparable properties in each analysis and most closely reflect the units of comparison used by buyers and sellers in a particular market.**

5.22 *Elements of comparison* identify specific characteristics of properties and transactions that may explain price variations. Market analysis identifies which elements are especially sensitive. **The following elements of comparison are considered as basic in comparable sales analysis.**

5.22.1 *Real property rights conveyed.* A precise identification of the real property rights conveyed in each comparable transaction, selected for analysis, is essential because the transaction price is always predicated on the property interest conveyed.

5.22.2 *Financing terms.* Where different financing arrangements can cause the price paid for one property to differ from that of another identical property, the types and conditions of financing arrangements in the transaction shall be fully understood, analysed, and accounted for.

5.22.3 *Conditions of sale.* The special motivations of the parties to the transaction in many situations can affect the prices paid and even render some transactions as non-market. Examples of special conditions of sale include a higher price paid by a buyer because the parcel had synergistic, or marriage, value; a lower price paid because a seller was in a hurry to conclude the sale; a financial, business, or family relationship between the parties involved in the transaction; unusual tax considerations; lack of exposure of the property in the (open) market; or the prospect of lengthy litigation proceedings.

5.22.4 *Expenditures made immediately after the purchase* are expenditures that would have to be made upon purchase of the property and that a knowledgeable buyer may negotiate into the purchase price. Examples include the cost to repair or replace structures or parts of structures, the cost to remediate environmental contamination, or the costs associated with zoning changes to permit development.

5.22.5 *Market conditions.* Market conditions at the time of the sales transaction of a comparable property may differ from those on the valuation date of the property being valued. Factors that impact market conditions include rapidly appreciating or depreciating property values, changes in tax laws, building restrictions or moratoriums, fluctuations in supply and demand, or any combination of forces working in concert to alter market conditions from one date to another.

5.22.6 *Location.* The locations of the comparable sale properties and the subject property are compared to ascertain whether location and the immediate environs are influencing the prices paid. Extreme locational differences may indicate that a transaction is not truly comparable and should be disqualified.

5.22.7 *Physical characteristics.* Attributes such as the size, construction quality, and physical condition of the subject property and the comparable properties are described and analysed by the Valuer. If the physical characteristics of a comparable property vary from those of the subject property, each of the differences is considered, and the Valuer shall adjust for the impact of each of these differences on value.

5.22.8 *Economic characteristics.* Qualities such as income, operating expenses, lease provisions, management, and tenant mix are used to analyse income-producing properties.

5.22.9 *Use.* Zoning and other restrictions or limitations affect the use of a property. If there is a difference in the current use or *highest and best use* of a comparable property and that of the subject property, its impact on value shall be carefully considered. Generally, only properties with the same or similar *highest and best uses* are used in comparable analysis.

5.22.10 *Non-realty components of sale.* Personal property, business interests, or other items that do not constitute real property may be included in either the transaction price or the ownership interest in the property being valued. These components shall be analysed separately from the real property. Typical examples of personal property are furniture, fixtures, and equipment (FF&E) in a hotel or restaurant.

5.23 In applying the *sales comparison approach,* a Valuer follows a systematic procedure. The Valuer will:

5.23.1 Research the market to develop appropriate market information for similar properties that compete with the subject for market share; this information will vary among different property types but will commonly include the property type, date of sale, size, location, zoning, and other relevant information.

5.23.2 Verify the information by confirming that it is accurate and that the terms and conditions of sale are consistent with *Market Value* requirements; where differences occur, the Valuer will determine whether the data warrant only general consideration.

5.23.3 Select relevant units of comparison (e.g., price per metre or per square square foot; price per room; income multiplier, or years' purchase; or others) and develop a comparative analysis for each unit.

5.23.4 Compare the sale properties with the subject property using the elements of comparison and adjusting the sale price of each comparable property when data are available to support such adjustments. As an alternative, the Valuer may use the sales data to bracket or determine a probable range of values for the property. If the data are found not to be sufficiently comparable, the sale property shall be eliminated as a comparable.

5.23.5 **Reconcile the results into a value indication.** Where market conditions are indefinite, or when an array of the sales data shows varying degrees of comparability, it may be advisable to develop a range of value indications.

5.24 *Highest and best use* **underlies the analysis for all** *Market Value* **assignments.** An understanding of real estate market behaviour and dynamics is essential to the determination of a property's *highest and best use.* Since market forces create *Market Value,* the interaction between market forces and *highest and best use is* of fundamental importance. **Highest and best use identifies the most profitable use among potential uses to which the property can be put, and is, therefore, market-driven.**

5.24.1 It is possible that the *highest and best use* (HABU) of land as though it were vacant and the HABU of an improved parcel of land are different. In many States, it may be illegal to demolish buildings even if a more productive use is possible. Where demolition and site clearance are legal and possible, the costs associated with them might make new construction economically unfeasible. Thus, it is possible that there is a difference between the HABU of land as though vacant and that of the property as improved. The Valuer must analyse and report these considerations, and clearly distinguish which HABU was selected. The Valuer must also provide support for the HABU selection.

5.24.2 In many States, it is necessary to make a land value estimate based on the HABU as though there were no improvements on the land. This HABU determination is, of course, necessary if the land is vacant, but it also provides an economic basis for judging the productivity of the improvements when they are present. The practice also involves analysing market information to determine the extent of accrued depreciation that may be present in the improvements. In other States, or in situations where there is little, if any, market information on vacant land sales, it is possible that land value may not be estimated. Local standards within each State prescribe practice in these situations, but in any event such restrictions shall be fully and clearly understood.

5.25 **The primary methods of valuing land are:**

5.25.1 A *sales comparison* **technique** for land valuation involves direct comparison of the subject property with similar land parcels for which actual data on recent market transactions are available. Although sales are the most important, analysis of listings and prices offered for similar parcels that compete with the subject may contribute to greater understanding of the market.

5.25.2 A *subdivision development* **technique** may also be applied to land valuation. This process entails projecting the subdivision of a particular property into a series of lots, developing incomes and expenses associated with the process, and discounting the resulting net incomes into an indication of value. This technique may be supportable in some situations, but is subject to a number of assumptions that may be exceedingly difficult to associate with the *Market Value* definition. Caution is advised in the development of supportable assumptions, of which the Valuer is advised to make full disclosure.

Where direct land comparisons are not available, the following methods can be applied with caution.

5.25.3 *Allocation* is an indirect comparison technique that develops a ratio between land value and improvement value or some other relationship between property components. The result is a measure that allocates a total market price between the land and improvements for comparative purposes.

5.25.4 *Extraction* is another indirect comparison technique (sometimes called *abstraction*). It provides a value estimate of improvements by applying a cost less depreciation analysis and extracting the result from the total price of otherwise comparable properties. The residual is an indication of possible land value.

5.25.5 The *land residual* **technique** for land valuation also applies income and expense data as elements in its analysis. A financial analysis is made of the net income that can be obtained by an income-producing use and a deduction from the net income is made for the financial return required by the improvements. The remaining income is considered residual to the land and is capitalised into a value indication. The method is limited to income-producing properties and is most applicable to newer properties for which fewer assumptions are required.

5.25.6 Land can also be valued by *ground rent capitalisation.* **If the** land is capable of independently producing a ground rental, that rent may be capitalised into a *Market Value* indication where sufficient market data are available. Care must be taken, however, not to be misled by special terms and conditions in a ground-rent lease that may not necessarily be representative of the particular market. In addition, since ground leases may have been drawn up many years before the valuation date, the rents quoted therein may be outdated, and current income capitalisation rates may be hard to obtain.

5.26 A real estate market may be defined as the interaction of individuals or entities that exchange real property rights for other assets, typically *money*. **Specific real estate markets** are defined by the property type, location, income-producing potential, typical tenant characteristics, attitudes and motivations of typical investors, or other attributes recognised by those individuals or entities participating in the exchange of real property. In turn, **real estate markets** are subject to a broad variety of social, economic, governmental, and environmental influences.

5.26.1 In comparison to markets in goods, securities, or commodities, **real estate markets are still considered inefficient.** This feature is attributable to a variety of factors including the relatively inelastic supply and the fixed location of real estate. Consequently, the supply of real estate does not adjust quickly in response to changes in market demand.

5.26.2 Investment in real estate, which is relatively illiquid, involves large sums of money for which appropriate financing might not be readily available. Valuers shall recognize these inefficiencies, and their understanding of the particular characteristics of a real estate market and/or sub-market shall produce a credible and objective analysis for the clients they serve.

5.27 The use of the *cost approach* can be appropriate when properties are new or of relatively new construction, provided estimates of items such as land value and depreciation are validated by market evidence. In depressed markets, economic or external obsolescence must be factored into the indication of value derived from the *cost approach*.

6.0 Effective Date

6.1 This International Valuation Guidance Note became effective 31 January 2005.

International Valuation Guidance Note No. 2

Valuation of Lease Interests (Revised 2007)

1.0 Introduction

1.1 International Valuation Standards (IVSs) Concepts Fundamental to Generally Accepted Valuation Principles distinguish between *real estate,* the physical tangible "thing" (see Concepts Fundamental to GAVP 3.0), and *real property* which pertains to the rights, interests, and benefits related to the ownership of real estate. *Lease interests* are a form of real property, arising from the contractual relationship (the terms of which are conveyed by a *lease*) between a *lessor,* one who owns the property leased to another, and a *lessee,* or tenant, one who typically receives a non-permanent right to use the leased property in return for rental payments or other valuable economic consideration.

1.2 To avoid misunderstandings or misrepresentations, Valuers and users of valuation services should recognise the important distinction between the physical and the legal issues involved in considering the value of lease interests.

1.3 This class of ownership is, as for the fee simple or freehold interest, common to all types of property assets valued. A piece of real estate may comprise one or more property interests, each of which will have a *Market Value* providing it is capable of being freely exchanged.

1.4 In no circumstances is it considered proper to value different property interests in the same piece of *real estate* separately and then to aggregate their values as an indication of the *real estate's* total value. Lease contracts establish unique legal estates that are different from fee simple, or freehold, ownership.

1.5 International Financial Reporting Standards (IFRSs) (including International Accounting Standards (IASs)) contain specific accounting requirements for property that is either held under a lease, or subject to a lease.

1.6 The relationships between different legal interests in the same property can be complex and can be made more confusing by the different terminology used to describe the various interests. This Guidance Note (GN) seeks to address and clarify these issues. The diagram on the following page illustrates the relationship between lease interests.

2.0 Scope

2.1 This GN sets out definitions, principles, and important considerations in the valuation of and related reporting for lease interests.

2.2 This GN is to be applied with particular reference to IVSs Concepts Fundamental to Generally Accepted Valuation Principles and to IVSs 1 and 2, and IVAs 1, 2 and 3.

2.3 This GN applies in States where a lessee holds an interest in land and/or buildings, which is regarded as a separate legal estate. A lease interest is subordinate to a superior interest, which itself may be either another lease interest for a longer term or the ultimate fee simple, or freehold, interest.

3.0 Definitions

3.1 Terms basic to the definition and valuation of legal interests include the following:

3.1.1 *Freehold Interest.* A *fee simple* estate, representing the perpetual ownership in land.

3.1.2 *Freehold subject to Lease Interest/s,* has the same meaning as Leased Fee Interest, representing the ownership interest of a lessor owning real estate that is subject to (a) lease(s) to others.

3.1.3 *Ground Lease.* Usually a long-term lease of land with the lessee permitted to improve or build on the land and to enjoy those benefits for the term of the lease.

3.1.4 *Headlease*, or *Master Lease.* A lease to a single entity that is intended to be the holder of subsequent leases to sublessees that will be the tenants in possession of the leased premises.

3.1.5 *Headleasehold Interest* has the same meaning as *Sandwich Lessor Interest.* The holder of a headlease or master lease.

Hierarchy of Property Rights

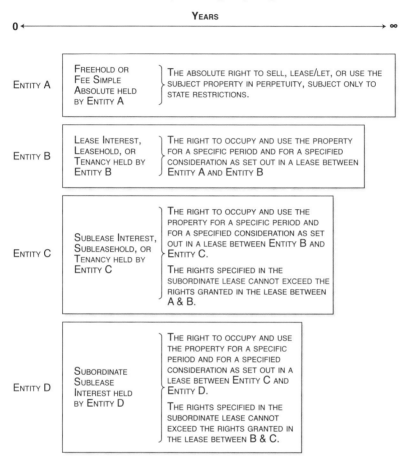

Years

0 ←————————————————————→ ∞

| ENTITY A | FREEHOLD OR FEE SIMPLE ABSOLUTE HELD BY ENTITY A | THE ABSOLUTE RIGHT TO SELL, LEASE/LET, OR USE THE SUBJECT PROPERTY IN PERPETUITY, SUBJECT ONLY TO STATE RESTRICTIONS. |

| ENTITY B | LEASE INTEREST, LEASEHOLD, OR TENANCY HELD BY ENTITY B | THE RIGHT TO OCCUPY AND USE THE PROPERTY FOR A SPECIFIC PERIOD AND FOR A SPECIFIED CONSIDERATION AS SET OUT IN A LEASE BETWEEN ENTITY A AND ENTITY B |

| ENTITY C | SUBLEASE INTEREST, SUBLEASEHOLD, OR TENANCY HELD BY ENTITY C | THE RIGHT TO OCCUPY AND USE THE PROPERTY FOR A SPECIFIC PERIOD AND FOR A SPECIFIED CONSIDERATION AS SET OUT IN A LEASE BETWEEN ENTITY B AND ENTITY C. THE RIGHTS SPECIFIED IN THE SUBORDINATE LEASE CANNOT EXCEED THE RIGHTS GRANTED IN THE LEASE BETWEEN A & B. |

| ENTITY D | SUBORDINATE SUBLEASE INTEREST HELD BY ENTITY D | THE RIGHT TO OCCUPY AND USE THE PROPERTY FOR A SPECIFIC PERIOD AND FOR A SPECIFIED CONSIDERATION AS SET OUT IN A LEASE BETWEEN ENTITY C AND ENTITY D. THE RIGHTS SPECIFIED IN THE SUBORDINATE LEASE CANNOT EXCEED THE RIGHTS GRANTED IN THE LEASE BETWEEN B & C. |

THE VALUER MUST IDENTIFY THE PROPERTY INTEREST TO BE VALUED ALONG WITH THE PERTINENT RIGHTS AND RESTRICTIONS.

3.1.6 *Lease*. A contract arrangement in which rights of use and possession are conveyed from a property's title owner (called the landlord, or lessor) in return for a promise by another (called a tenant, or lessee) to pay rents as prescribed by the lease. In practice the rights and the duties of the parties can be complex, and are dependent on the specified terms of their contract.

3.1.7 *Lease Interest,* also known as *Lessee Interest, Tenant's Interest,* or *Leasehold Estate.* The ownership interest that is created by the terms of a lease rather than the underlying rights of real estate ownership. The lease interest is subject to the terms of a specific lease arrangement, expires within a specified time, and may be capable of subdivision, or subleasing to other parties.

3.1.8 *Lessor Interest.* The interest held by the lessor in any of the circumstances set out in paras. 3.1.2, 3.1.4, or 3.1.5 above.

3.1.9 *Marriage Value,* or *Merged Interests Value.* The excess value, if any, produced by a merging of two or more interests in a property, over-and-above the sum of the values of those individual interests.

3.1.10 Rent Types

3.1.10.1 *Market Rent.* The estimated amount for which a property, or space within a property, should lease on the date of valuation between a willing lessor and a willing lessee on appropriate lease terms in an arm's-length transaction, after proper marketing wherein the parties had each acted knowledgeably, prudently, and without compulsion.

Whenever *Market Rent* is provided, the "appropriate lease terms" which it reflects should also be stated.

3.1.10.2 *Contract Rent,* or *Passing Rent.* The rent specified by a given lease arrangement; although a given contract rent may equate to the *Market Rent,* in practice they may differ substantially, particularly for older leases with fixed rental terms.

3.1.10.3 *Turnover Rent,* or *Participation Rent.* Any form of lease rental arrangement in which the lessor receives a form of rental that is based on the earnings of the lessee. Percentage rent is an example of a turnover rent.

3.1.11 *Sale and Leaseback.* A simultaneous sale of real estate and lease of the same property to the seller. The buyer becomes the lessor, or landlord, and the seller becomes the lessee, or tenant. Because there may be unique circumstances or relationships between the parties, sale and leaseback transactions may or may not involve typical market terms.

4.0 Relationship to Accounting Standards

4.1 Leased property is accounted for differently from freehold property, plant and equipment under IFRSs/IASs. The valuation requirements are summarized in IVA 1 and Addendum A to IVA 1.

5.0 Guidance

5.1 Lease interests are valued on the same general principles as freeholds, but with recognition of the differences created by the lease contract encumbering the freehold interest, which may cause the interest to be unmarketable or restricted.

5.2 Lease interests, in particular, are often subject to restrictive covenants or alienation provisions.

5.3 Freeholds subject to an *operating lease* are for accounting purposes generally considered *investment property,* and as such are valued on the basis of *Market Value*. Headleasehold interests are also commonly valued on the basis of *Market Value*.

5.4 In some States a lessee may have a statutory right to purchase the lessor's interest, usually the freehold, or may have an absolute or conditional right to a renewal of the lease for a term of years. The Valuer should draw attention to the existence of statutory rights and indicate in the Valuation Report whether or not regard has been paid to them.

5.5 The importance of the distinction between the physical matter and the legal interest in it is critical to valuation. For example, a lease might specify that the lessee has no right to sell or transfer the leasehold interest, causing it to be unmarketable during the term of the lease. Its value to the lessee, therefore, lies solely in the rights of use and occupancy**. The leasehold value may be expressed in monetary terms but is not a *Market Value* as the interest cannot be sold in the market. However, the lessor's interest (leased fee value) does have a *Market Value,* based on the value of the rental income during the lease together with any residual value remaining at the end of the lease.**

5.6 Each legal interest in a property shall be valued as a separate entity and not treated as though merged with another interest. Any calculation of *merged interests value* or *marriage value* should be referred to in supplementary advice only and may be undertaken as a valuation based on specific assumptions only and where the Valuer's Report is appropriately qualified.

5.7 Onerous lease covenants may adversely affect the *Market Value* of a lease interest. The Valuer must draw attention in the Valuation Report to the existence of such circumstances. The most common situation where this adverse effect arises involves restrictions on assignment, or on the right to sublet.

5.8 Inter-Company Leases

5.8.1 Where a property is subject to a lease or tenancy agreement between two companies in the same group, it is acceptable to take account of the existence of that agreement, providing the relationship between the parties is disclosed in the report, and that the agreement is on arm's-length terms in accordance with normal commercial practice. When the valuation is being undertaken for inclusion in a financial statement, it is acceptable to reflect any inter-company leases, providing the interests of one of the parties to the lease are being valued. However, if the interest of the group is being valued for inclusion in its consolidated accounts, the existence of any inter-company leases should be disregarded. (International Accounting Standard 40, para B21)

5.9 Leasehold Alterations

5.9.1 When valuing any property interest that is subject to a lease, it is important that Valuers establish whether any alterations or adaptations have been made to the property by the lessee. If so the following questions need to be addressed:

   a) **has the lessee complied with any lease conditions or restrictions relating to the alterations?**

   b) **what is the impact of any state laws on the rights of the parties in relation to the alterations?**

   c) **are the alterations obligatory or voluntary? (see below)**

   d) **is there any obligation on the lessor to compensate the lessee for the cost or value of the work, or on the lessee to remove the alterations at the lease end?**

5.9.2 Leasehold alterations fall into two main categories:

a) *Obligatory alterations:* **These usually arise where a property is leased in a basic state or constructed to a "shell" specification that is not suitable for occupation without the lessee undertaking further building or fitting-out work**. The lease will often impose a condition that such work be carried out by the lessee within a certain timescale

b) *Voluntary alterations:* **Typically these arise where a property is leased in a completed state ready for immediate occupation, but where the lessee elects to undertake work to improve or adapt the accommodation to suit the lessee's own particular requirements.** Although the tenant may regard these as alterations, the general market may not.

5.9.3 Obligatory alterations will usually have a beneficial impact on the *Market Rent*. Voluntary alterations may have a beneficial, neutral or detrimental effect on the *Market Rent,* depending upon their nature and degree of specialisation. The degree to which the impact on the *Market Rent* is reflected in the value of either the lessor's or the lessee's interest will depend upon the answers to the questions in 5.9.1.

5.10 Negative *Market Values*

5.10.1 Where lease interests are liabilities to an undertaking, they may have a negative *Market Value*.

5.11 *General*

Due to the relative complexity of lease interest valuations, it is essential that the client or the client's legal advisor provide the Valuer with either copies of all the leases or, for multitenanted property, typical sample leases together with a summary of lease terms on the other leases.

6.0 Effective Date

6.1 This International Valuation Guidance Note became effective 31 July 2007.

International Valuation Guidance Note No. 3

Valuation of Plant and Equipment (Revised 2007)

1.0 Introduction

1.1 Plant and equipment collectively constitute a general class of tangible property assets. International Valuation Application 1 (IVA 1) deals with valuation requirements for financial reporting purposes. This Guidance Note provides additional information to assist in the application of the International Valuation Standards to plant and equipment assets.

1.2 Plant and equipment assets have particular characteristics that distinguish them from most types of real property and that influence both the approach to and reporting of their value. Plant and equipment are normally capable of being moved or relocated and often will depreciate at a significantly faster rate than real property. Frequently, the value will differ notably depending on whether an item of plant or equipment is valued in combination with other assets within an operational unit or whether it is valued as an individual item for exchange, and where it may be considered as either in-situ (in place) or for removal.

2.0 Scope

2.1 This Guidance Note focuses on the application of the approaches, principles and bases described in the Standards to the valuation of plant and equipment. The following Guidance Notes may also be relevant to the valuation of plant and equipment:

GN 4, Valuation of Intangible Assets

GN 5, Valuation of Personal Property

GN 6, Business Valuation

GN 7, Consideration of Hazardous and Toxic Substances in Valuation

GN 8, Cost Approach for Financial Reporting—(DRC)

2.2 This Guidance Note applies to the valuation of the plant and equipment assets of both private-sector and public-sector entities.

3.0 Definitions

International Valuation Standards Definitions

3.1 *Fair Value*. The amount for which an asset could be exchanged between knowledgeable willing parties in an arm's length transaction.

3.2 *Market Value*. The estimated amount for which a property should exchange on the date of valuation between a willing buyer and a willing seller in an arm's-length transaction after proper marketing wherein the parties had each acted knowledgeably, prudently, and without compulsion.

3.3 *Plant and Equipment*. Tangible assets, other than *realty,* that:

(a)   are held by an entity for use in the production or supply of goods or services, for rental by others, or for administrative purposes; and

(b)   are expected to be used over a period of time.

The categories of plant and equipment are:

Plant. Assets that are inextricably combined with others and that may include specialised buildings, machinery, and equipment.

Machinery. Individual machines or a collection of machines. A machine is an apparatus used for a specific process in connection with the operation of the entity.

Equipment. Other assets that are used to assist the operation of the enterprise or entity.

International Financial Reporting Standards Definitions

3.3 *Finance Lease*. A lease that transfers substantially all the risks and rewards incidental to ownership of an asset. Title may or may not be eventually transferred. (IAS 17, para. 4)

3.4 *Operating Lease*. A lease other than a finance lease. (IAS 17, para. 4)

3.5 *Property, Plant and Equipment.* Tangible items that:

a) are held for use in the production or supply of goods or services, for rental to others, or for administrative purposes; and

b) are expected to be used during more than one (accounting) period. (IAS 16, para. 6)

4.0 Relationship to Accounting Standards

4.1 Under International Financial Reporting Standards (IFRSs), *Property Plant and Equipment* may be included on an entity's balance sheet at either cost less depreciation less impairment or at fair value at the date of revaluation less depreciation less impairment. (IAS 16, paras. 29, 30 and 31). The fair value of items of plant and equipment is usually their market value determined by appraisal (IAS 16, para. 32). Plant and equipment, together with other fixed assets, may be subject to other IFRSs, including IAS 2, Inventories; IAS 17, Leases; IAS 36, Impairment of Assets; IFRS 3, Business Combinations; and IFRS 5, Non-Current Assets Held for Sale and Discontinued Operations.

4.2 International Valuation Application (IVA) 1, Valuation for Financial Reporting, sets out the valuation and valuation reporting requirements under the various IFRSs referred to above.

4.3 International Public Sector Accounting Standards (IPSASs) require that after recognition, items of *Property, Plant and Equipment* be carried at either cost less any accumulated depreciation and any accumulated impairment losses, or at a revalued amount being the fair value at the date of revaluation less any subsequent accumulated depreciation and subsequent accumulated impairment losses (IPSAS 17, paras. 43 and 44). IPSAS 21, Impairment of Non-Cash-Generating Assets, may also apply to plant and equipment, together with other fixed assets. International Valuation Application 3, Valuation of Public Sector Assets for Financial Reporting, sets out the valuation and valuation reporting requirements under IPSASs.

4.4 The valuation approach and assumptions applicable to a valuation of plant and equipment for inclusion in a financial statement may be very different from those appropriate for another purpose. A clear distinction should be made if values for different purposes are reported in the same document.

Different valuation assumptions may be appropriate under different IFRSs and IPSASs and therefore it is important for the Valuer to be familiar with the basic requirements of the relevant standard, and to discuss the appropriate assumptions with the client before proceeding.

5.0 Guidance

5.1 Valuations of plant and equipment can be carried out using any of the following approaches:

5.1.1 *sales comparison approach.*

5.1.2 *cost approach (depreciated replacement cost)* (See GN 8); and

5.1.3 *income capitalisation approach.*

5.2 For many purposes, including compliance with IFRSs, the most appropriate basis of value is *Market Value*. However, *Market Value* simply stipulates that an exchange is assumed to take place on an arm's-length basis between knowledgeable and willing parties; it is silent as to how the particular asset is to be presented for sale or any of the other specific circumstances that could have a fundamental effect on the valuation. When undertaking a valuation of plant and equipment, the Valuer must therefore establish and state the additional assumptions that are appropriate, having regard to the nature of the asset and the purpose of the valuation. These assumptions may include the state of the business in which the plant and equipment are currently utilized, or the extent to which individual items are aggregated with other assets. Examples of assumptions that may be appropriate in different circumstances, or for different valuation purposes include:

5.2.1 that the plant and equipment are valued as a whole, in-situ (in place) and as part of the business considered as a going concern;

5.2.2 that the plant and equipment are valued in-situ but on the assumption that the business is closed; or

5.2.3 that the plant and equipment are valued as individual items for removal from their current location.

For assets in the public sector, the assumption equivalent to a business continuing as a going concern is that the public sector assets will continue to be used for the provision of the relevant public good or service.

5.3 The list of assumptions above is not comprehensive. Because of the diverse nature and transportability of much plant and equipment, *Market Value* will need appropriate qualifying assumptions to describe the state and circumstances in which the asset is offered to the market. These assumptions should be discussed with the client and must be included in the report. Frequently, it may be appropriate to report on more than one set of assumptions, e.g., in order to illustrate the effect of business closure or cessation of operations on the *Market Value* of plant and equipment assets, where closure or cessation is not yet definite.

5.4 Other factors that can affect the *Market Value* of plant and equipment include:

5.4.1 the costs of installation and commissioning where plant and equipment are valued in situ;

5.4.2 where they are valued for removal, any allowance made for the costs of decommissioning, removal, and possible reinstatement following removal, and which party is to bear those costs. In some cases, these costs can be substantial and therefore the Valuer should reach an agreement with the client as to how they should be reflected and which specific assumption(s) are to be made.

5.5 Factors such as finite sources of raw materials, the limited life of the buildings or limited tenure of the land and buildings housing the plant, and statutory restrictions or environmental legislation can also have a significant impact on the value of plant and equipment. These factors will need to be taken into account by the Valuer and any necessary assumptions will have to be made.

5.6 Some plant and equipment connected with the supply or provision of services to a building will normally be included in any exchange of the real estate interest. Examples include plant for the supply of electricity, gas, heating, cooling or ventilation and equipment such as elevators. Although the value of these items would normally be reflected in the value of the real estate interest, for certain purposes, such as depreciation accounting, it may be necessary to value these items separately. **Where this is the case, the Valuer should make it clear that the separate valuation and treatment of these items will affect the value of the real estate interest. When different Valuers are employed to carry out valuations of real estate assets and plant and equipment assets at the same location, careful liaison is necessary to avoid either omissions or double counting.**

5.7 **Intangible assets fall outside the definition of plant and equipment. However, intangible assets may have an impact on the value of plant and equipment;** for example, the value of patterns and dies is often inextricably linked to associated intellectual property rights. **In such cases the Valuer should establish what assumptions are appropriate as to the availability of those intangible assets before reporting a valuation.** Operating software, technical data, production records and patents are examples of intangible assets that can have an impact on the value of plant and equipment, depending on whether or not they are included in the transfer.

5.8 **An item of plant and equipment may be subject to a financing arrangement, such as a finance lease. Accordingly, the asset cannot be sold without the lender or lessor being paid any balance outstanding under the arrangement.** This payment may or may not exceed the unencumbered value of the item. **Items of plant and equipment subject to such arrangements should be separately identified from assets that are unencumbered, and their value separately reported. Items, which are subject to operating leases or are otherwise the property of third parties, are normally excluded as the benefits of ownership are not transferred to the lessee. Guidance on Finance and Operating Leases is included in Addendum 1 to IVA 1.**

5.9 *Market Value* does not imply any particular method of sale, as for example, by private treaty, tender, auction, etc. The conceptual framework in IVS 1 makes it clear that *Market Value* assumes a sale after proper marketing in the most appropriate manner. It is implicit in this definition that the method of sale will be the one that will achieve the highest price for the asset or the defined group of assets in a given set of circumstances. A willing and knowledgeable seller would not voluntarily choose a method of sale that did not maximize the price. However, **if the exchange is to take place under circumstances that prevented the seller from choosing the optimal method of disposal, the anticipated realisation will not be the** *Market Value* **unless the constraint on the seller was one common to all** sales in that particular market at that time. **A constraint specific to a particular seller or asset, coupled with a requirement to sell subject to that constraint, will result in a forced sale.**

5.10 **Plant and equipment assets are more likely to be subject to forced sale circumstances than real estate interests.** For example, assets sometimes have to be disposed of in a time frame that precludes proper marketing because the current owner of the assets has to vacate or surrender the land and buildings where they are located. **If such a scenario has actually arisen, or is reasonably foreseeable, it may be appropriate for the Valuer to provide advice on the price that could be anticipated or that should be accepted, although before doing so the Valuer will need to establish the exact nature of the constraint on the vendor and understand the consequences for the vendor of failing to dispose of the assets within the stipulated time limit.** For example, the assets may be subject to forfeit or the owner may be subject to a specific financial penalty. It may also be necessary to consider any alternatives to sale, for example, the practicality and cost of removing the items to another location for disposal. **Without knowledge of the actual or anticipated circumstances, the Valuer cannot give meaningful advice since the exchange may fall outside the definition of** *Market Value*. **Assumptions regarding realisation of a transfer under forced sale circumstances must be carefully considered and clearly stipulated.**

6.0 Effective Date

6.1 This Guidance Note became effective 31 July 2007.

International Valuation Guidance Note No. 4

Valuation of Intangible Assets (Revised 2007)

1.0 Introduction

1.1 The International Valuation Standards Committee (IVSC) adopted this Guidance Note (GN) to improve the consistency and quality of intangible asset valuations among the international community for the benefit of users of financial statements and users of intangible asset valuations.

1.2 Intangible asset valuations are commonly sought and performed on the *Market Value* basis of valuation applying the provisions of International Valuation Standard 1 (IVS 1). Where other bases of valuation are used with proper explanation and disclosure, the provisions of IVS 2 are applied.

1.3 In general, the concepts, processes, and methods applied in the valuation of intangible assets are the same as those for other types of valuations. Certain terms may have different meanings or uses. Those differences become important disclosures wherever they are used. This GN sets forth important definitions used in valuations of intangible assets.

1.4 Care should be taken by Valuers and users of valuation services to distinguish between the value of individual, identifiable intangible assets and going concern considerations, including those encountered in the valuation of real property interests. An example of the latter is valuations of trade related property.

2.0 Scope

2.1 This GN is provided to assist in the course of rendering or using valuations of intangible assets.

2.2 In addition to the elements that are common to other GNs to the International Valuation Standards, this GN contains a more expansive discussion of the intangible asset valuation process. This is included to typify what is commonly involved in valuations of intangible assets and to provide a basis of comparison with other types of valuations, but the discussion should not be considered as either mandatory or limiting except as provided in this GN or otherwise in the IVSs.

2.3 Because other basic valuation principles, the International Valuation Standards, and Guidance Notes are also applicable to valuations of intangible assets, this GN should be understood to incorporate all other applicable portions of the IVSs.

3.0 Definitions

3.1 *Book Value*

3.1.1 With respect to assets, the capitalised cost of an asset less accumulated depreciation, depletion, or amortisation as it appears on the account books of the business.

3.1.2 With respect to a business entity, the difference between total assets (net of depreciation, depletion, and amortisation) and total liabilities of a business as they appear on the balance sheet. In this case, *book value* is synonymous with *net book value, net worth,* and *shareholder's equity.*

3.2 *Business Entity.* A commercial, industrial, or service organisation pursuing an economic activity.

3.3 *Capitalisation*

3.3.1 At a given date, the conversion into the equivalent capital value of net income or a series of net receipts, actual or estimated, over a period.

3.3.2 In business valuation, the term refers to the capital structure of a business of a business entity.

3.3.3 In business valuation, this term also refers to the recognition of an expenditure as a capital asset rather than a periodic expense.

3.4 *Capitalisation Factor.* Any multiple or divisor used to convert income into capital value.

3.5 *Capitalisation Rate.* Any divisor (usually expressed as a percentage) that is used to convert income into capital value.

3.6 *Cash Flow*

3.6.1 *Gross Cash Flow:* Net income after taxes, plus non-cash items such as depreciation and amortisation.

3.6.2 *Net Cash Flow:* During an operating period, that amount of cash that remains after all cash needs of the business have been satisfied. *Net cash flow* is typically defined as being cash available to equity or invested capital.

3.6.3 *Equity Net Cash Flow:* Net income after taxes, plus depreciation and other non-cash charges, less increases in working capital, less capital expenditures, less decreases in invested capital debt principal, plus increases in invested capital debt principal.

3.6.4 *Invested Capital Net Cash Flow: Equity net cash flow,* plus interest payments net of tax adjustment, less net increases in debt principal.

3.7 *Discount Rate.* A rate of return used to convert a monetary sum, payable or receivable in the future, into present value. A weighted average of the discount rate applied to intangibles and the discount rate applied to tangibles should correlate with the weighted average cost of capital for the business.

3.8 *Economic Life.* The period over which property may be profitably used. Economic life may vary by State depending on the level of industrial development and regulatory atmosphere in each State.

3.9 *Effective Date.* The date as of which the Valuer's opinion of value applies. (Also referred to as *Valuation Date*, and/or *As Of Date*.)

3.10 *Enterprise.* See Business Entity.

3.11 *Going Concern.* An operating business.

The entity is normally viewed as a going concern, that is, as continuing in operation for the foreseeable future. It is assumed that the entity has neither the intention nor the necessity of liquidation or of curtailing materially the scale of its operations. (IAS 1, 23-24, Framework, 23)

3.12 *Goodwill.*

3.12.1 Future economic benefits arising from assets that are not capable of being individually identified and separately recognised. (IFRS 3, Appendix A)

3.12.2 *Personal Goodwill.* The value of profit over and above market expectations, which would be extinguished upon sale of the trade related property, together with those financial factors related specifically to the current operator of the business, such as taxation, depreciation policy, borrowing costs and the capital invested in the business.

3.12.3 *Transferable Goodwill.* That intangible asset that arises as a result of property-specific name and reputation, customer patronage, location, products, and similar factors, which generate economic benefits. It is inherent to the trade related property, and will transfer to a new owner on sale.

3.13 *Income Capitalisation Approach.* A general way of estimating a value indication of an intangible asset using one or more methods wherein a value is estimated by converting anticipated benefits into capital value.

3.14 *Intangible Assets.* Assets that manifest themselves by their economic properties. They do not have physical substance; they grant rights and privileges to their owner and usually generate income for their owner. Intangible Assets can be categorised as arising from *Rights, Relationships, Grouped Intangibles,* or *Intellectual Property.*

3.14.1 *Rights* exist according to the terms of a contract, written or unwritten, that is of economic benefit to the parties. Examples are supply contracts, distribution contracts, providing contracts, and licensing permits, among others.

3.14.2 *Relationships* between parties are normally non-contractual, can be short-lived, and can have great value to the parties. Examples are assembled workforce, customer relationships, supplier relationships, distributor relationships, and structural relationships between parties, among others.

3.14.3 *Grouped Intangibles* are the residual *intangible asset* value left after all identifiable *intangible assets* have been valued and deducted from total *intangible asset* value. Alternative concepts include patronage, excess earnings, and residual value. *Grouped intangibles* are often called *goodwill*. *Goodwill* has, at various times, been said to be the tendency for customers to return to a place of business, the extra income generated by a business over and above a fair return to the identified assets, and/or the extra value of the entity as a whole over and above the aggregate value of its constituent identifiable assets.

3.14.4 *Intellectual Property* is a special classification of *intangible assets* because it is usually protected by law from unauthorised use by others. Examples are brand names, or tradenames; copyrights; patents; trademarks; trade secrets, or know-how; among others.

3.14.5 In general, the accounting profession limits the recognition of individual *intangible assets* to those that are commonly recognisable, have a statutory or contractual remaining life, and/or must be individually transferable and separable from the business.

3.15 *Intangible Property*. The rights and privileges granted to the owner of intangible assets.

3.16 *Legal Life*. The life of the *intangible assets* allowed by law.

3.17 *Market Approach*. A general way of estimating a value indication for an intangible asset using one or more methods that compare the subject to similar assets that have been sold.

3.18 *Market Value*. See IVS 1, para. 3.1.

3.19 *Rate of Return*. An amount of income (loss) and/or change in value realised or anticipated on an investment, expressed as a percentage of that investment.

3.20 *Replacement Cost New*. The current cost of a similar new item having the nearest equivalent utility as the item being appraised.

3.21 *Report Date*. The date of the Valuation Report. May be the same as or different from the valuation date.

3.22 *Reproduction Cost New*. The current cost of an identical new item.

3.23 *Valuation Approach.* In general, a way of estimating value using one or more specific valuation methods. (See *Asset Based Approach, Market Approach,* and *Income Capitalisation Approach* definitions).

3.24 *Valuation Method.* Within valuation approaches, a specific way to estimate a value.

3.25 *Valuation Procedure.* The act, manner, and technique of performing the steps of a valuation method.

3.26 *Valuation Ratio.* A factor wherein a value or price serves as the numerator and financial, operating, or physical data serve as the denominator.

3.27 *Value in Use.* This value type focuses on the value that specific property contributes to the entity of which it is a part without regard to the property's *highest and best use* or the monetary amount that might be realised upon its sale. Value in use is the value a specific property has for a specific use to a specific user and is, therefore, non-market related.

4.0 Relationship to Accounting Standards

4.1 Intangible asset valuations are commonly used as a basis for making allocations of value for various assets to aid in the establishment or restatement of financial statements. In this context, Intangible Asset Valuers reflect the *Market Value* of all components of a business's balance sheet in order to meet accounting Standards, having regard to the convention that reflects the effect of changing prices.

4.2 International Accounting Standard 38 (IAS 38) prescribes the accounting treatment for intangible assets, discusses the criteria an intangible asset must meet for recognition, specifies the carrying amount of intangible assets, and sets forth requirements for disclosures about intangible assets.

5.0 Guidance

5.1 Valuations of intangible assets may be required for a number of possible uses including acquisitions and dispositions of businesses or parts of businesses, mergers, sale of an intangible asset, financial reporting and the like.

5.1.1 Where the purpose of the valuation requires a *Market Value* estimate, the Valuer shall apply definitions, processes, and methodologies consistent with their provision in IVS 1.

5.1.2 When an engagement calls for a value basis other than *Market Value*, the Valuer shall clearly identify the type of value involved, define such value, and take steps necessary to distinguish the value estimate from a *Market Value* estimate.

5.2 If, in the opinion of the Valuer, certain aspects of an engagement indicate that a departure from any provision of the International Valuation Standards or of this GN is necessary and appropriate, such departure should be considered for disclosure along with the reason for invoking the departure.

5.3 The Valuer shall take steps to assure that all data sources relied on are reliable and appropriate to the valuation undertaking. In many instances it will be beyond the scope of the Valuer's services to perform a complete verification of secondary or tertiary data sources. Accordingly, the Valuer shall verify the accuracy and reasonableness of data sources as are customary in the markets and locale of the valuation.

5.4 Valuers of intangible assets must frequently rely on information received from a client or from a client's representatives. The source of any such data relied upon must be cited by the Valuer in oral or written reports, and the data shall be reasonably verified wherever possible. The requirements for Valuation Reports are addressed in the IVSC Code of Conduct (section 7), and IVS 3, Valuation Reporting.

5.5 Although many of the principles, methods, and techniques of intangible asset valuation are similar to those used in other fields of valuation, valuations of intangible assets require special education, training, skills, and experience.

5.6 A description of the valuation assignment must include

5.6.1 identification of the intangible asset(s), or the ownership interest in the intangible asset(s), to be valued;

5.6.2 the effective date of the valuation;

5.6.3 the definition of value;

5.6.4 the owner of the interest; and

5.6.5 the purpose and use of the valuation.

5.7 Factors to be considered by the Intangible Asset Valuer include:

5.7.1 The rights, privileges, or conditions that attach to the ownership interest

5.7.1.1 Ownership rights are set forth in various legal documents. In various States, or in some legal jurisdictions, these documents may be called patents, trademarks, brands, know-how, databases, and copyrights, to name a few.

5.7.1.2 Whoever owns the interest is bound by the documents that record such interest in the intangible assets. There may be rights and conditions contained in an agreement or exchange of correspondence, and these rights may or may not be transferable to a new owner of the interest.

5.7.2 Remaining economic life and/or legal life of the intangible asset

5.7.3 The earnings capacity of the intangible assets

5.7.4 The nature and history of the intangible assets. Since value resides in the benefits of future ownership, history is valuable in that it may give a guide to the expectations of the intangible assets for the future.

5.7.5 The economic outlook that may affect the subject intangible assets, including political outlook and government policy. Matters such as the exchange rate and inflation and interest rates may affect intangible assets that operate in different sectors of the economy quite differently.

5.7.6 The condition and outlook of the specific industry, which may affect the subject intangible assets

5.7.7 Intangible value may also be contained in undifferentiated assets, often called *goodwill.* Note that goodwill value in this context is similar to goodwill in the accounting sense in that both are the residual value (historical cost in accounting terms) after all other assets have been taken into account.

5.7.8 Prior transactions in ownership interests of the subject intangible assets

5.7.9 Other market data, e.g., rates of return on alternative investments, etc.

5.7.10 The market prices for acquisition of similar intangible assets interests or intangible assets

5.7.10.1 Often, particularly in the use of acquisition transactions, adequate information is difficult or impossible to obtain. While the actual transaction price may be known, the Valuer may not know what warranties and indemnities were given by the seller, what terms were given or received, or what impact taxation planning had on the transaction.

5.7.10.2 Comparable data should always be used with care, and numerous adjustments may need to be made.

5.7.11 Adjustment of historical financial statements to estimate the economic abilities of and prospects for the intangible assets

5.7.12 Any other information the Valuer believes to be relevant

5.8 Intangible asset valuation approaches

5.8.1 *Market (sales comparison) approach* to intangible asset valuation

5.8.1.1 The *market approach* compares the subject to similar intangible assets or intangible asset ownership interests and securities that have been sold in the open market.

5.8.1.2 The two most common sources of data used in the *market approach* are markets in which ownership interests of similar intangible assets are traded and prior transactions in the ownership of the subject intangible assets.

5.8.1.2.1 There must be a reasonable basis for comparison with and reliance upon the similar intangible assets in the market approach. These similar intangible assets should be in the same industry as the subject or in an industry that responds to the same economic variables. The comparison must be made in a meaningful manner and must not be misleading.

5.8.1.3 Through analysis of acquisitions of intangible assets, the Valuer often computes valuation ratios, which are usually price divided by some measure of income or net assets. Care must be used in calculating and selecting these ratios.

5.8.1.3.1 The ratio(s) selected must provide meaningful information about the value of the intangible assets.

5.8.1.3.2 The data on the similar intangible assets used to compute the ratio must be accurate.

5.8.1.3.3 The calculation of ratios must be accurate.

5.8.1.3.4 If the data are averaged, the time period considered and the averaging method must be appropriate.

5.8.1.3.5 All calculations must be done in the same way for both the similar intangible assets and the subject intangible assets.

5.8.1.3.6 The price data used in the ratio(s) must be valid as of the valuation date and representative of the market at that time.

5.8.1.3.7 Where appropriate, adjustments may need to be made to render the similar intangible assets and the subject intangible assets more comparable.

5.8.1.3.8 Adjustments may need to be made for unusual, non-recurring, and non-operating items.

5.8.1.3.9 The selected ratios must be appropriate given the differences in risk and expectations of the similar intangible assets and the subject intangible assets.

5.8.1.3.10 Several value indications may be calculated since several valuation multiples may be selected and applied to the subject intangible assets.

5.8.1.4 When prior transactions in the subject intangible assets are used to provide valuation guidance, adjustments may need to be made for the passage of time and for changed circumstances in the economy, the industry, and the intangible assets.

5.8.2 *Income capitalisation approach* to intangible asset valuation

5.8.2.1 The *income approach* estimates the value of an intangible asset or of intangible asset ownership interests by calculating the present value of anticipated benefits. The two most common *income approach* methods are *(direct) capitalisation* of income and *discounted cash flow analysis* (DCF).

5.8.2.1.1 In *(direct) capitalisation* of income, a representative income level is divided by a capitalisation rate or multiplied by an income multiple (capitalisation factor) to convert the income into value.

5.8.2.1.2 Income is typically allocated to the various intangible assets by the Valuer. Care must be taken so that the income allocated to all of the individual assets does not exceed the income available to all assets.

5.8.2.1.3 In theory, income can consist of a variety of types of income and cash flow. In practice, the income measure is usually pre-tax income or post-tax income. If capitalisation methods are used, the economic life of the assets must be infinite, or very long.

5.8.2.1.4 In DCF *analysis* and/or *dividend method,* cash receipts are estimated for each of several future periods. These receipts are converted to value by the application of a discount rate, using present value techniques. Many definitions of *cash flow* could be used. Discounting methods are most commonly used for intangible assets with finite economic lives. **The time period covered by the discounting methods is normally the shorter of the economic life or the legal life (the definable period over which the asset or interest therein is legally protected).**

5.8.2.1.4.1 Economic life is measured as the period when the intangible assets can be expected to give the owner an economic return on the assets. An example is computer software that may have an expected life of 36 months before it is necessary to replace it with an updated version.

5.8.2.1.4.2 Legal life is measured as the period when the intangible asset can be protected by law. An example is a patent that has a definable life at its inception and that slowly, over time, goes to zero.

5.8.2.1.5 Capitalisation rates and discount rates are derived from the market and are expressed as price multiples (derived from data on publicly traded businesses or transactions) or an interest rate (derived from data on alternative investments).

5.8.2.2 Anticipated income or benefits are converted to value using calculations that consider the expected growth and timing of the benefits, the risk associated with the benefit stream, and the time value of money.

5.8.3 *The cost approach,* often called the cost to recreate, is also known as the *adjusted asset approach.*

5.8.3.1 A cost-based approach is founded on the Principle of Substitution, i.e., an asset is worth no more than it would cost to replace all of its constituent parts.

5.8.3.2 In the execution of the cost approach, **the cost of each item in the creation of the assets, including developer's profit, must be estimated using the knowledge possessed as of the valuation date.**

5.9 Reconciliation processes

5.9.1 The value conclusion shall be based upon

5.9.1.1 the definition of value, and

5.9.1.2 all relevant information as of the valuation date necessary in view of the scope of the assignment.

5.9.2 The value conclusion shall also be based on value indications from the valuation methods performed.

5.9.2.1 The selection of and reliance on the appropriate approaches, methods, and procedures depend on the judgment of the Valuer.

5.9.2.2 The Valuer must use judgment when determining the relative weight to be given to each of the value indications derived during application of the Valuation Process. The Valuer should provide the rationale and justification for the valuation methods used and for the weighting of the methods relied on in reaching the reconciled value conclusion.

6.0 Effective Date

6.1 This International Valuation Guidance Note became effective 31 July 2007.

International Valuation Guidance Note No. 5

Valuation of Personal Property (Revised 2007)

1.0 Introduction

1.1 The objective of this Guidance Note (GN) is to improve the consistency and quality of personal property valuations for the benefit of users of personal property valuation services.

1.2 Personal property valuations are commonly sought and performed on the *Market Value* basis of valuation, applying the provisions of International Valuation Standard 1 (IVS 1). Where other bases of valuation are used, the provisions of IVS 2 are applied, subject to proper disclosure and explanation.

1.3 While certain terms may have alternative definitions, and the applicability of specific methods may diverge, the theory, concepts, and processes applied in the valuation of personal property are fundamentally the same as those for other types of valuations. Whenever terms that have different meanings are used, it is important that those differences be disclosed. This GN sets forth important definitions used in personal property valuations.

1.4 Care should be taken by Valuers and users of valuation services to distinguish among the market components and corresponding *Market Values* of personal properties. One example of such differentiation is the *Market Value* of properties sold at auction vs that of properties sold by or acquired from private dealers where the negotiated price is not publicly disclosed. Another example would be the *Market Value* of personal property sold wholesale vs the market value of the same item(s) sold retail.

2.0 Scope

2.1 This GN is provided to assist in the course of rendering or using personal property valuations.

2.2 In addition to the elements that are common to other Applications and Guidance Notes in the International Valuation Standards, this GN contains an expanded discussion of the Valuation Process for personal properties. This is included to typify what is commonly involved in personal property valuations and to provide a basis of comparison with other types of valuations.

2.3 Plant and equipment (P&E) is a category of personal property, but P&E valuation is dealt with under GN 3.

3.0 Definitions

3.1 *Auction Price*. The price that is the final accepted bid at a public auction; may or may not include any fees or commissions. See also Hammer Price, Private Treaty Sale.

3.2 *Collectibles*. Broad descriptive term for objects collected because of the interest they arouse owing to their rarity, novelty, or uniqueness. In some States, the term may be applied to fine art, antiques, gems and jewelry, musical instruments, numismatic and philatelic collections, rare books, and archival materials, among others. Elsewhere the term is normally used for these and a wide variety of other items not found in any other category.

3.3 *Cost Approach*. A comparative approach to the value of property or another asset that considers as a substitute for the purchase of a given property, the possibility of constructing another property that is equivalent to the original or one that could furnish equal utility with no undue cost resulting from delay. The Valuer's estimate is based on the reproduction or replacement cost of the subject property or asset, less total (accrued) depreciation.

3.4 *Cost Approach for Valuing Fine Art*. A comparative approach to the value of fine art that considers as a substitute for the purchase of a given work of fine art the possibility of creating another work of fine art that replaces the original. The Valuer's estimate is based on the reproduction or replacement cost of the subject work of fine art, and the nature of the replacement, i.e., whether it be *new for old*, *indemnity basis*, a *replica,* or a *facsimile.*

> *New for old* refers to the cost of purchasing the same item or, if unavailable, an item similar in nature and condition in the retail market for new works of fine art.

> *Indemnity basis* refers to the cost of replacing an item with a similar item in similar condition in the second-hand retail market for art and antiques.

A *replica* is a copy of the original item, as near as possible to the original in terms of nature, quality, and age of materials but created by means of modern construction methods.

A *facsimile* is an exact copy of the original item, created with materials of a closely similar nature, quality, and age and using construction methods of the original period.

3.5 *Fixtures and Fittings*. The totality of improvements integral to a property, valued collectively. See Trade Fixtures or Tenant's Fixtures.

3.6 *Furniture, Fixtures and Equipment*. (FF&E) A term used in North America to refer to tangible personal property plus trade fixtures and leasehold improvements. See also Personal Property.

3.7 *Goods and Chattels Personal*. In certain States, a term used for identifiable, portable, and tangible objects considered by the public to be personal property. See also Personal Property.

3.8 *Hammer Price*. The accepted and announced bid, exclusive of any fees or commissions and, therefore, not necessarily the purchase price. See also Auction Price, Private Treaty Sale.

3.9 *Income Capitalisation Approach*. A comparative approach to value that considers income and expense data relating to the property being valued and estimates value through a capitalisation process.

3.10 *Intrinsic Value*. The amount considered, on the basis of an evaluation of available facts, to be the "true" or "real" worth of an item. A long-term, *Non-Market Value* concept that smoothes short-term price fluctuations.

3.11 *Leasehold Improvements or Tenant's Improvements*. Fixed improvements or additions to land or buildings, installed by and paid for by the tenant to meet the tenant's needs; typically removable by the tenant upon expiration of the lease; removal causes no material damage to the real estate. See also Personal Property, Trade Fixtures or Tenant's Fixtures.

3.12 *Market Value*. See IVS 1, para. 3.1.

3.13 *Personal Property*. A legal concept referring to all rights, interests, and benefits related to ownership of items other than real estate. In certain

States, items of personal property are legally designated as personalty in distinction to realty, which may either refer to real property or real estate. Items of personal property can be tangible, such as a chattel, or intangible, such as a debt or patent. Items of tangible personal property typically are not permanently affixed to real estate and are generally characterized by their movability. See also Collectibles; Fixtures and Fittings; Furniture, Fixtures and Equipment (FF&E); Goods and Chattels Personal; Leasehold Improvements or Tenant's Improvements; Plant and Equipment; Trade Fixtures or Tenant's Fixtures.

3.14 *Personalty.* A legal term used in certain States to designate items of personal property in distinction to realty, which may either refer to real property or real estate. Personalty includes tangible and intangible items that are not real estate. See also Personal Property.

3.15 *Plant and Equipment.* Tangible assets, other than realty, that:

(a) are held by an entity for use in the production or supply of goods or services, for rental by others, or for administrative purposes; and

(b) are expected to be used over a period of time.

The categories of plant and equipment are:

Plant. Assets that are inextricably combined with others and that may include specialised buildings, machinery, and equipment.

Machinery. Individual machines or a collection of machines. A machine is an apparatus used for a specific process in connection with the operation of the entity.

Equipment. Other assets that are used to assist the operation of the enterprise or entity.

3.16 *Private Treaty Sale.* A sale negotiated and transacted between persons rather than by public auction or another method. The sale price paid in a private treaty sale is generally not known except by the parties to the transaction. See also Auction Price, Hammer Price.

3.17 *Professional Property Valuer.* A person who possesses necessary qualifications, ability, and experience to estimate property value for a diversity of purposes including transactions involving transfers of property ownership, property considered as collateral to secure loans and mortgages, property subject to litigation or pending settlement on taxes, and property treated as fixed assets in financial reporting.

3.18 *Sales Comparison Approach*. A general way of estimating a value indication for personal property or an ownership interest in personal property, using one or more methods that compare the subject to similar properties or to ownership interests in similar properties. This approach to the valuation of personal property is dependent upon the Valuer's market knowledge and experience as well as recorded data on comparable items.

3.19 *Trade Fixtures or Tenant's Fixtures*. Non-realty fixtures attached to property by the tenant and used in conducting the trade or business. See also Leasehold Improvements or Tenant's Improvements, Personal Property.

3.20 *Valuation Approach*. In general, a way of estimating value that employs one or more specific valuation methods. Depending on the nature and purpose of the property, three valuation approaches may be applied. These are the *sales comparison, income capitalisation, and cost approaches*. Their application will enable the Valuer to determine *Market Value* or a value other than *Market Value*.

3.21 *Valuation Method*. Within the valuation approaches, a specific way to estimate value.

3.22 *Valuation Procedure*. The act, manner, and technique of performing the steps of a valuation method.

4.0 Relationship to Accounting Standards

4.1 In some instances the valuation of personal property undertaken in conjunction with the valuation of real property and/or a business provides a basis for determining the extent of depreciation or obsolescence of certain fixed assets. In this application, the personal property valuation *per se* may or may not be the principal reason for the valuation, but the combination of services by a Personal Property Valuer, a Business Valuer and/or a Real Property Valuer, is necessary to properly allocate and reflect the *Market Value* of assets to be included in a financial statement.

5.0 Guidance

5.1 Personal property valuations may be required for a number of possible uses including financial reporting, acquisitions and disposals/dispositions, insurance, and taxation.

> 5.1.1 Where the purpose of the valuation requires **a *Market Value* estimate,** the Valuer shall apply definitions, processes, and methodologies consistent with their provision in IVS 1.

> 5.1.2 When an engagement calls for a value basis **other than *Market Value,*** e.g., insurable value, the Valuer shall clearly identify the type of value involved, define such value, and take steps necessary to distinguish the value estimate from a *Market Value* estimate as consistent with IVS 2.

5.2 Steps shall be taken by the Valuer to assure that all data sources relied upon are reliable and appropriate to the valuation undertaking. In many instances, it will be beyond the scope of the Valuer's services to perform a complete verification of secondary or tertiary data sources. Accordingly, the Valuer shall take reasonable steps to verify the accuracy and reasonableness of data sources as is customary in the market(s) and locale of the valuation.

5.3 It is not uncommon for personal property valuations to require that the Personal Property Valuer call for and rely upon the services of other Professional Property Valuers and/or other professionals. Thus, **the parameters of responsibility relating to the classification of property items must be established between Valuers of different disciplines to ensure that nothing has been omitted or double entered.** A common example is reliance upon a Real Property Valuer to value the real estate components of a property. **Where the services of other experts are relied upon, the Personal Property Valuer shall**

> **5.3.1 take verification steps as are reasonably necessary to ensure that such services are competently performed and that the conclusions relied upon are reasonable and credible, or**

> **5.3.2 disclose the fact that no such verification steps were taken.**

5.4 Personal Property Valuers must frequently rely upon information received from a client or from a client's representatives. The source of

any such data relied upon shall be cited by the Valuer in oral or written reports, and the data shall be reasonably verified wherever possible.

5.5 Although many of the principles, methods, and techniques of personal property valuation are similar to those in other fields of valuation, **personal property valuations require special education, training, skill, and experience.**

5.6 Requirements for Valuation Reports are addressed in the IVSC Code of Conduct, and IVS 3, Valuation Reporting. For personal property the Valuation Report must include

5.6.1 Identification of the property and owner or ownership interest to be valued (location of the object of personal property and address of the owner);

5.6.2 The effective date of the valuation;

5 6.3 The basis or definition of value;

5.6.4 Identification of the owner of interest or instructing party (n.b., in some States, the identity of the owner of interest may not be made known for reason of confidentiality);

5.6.5 The purpose and use of the valuation;

5.6.6 The conditions of the valuation;

5.6.7 Liens and encumbrances on the property; and

5.6.8 A Compliance Statement (signed and dated).

5.7 Factors to be considered (but not necessarily reported) by the Personal Property Valuer include:

5.7.1 Rights, privileges, or conditions that attach to the ownership of the subject property

5.7.1.1 Ownership rights are set forth in various legal documents

5.7.1.2 Rights and conditions contained in an owner's agreement or exchange of correspondence; these rights may or may not be transferable to a new owner of the subject property.

5.7.1.3 The documents may contain restrictions on the transfer of the property and may contain provisions governing the basis of valuation that has to be adopted in the event of transfer of the property.

5.7.2 The nature of the property and history of its ownership (provenance)

5.7.2.1 Previous sales or transfers of the property

5.7.3 The economic outlook that may affect the subject property, including political outlook and government policy

5.7.4 The condition and outlook of a market specific to the trade of personal properties that may affect the subject property

5.7.5 Whether or not the subject property has intangible value

5.7.5.1 If intangible value is inherent in the personal property, the Valuer must ensure that the intangible value is fully reflected, whether the identifiable intangible has been valued separately or not.

5.7.5.1.1 Intangible value, insofar as can be reasoned, should be distinguished from the value of the tangible property.

5.7.5.2 It is essential that the Valuer be aware of the legal restrictions and conditions that arise through the laws of the State in which the property exists.

5.7.5.3 Often, particularly in the use of acquisition transactions, adequate information is difficult to obtain. While the actual transaction price may be known, the Valuer may not know what warranties and indemnities were given by the seller, whether cash or other assets were taken from the seller prior to acquisition, how value should be allocated among the assets acquired, or what impact taxation planning had on the transaction.

5.7.5.4 For the reasons explained in para. 5.7.5.3, comparable data should always be used with care, and adjustments may need to be made. When using published auction results, it must be borne in mind that those results may represent transactions for a small market sector. Adjustments may be needed for differences due to differing market levels.

5.7.6 Any other information the Valuer believes is relevant.

5.8 Personal property valuations performed by means of the *sales comparison approach*

5.8.1 The *sales comparison approach* compares the subject property to similar properties and/or property ownership interests that have been sold in open markets.

5.8.2 The two most common sources of data used in the *sales comparison approach* are published auction results and transactions reported by firms regularly engaged in the trade of similar properties.

5.8.3 There must be a reasonable basis for comparison with and reliance upon the similar properties in the *sales comparison approach*. These similar properties should be regularly traded in the same market as the subject or in a market that responds to the same economic variables. The comparison must be made in a meaningful manner and must not be misleading. Factors to be considered in whether a reasonable basis for comparison exists include:

5.8.3.1 Similarity to the subject property in terms of qualitative and quantitative descriptive characteristics

5.8.3.2 Amount and verifiability of data on the similar property

5.8.3.3 Whether the price of the similar property represents an arm's-length transaction

5.8.3.4 A thorough, unbiased search for similar properties is necessary to establish the independence and reliability of the valuation. The search should include simple, objective criteria for selecting similar properties

5.8.3.5 A comparative analysis of qualitative and quantitative similarities and differences between similar properties and the subject property must be made

5.8.3.6 Where appropriate, adjustments may need to be made to render the value of the similar properties more comparable to the subject property. Adjustments may need to be made for unusual, non-recurring and unique items.

5.8.3.7 Appropriate adjustments for differences in the subject property's ownership and the ownership of similar properties with regard to the character and influence of such provenance or marketability/saleability or lack thereof, must be made, if applicable.

5.8.4 When prior transactions of the subject property are used to provide valuation guidance, adjustments may need to be made for the passage of time, for changes in the subject property, and for changed circumstances in the economy, industry, scholarly appreciation, and the business in which such properties are traded.

5.8.5 Anecdotal valuation rules, or rules of thumb, may be useful in the valuation of a property or ownership interest in an item of personal property. However, value indications derived from the use of such rules should not be given substantial weight unless it can be shown that buyers and sellers place substantial reliance on them.

5.9 Personal property valuations performed by means of the *income capitalisation approach*

5.9.1 The Income Capitalisation Approach to value considers income and expense data relating to the property being valued and estimates value through a capitalisation process.

5.9.2 The application of *the income capitalisation approach* may be appropriate in the valuation of furniture, fixtures, and equipment (FF&E) essential to the operation of properties such as hotels, furnished apartments, and care facilities.

5.9.2.1 FF&E may be subject to heavy use and, therefore, require periodic replacement to maintain the attractiveness and utility of the facility.

5.9.2.2 The useful lives of items of FF&E are estimated on the basis of their quality, durability, and the amount of use they receive. A weighted average for the useful lives of items of FF&E may then be calculated.

5.9.2.3 An estimate of the future replacement cost of the items of FF&E is divided by this figure to arrive at an annual replacement allowance/renewal fund. The replacement allowance/renewal fund is included among the entity's operating expenses/outgoings.

5.10 Personal property valuations performed by means of the cost approach

5.10.1 The *cost approach* considers as a substitute for the purchase of a given item of personal property, the possibility of creating another item equivalent to the original or one that could furnish equal utility with no undue cost resulting from delay.

5.10.2 The Valuer's estimate is based on the reproduction or replacement cost of the subject property or asset.

5.10.2.1 Replacement cost refers to what one might expect to pay for an object of similar age, size, color, and condition. Generally, it seeks to establish the cost of an alternative example or of a *replica,* or copy, of the original item, as near as possible to the original in terms of nature, quality, and age of materials but created by means of modern construction methods.

5.10.2.1.1 In the case of assets such as valuable antiques or paintings, replacement may be impractical regardless of the cost.

5.10.2.1.2 Reproduction cost refers to what one might expect to pay for a *facsimile,* or exact copy, of the original item, created with materials of a closely similar nature, quality, and age and using construction methods of the original period.

5.10.2.1.3 Over time some items of personal property that do not suffer physical depreciation may appreciate since current cost to replace or reproduce such items typically outpaces increases in their current price.

5.10.3 The application of the *cost approach* is especially appropriate in valuations of personal property such as manufactured products or items for which multiple copies exist, e.g., prints, porcelain figurines, or products turned out by a mint.

5.11 Reconciliation processes

5.11.1 The value conclusion shall be based upon

5.11.1.1 the definition of value;

5.11.1.2 the purpose and intended use of the valuation; and

5.11.1.3 all relevant information as of the valuation date necessary in view of the scope of the assignment.

5.11.2 The value conclusion shall also be based on value estimates from the valuation methods performed.

5.11.2.1 The selection of and reliance on the appropriate approaches, methods, and procedures depend on the judgment of the Valuer.

5.11.2.2 The Valuer must use judgment when determining the relative weight to be given to each of the value estimates during the Valuation Process. The Valuer should provide the rationale and justification for the valuation methods used and for the weighting of the methods relied on in reaching the value reconciliation when requested.

6.0 Effective Date

6.1 This International Valuation Guidance Note became effective 31 July 2007.

International Valuation Guidance Note No. 6

Business Valuation (Revised 2007)

1.0 Introduction

1.1 The International Valuation Standards Committee (IVSC) adopted this Guidance Note (GN) to improve the consistency and quality of business valuations among the international community for the benefit of users of financial statements and users of business valuations.

1.2 Business valuations are commonly sought and performed on the *Market Value* basis of valuation applying the provisions of International Valuation Standard 1 (IVS 1). Where other bases of valuation are used, with proper explanation and disclosure, the provisions of IVS 2 are applied.

1.3 In general the concepts, processes, and methods applied in the valuation of businesses are the same as those for other types of valuations. Certain terms may have different meanings or uses. Those differences become important disclosures wherever they are used. This GN sets forth important definitions used in business valuations.

1.4 Care should be taken by Valuers and users of valuation services to distinguish between the value of a business entity or trade related property, the valuation of assets owned by such an entity, and various possible applications of business or going concern considerations encountered in the valuation of real property interests. An example of the latter is valuations of trade related property. (See Property Types, para. 4.3.2.)

2.0 Scope

2.1 This GN is provided to assist in the course of rendering or using business valuations.

2.2 In addition to the elements that are common to other GNs to the International Valuation Standards, this GN contains a more expansive discussion of the business valuation process. This is included to typify what is commonly involved in business valuations and to provide a basis of comparison with other types of valuations, but the discussion should not be considered as either mandatory or limiting except as provided in this GN or otherwise in the International Valuation Standards.

2.3 Because other basic valuation principles, International Valuation Standards, and Guidance Notes are also applicable to business valuations, this GN should be understood to incorporate all other applicable portions of the IVSs.

3.0 Definitions

3.1 *Adjusted Book Value.* The book value that results when one or more asset or liability amounts are added, deleted or changed from the reported book amounts.

3.2 *Asset-based Approach.* A means of estimating the value of a business and/or equity interest using methods based on the *Market Value* of individual business assets less liabilities.

3.3 *Book Value*

3.3.1 With respect to assets, the capitalised cost of an asset less accumulated depreciation, depletion, or amortisation as it appears on the account books of the business.

3.3.2 With respect to a business entity, the difference between total assets (net of depreciation, depletion, and amortisation) and total liabilities of a business as they appear on the balance sheet. In this case, *book value* is synonymous with *net book value, net worth,* and *shareholder's equity.*

3.4 *Business Entity.* A commercial, industrial, service, or investment entity pursuing an economic activity.

3.5 *Business Valuation.* The act or process of arriving at an opinion or estimation of the value of a business or entity or an interest therein.

3.6 *Business Valuer.* A person who, by education, training, and experience is qualified to perform a valuation of a business, business ownership interest, security and/or intangible assets.

3.7 *Capitalisation*

3.7.1 At a given date, the conversion into the equivalent capital value of net income or a series of net receipts, actual or estimated, over a period.

3.7.2 In business valuation, the term refers to the capital structure of a business entity.

3.7.3 In business valuation, this term also refers to the recognition of an expenditure as a capital asset rather than a periodic expense.

3.8 *Capitalisation Factor.* Any multiple used to convert income into value.

3.9 *Capitalisation Rate.* Any divisor (usually expressed as a percentage) that is used to convert income into value.

3.10 *Capital Structure.* The composition of the invested capital.

3.11 *Cash Flow.*

3.11.1 *Gross Cash Flow:* Net income after taxes, plus non-cash items such as depreciation and amortisation.

3.11.2 *Net Cash Flow:* During an operating period, that amount of cash that remains after all cash needs of the business have been satisfied. *Net cash flow* is typically defined as being cash available to equity or invested capital.

3.11.3 *Equity Net Cash Flow*: Net income after taxes, plus depreciation and other non-cash charges, less increases in working capital, less capital expenditures, less decreases in invested capital debt principal, plus increases in invested capital debt principal.

3.11.4 *Invested Capital Net Cash Flow: Equity net cash flow,* plus interest payments net of tax adjustment, less net increases in debt principal.

3.12 *Control.* The power to direct the management and policies of a business.

3.13 *Control Premium.* The additional value inherent in the control interest that reflects its power of control, as contrasted to a minority interest.

3.14 *Discount for Lack of Control.* An amount or percentage deducted from a pro rata share of the value of 100 % of an equity interest in a business to reflect the absence of some or all of the powers of control.

3.15 *Discount Rate.* A rate of return used to convert a monetary sum, payable or receivable in the future, into present value.

3.16 *Economic Life.* The period over which property may be profitably used.

3.17 *Effective Date.* The date as of which the Valuer's opinion of value applies (Also referred to as *Valuation Date,* and/or *As Of Date*).

3.18 *Enterprise.* See Business Entity.

3.19 *Going Concern*

3.19.1 An operating business.

3.19.2 A premise of valuation, under which Valuers and accountants consider a business as an established entity that will continue in operation indefinitely. The premise of a going concern serves as an alternative to the premise of liquidation.

Adoption of a going concern premise allows the business to be valued above liquidation value and is essential to the development of *Market Value* for the business.

3.19.3 The entity is normally viewed as a going concern, that is, as continuing in operation in the foreseeable future. It is assumed that the entity has neither the intention nor the necessity of liquidation or of curtailing materially the scope of its operations. (IAS 1, 23-24, Framework, 23)

3.20 *Goodwill.*

3.21.1 Future economic benefits arising from assets that are not capable of being individually identified and separately recognised. (IFRS 3, Appendix A)

3.21.2 *Personal Goodwill*. The value of profit over and above market expectations, which could be extinguished upon sale of the trade related property, together with those financial factors related specifically to the current operator of the business, such as taxation, depreciation policy, borrowing costs and the capital invested in the business.

3.21.3 Transferable Goodwill. That intangible asset that arises as a result of property-specific name and reputation, customer patronage, location, products, and similar factors, which generate economic benefits. It is inherent to the trade related property, and will transfer to a new owner on sale.

3.21 *Holding Company*. A business that receives returns on its assets.

3.22 *Income Capitalisation Approach*. A general way of estimating a value indication of a business, business ownership interest, or security using one or more methods wherein a value is estimated by converting anticipated benefits into capital value.

3.23 *Invested Capital*. The sum of the debt and equity in a business on a long-term basis.

3.24 *Majority Control*. The degree of control provided by a majority position.

3.25 *Majority Interest*. Ownership position greater than 50% of the voting interest in a business

3.26 *Market Approach*. A general way of estimating a value indication of a business, business ownership interest, or security using one or more methods that compare the subject to similar businesses, business ownership interests, or securities that have been sold.

3.27 *Market Value*. See IVS 1, para. 3.1.

3.28 *Marketability Discount*. An amount or percentage deducted from an equity interest to reflect lack of marketability.

3.29 *Minority Discount*. A Discount for lack of control applicable to a minority interest.

3.30 *Minority Interest.* Ownership position less than 50% of the voting interest in a business.

3.31 *Net Assets.* Total assets less total liabilities.

3.32 *Net Income.* Revenue less expenses, including taxes.

3.33 *Operating Company.* A business that performs an economic activity by making, selling, or trading a product or service.

3.34 *Rate of Return.* An amount of income (loss) and/or change in value realised or anticipated on an investment, expressed as a percentage of that investment.

3.35 *Replacement Cost New.* The current cost of a similar new item having the nearest equivalent utility as the item being appraised.

3.36 *Report Date.* The date of the Valuation Report. May be the same as or different from the Valuation date.

3.37 *Reproduction Cost New.* The current cost of an identical new item.

3.38 *Valuation Approach.* In general, a way of estimating value using one or more specific valuation methods. (See *Market Approach, Income Capitalisation Approach,* and *Asset Based Approach* definitions.)

3.39 *Valuation Method.* Within approaches, a specific way to estimate value.

3.40 *Valuation Procedure.* The act, manner, and technique of performing the steps of a valuation method.

3.41 *Valuation Ratio.* A factor wherein a value or price serves as the numerator and financial, operating, or physical data serve as the denominator.

3.42 *Working Capital.* The amount by which current assets exceed current liabilities.

4.0 Relationship to Accounting Standards

4.1 Business valuations are commonly used as a basis for making allocations of various assets to aid in the establishment or restatement of financial statements. In this context, business Valuers reflect the *Market Value* of all components of a business's balance sheet in order to meet Accounting Standards, having regard to the convention that reflects the effect of changing prices.

4.2 In some instances the business valuation provides a basis for estimating the extent of obsolescence of certain fixed assets. In this application the business valuation may or may not be the principal reason for the valuation, but the combination of services by the Business Valuer and, for example, a Real Property Valuer, is necessary to properly allocate and reflect the *Market Value* of assets to appear in a financial statement.

4.3 Other considerations relative to the relationship of business valuations and Accounting Standards are similar to the provisions discussed in International Valuation Application 1 (IVA 1).

5.0 Guidance

5.1 Business valuations may be required for a number of possible uses, including acquisitions and dispositions of individual businesses, mergers, valuation of shareholder ownings, and the like.

5.1.1 Where the purpose of the valuation requires a *Market Value* estimate, the Valuer shall apply definitions, processes, and methodologies consistent with their provision in IVS 1.

5.1.2 When an engagement calls for a value basis other than *Market Value,* the Valuer shall clearly identify the type of value involved, define such value, and take steps necessary to distinguish the value estimate from a *Market Value* estimate.

5.2 If, in the opinion of the Valuer, certain aspects of an engagement indicate that a departure from any provision of IVSs or of this Guidance, is necessary and appropriate, such departure shall be disclosed and the reason for invoking the departure clearly set forth in all Valuation Reports (oral or written) issued by the Valuer. The requirements for Valuation Reports are addressed in the IVSC Code of Conduct and IVS 3, Valuation Reporting.

5.3 The Valuer shall take steps to assure that all data sources relied upon are reliable and appropriate to the valuation undertaking. In many instances it will be beyond the scope of the Valuer's services to perform a complete verification of secondary or tertiary data sources. Accordingly, the Valuer shall verify the accuracy and reasonableness of data sources as is customary in the markets and locale of the valuation.

5.4 Business Valuers must often rely upon the services of Professional Property Valuers and/or other experts. A common example is reliance upon a Real Property Valuer to value the real estate components owned by a business. **Where the services of other experts are relied upon, the Business Valuer shall**

5.4.1 take such verification steps as are necessary to assure that such services are competently performed and that the conclusions relied upon are reasonable and credible, or

5.4.2 disclose the fact that no such steps were taken.

5.5 Business Valuers must frequently rely upon information received from a client or from a client's representatives. The source of any such data relied upon shall be cited by the Valuer in oral or written Valuation Reports, and the data shall be reasonably verified wherever possible.

5.6 Although many of the principles, methods, and techniques of business valuation are similar to other fields of valuation, business valuations require special education, training, skills, and experience.

5.7 Going concern has several meanings in accounting and valuation. **In some contexts, going concern serves as a premise under which Valuers and accountants consider a business as an established entity that will continue in operation indefinitely.**

5.7.1 The premise of a going concern serves as an alternative to the premise of liquidation. Adoption of a going concern premise allows the business to be valued above liquidation value and is essential to the development of the *Market Value* of the business.

5.7.1.1 In liquidations, the value of most intangible assets (e.g., goodwill) tends toward zero, and the value of all tangible assets reflects the circumstance of liquidation. Expenses associated with liquidation (sales fee, commissions, taxes, other closing costs, administrative costs during close-out, and loss of value in inventory) are also calculated and deducted from the estimate of business value.

5.8 Awareness of current market activity, and knowledge about relevant economic developments and trends are essential for competent business valuations. In order to estimate the *Market Value* of a business, Business Valuers identify and assess the impact of such considerations in their valuations and Valuation Reports.

5.9 A description of the business valuation assignment must include

> **5.9.1 Identification of the business, business ownership interest, or security to be valued;**

> **5.9.2 the effective date of the valuation;**

> **5.9.3 the definition of value;**

> **5.9.4 the owner of the interest; and**

> **5.9.5 the purpose and use of the valuation.**

5.10 Factors to be considered by the Valuer in the valuation of a business include:

> **5.10.1 The rights, privileges, or conditions that attach to the ownership interest, whether held in corporate form, partnership form, or proprietorship**

>> 5.10.1.1 Ownership rights are set forth in various legal documents. In various States these documents may be called articles of association and/or the capital clause in the memorandum of the business, articles of incorporation, bylaws, partnership agreements, and shareholder agreements, to name a few.

>> 5.10.1.2 Whoever owns the interest is bound by the business's documents. There may be rights and conditions contained in an owner's agreement or exchange of correspondence, and these rights may or may not be transferable to a new owner of the interest.

>> 5.10.1.3 The documents may contain restrictions on the transfer of the interest and may contain provisions governing the basis of valuation that has to be adopted in the event of transfer of the interest. For example, the documents may stipulate that the interest to be transferred should be valued as a pro rata fraction of the value of the

entire issued share capital even though the interest to be transferred represents a minority interest. In each case the rights of the interest being valued and the rights attaching to any other class of interest must be considered at the outset.

5.10.2 The nature of the business and history of the business. Since value resides in the benefit of future ownership, history is valuable in that it may give guidance as to the expectations of the business for the future.

5.10.3 The economic outlook that may affect the subject business, including political outlook and government policy. Matters such as exchange rates, inflation and interest rates may affect businesses that operate in different sectors of the economy quite differently.

5.10.4 The condition and outlook of the specific industry that may affect the subject business

5.10.5 The assets, liabilities, and equity and financial condition of the business

5.10.6 The earnings and dividend paying capacity of the business

5.10.7 Whether or not the business has intangible value

5.10.7.1 Intangible value may be embodied in identifiable intangible assets such as patents, trademarks, copyrights, brands, know-how, databases, etc.

5.10.7.2 Intangible value may also be contained in undifferentiated assets, often called *"goodwill."* Note that goodwill value in this context is similar to goodwill in the accounting sense in that both are the residual value (historical cost in accounting terms) after all other assets have been taken into account.

5.10.7.3 If the business has intangible assets, the Valuer must ensure that the value of the intangibles is fully reflected, whether the identifiable intangible assets have been valued separately or not.

5.10.8 Prior transactions in ownership interests of the subject business

5.10.9 The relative size of the ownership interest to be valued

5.10.9.1 There are different levels of control or lack of control resulting from differences in the size of ownership interests. In some instances effective control may be obtained with less than 50% of the voting rights. Even if one person owns more than 50% of the voting rights and has operational control, there may be certain actions, such as winding the business up (i.e., putting everything in order before the business may be dissolved), that may require more than 50% affirmative vote, and may require an affirmative vote of all owners.

5.10.9.2 It is essential that the Valuer be aware of the legal restrictions and conditions that arise through the laws of the State in which the business exists.

5.10.10 Other market data, e.g., rates of return on alternative investments, advantages of control, disadvantages of lack of liquidity, etc.

5.10.11 The market prices of publicly traded stocks or partnership interests, acquisition prices for business interests, or businesses engaged in the same or similar lines of business.

5.10.11.1 Often, particularly in the use of acquisition transactions, adequate information is difficult or impossible to obtain. While the actual transaction price may be known, the Valuer may not know what warranties and indemnities were given by the seller, what terms were given or received, whether cash or other assets were taken from the business prior to acquisition, or what impact taxation planning had on the transaction.

5.10.11.2 Comparable data should always be used with care, and inevitably numerous adjustments need to be made. When using market prices that reflect public trading, the Valuer must bear in mind that the market prices are from transactions for small minority holdings. The price for the acquisition of an entire business represents 100% of the business. Adjustments must be made for differences arising due to different levels of control.

5.10.12 Any other information the Valuer believes to be relevant.

5.11 Use of financial statements

5.11.1 There are three goals of financial analysis and adjustment:

5.11.1.1 Understanding of the relationships existing in the profit and loss statement and the balance sheet, including trends over time, to assess the risk inherent in the business operations and the prospects for future performance

5.11.1.2 Comparison with similar businesses to assess risk and value parameters

5.11.1.3 Adjustment of historical financial statements to estimate the economic abilities of and prospects for the business

5.12 To aid in understanding the economics of and risk in a business interest, financial statements should be analysed in terms of 1) money, 2) percentages (percentage of sales for items in the income statement and percentage of total assets for items in the balance sheet), and 3) financial ratios.

5.12.1 Analysis in terms of money as stated in the financial statements is used to establish trends and relationships between income and expense accounts in a business interest over time. These trends and relationships are used to assess the expected income flow in the future, along with the capital needed to allow the business to provide that income flow.

5.12.2 Analysis in terms of percentages compares accounts in the profit and loss statement to revenues, and accounts in the balance sheets to total assets. Percentage analysis is used to compare the trends in relationships, i.e., between revenue and expense items, or between balance sheet amounts, for the subject business over time and among similar businesses.

5.12.3 Analysis in terms of financial ratios is used to compare the relative risk of the subject business over time and among similar businesses.

5.13 For estimates of the *Market Value* of a business, common adjustments to the financial record of the business are made to more closely approximate economic reality of both the income stream and the balance sheet.

5.13.1 Financial statement adjustments should be made to reported financial information for items that are relevant and significant to the valuation process. Adjustments may be appropriate for the following reasons:

5.13.1.1 To adjust revenues and expenses to levels that are reasonably representative of expected continuing operations

5.13.1.2 To present financial data of the subject and guideline comparison businesses on a consistent basis

5.13.1.3 To adjust from reported values to *Market Values*

5.13.1.4 To adjust for non-operating assets and liabilities and the related revenue and expenses

5.13.1.5 To adjust for non-economic revenue or expense

5.13.2 Whether an adjustment is appropriate, or not, may depend on the degree of control held by the ownership interest under valuation. For controlling interests, including an ownership interest of 100%, most adjustments may be appropriate if the owner could make the changes implied by the adjustment. For valuation of minority interests, whose owners do not have the ability to change most items, the Valuer should be careful to reflect reality when considering potential adjustments. **Common adjustments include:**

5.13.2.1 Elimination of the impact of non-recurring events from the income statement and balance sheet, if any. Since these events are not likely to recur, a buyer of the interest would not expect to incur them, and would not include them in the income stream. Adjustments may be required in taxes. These types of adjustments are typically appropriate for both majority and minority interest valuations. Examples of non-recurring items include:

5.13.2.1.1 Strikes, if unusual

5.13.2.1.2 New plant startup

5.13.2.1.3 Weather phenomena such as floods, cyclones, etc.

5.13.2.2 The Valuer should be wary of adjusting for non-recurring items whenever non-recurring items arise in most years, but in each year they appear to be the result of different events. Many businesses have non-recurring items every year, and the Valuer should make contingency provisions for these expenses.

5.13.2.3 **Elimination of the impact of non-operating items from the balance sheet and the income statement** in the context of valuation of a controlling shareholder's interest. In the context of valuation of a minority shareholder's interest, these adjustments may not be appropriate. If non-operating items are on the balance sheet, they should be removed and valued separately from the operating business. Non-operating items should be valued at *Market Value*. Tax adjustments may be required. Costs of sale should be taken into account. Adjustments to the income statement should include removal of both income and expense arising from the non-operating assets, including tax impacts. **Examples of non-operating items and the appropriate adjustments include:**

5.13.2.3.1 Non-essential personnel. Eliminate compensation expense and taxes related to compensation expense and adjust income taxes. The Valuer should be wary of adjusting for items such as non-essential personnel in arriving at a maintainable profits figure. Unless the Valuer knows that the acquirer, or whoever the Valuer is acting for, actually has the controlling power to make the change and intends of get rid of non-essential personnel, there is a danger of overvaluing the business if the expenses are added back to profit.

5.13.2.3.2 Non-essential assets (e.g., an airplane). Eliminate the value of the non-essential asset(s) and any associated assets and liabilities from the balance sheet. (After the business has been valued, the value of the non-essential asset(s) is added to reconciled business value net of costs of disposal, including taxes if any.). Eliminate income statement impact of owning the non-essential asset(s), including support expenses (in the case of an airplane, the fuel, crew, hanger, taxes, maintenance, etc.) and revenue (charter or rental income).

5.13.2.3.3 Redundant assets (surplus or not necessary to the requirements of the business) should be discussed in the Valuation Report similarly with non-operating items. Such redundant assets may principally include: unemployed licences, franchises, copyrights and patents; investments in land, rental buildings and excess equipment; investments in other businesses; a marketable securities portfolio; and, excess cash or term deposits. The net realisable value of redundant assets (net of income tax and selling costs) must be added as inflow to operating net cash flow, especially in the first year of the specified forecast period.

5.13.2.4 Depreciation may need to be adjusted from the tax or accounting depreciation shown in the reported financial statements to an estimate that compares more accurately to depreciation used in similar businesses. Tax adjustments may subsequently need to be made.

5.13.2.5 Inventory accounting may need to be adjusted to more accurately compare to similar businesses, whose accounts may be kept on a different basis from the subject business, or to more accurately reflect economic reality. **Inventory adjustments** may be different when considering the income statement and when considering the balance sheet. For example, first-in-first-out (a method of costing inventory that assumes the first acquired stock will be the first sold) may most accurately represent the value of the inventory when constructing a *Market Value* balance sheet. But, when examining the income statement, last-in-first-out (a method of costing inventory that assumes the most recently acquired stock will be the first sold) may more accurately represent the income level in times of inflation or deflation. Tax adjustments may subsequently need to be made.

5.13.2.6 Compensation of the owner(s) may need to be adjusted to reflect the market cost of replacing the labor of the owner(s). **Severence pay** for non-essential personnel may need to be considered. **Tax adjustments** may need to be made. **Service contracts** may need to be looked at carefully to adjust for the value (rather than the face amount of the cost) of terminating contracts with senior personnel.

5.13.2.7 Cost of items leased, rented or otherwise contracted from related parties may need to be adjusted to reflect *Market Value* payments. Tax adjustments may subsequently need to be made.

5.13.3 Some adjustments that would be made in the context of valuation of the entire business might not be made in the context of valuation of a non-controlling interest in that entity since the non-controlling interest would not have the ability to exert an influence that would warrent adjustment.

5.13.4 Financial statement adjustments are made for the purpose of assisting the Valuer in reaching a valuation conclusion. If the Valuer is acting as a consultant to either the buyer or seller in a proposed transaction, the adjustments should be understood by the client. For example, the proposing purchaser should understand that the value derived after adjustments may represent the maximum that should be paid. If the purchaser does not believe the financial or operational improvements can be made, a lesser price may be appropriate.

5.13.5 Adjustments made should be fully described and supported. The Valuer should be very careful in making adjustments to the historical record. Such adjustments should be discussed fully with the client. The Valuer should make adjustments only after sufficient access to the business to support their validity.

5.14 Business valuation approaches

5.14.1 *Market approach* **to business valuation**

5.14.1.1 The *market approach* **compares the subject to similar businesses, business ownership interests, and securities that have been sold in the market.**

5.14.1.2 The three most common sources of data used in the *market approach* **are public stock markets in which ownership interests of similar businesses are traded, the acquisition market in which entire businesses are bought and sold, and prior transactions in the ownership of the subject business.**

5.14.1.3 There must be a reasonable basis for comparison with and reliance upon the similar businesses in the *market approach.* These similar businesses should be in the same industry as the subject or in an industry that responds to the same economic variables. The comparison must be made in a meaningful manner and must not be misleading. Factors to be considered in whether a reasonable basis for comparison exists include:

5.14.1.3.1 Similarity to the subject business in terms of qualitative and quantitative business characteristics

5.14.1.3.2 Amount and verifiability of data on the similar business

5.14.1.3.3 Whether the price of the similar business represents an arm's-length transaction

5.14.1.3.3.1 A thorough, unbiased search for similar businesses is necessary to establish the independence and reliability of the valuation. The search should include simple, objective criteria for selecting similar businesses.

5.14.1.3.3.2 A comparative analysis of qualitative and quantitative similarities and differences between similar businesses and the subject business must be made.

5.14.1.4 Through analysis of the publicly traded businesses or acquisitions, the Valuer often computes valuation ratios, which are usually price divided by some measure of income or net assets. Care must be used in calculating and selecting these ratios.

5.14.1.4.1 The ratio must provide meaningful information about the value of the business.

5.14.1.4.2 The data from the similar businesses used to compute the ratio must be accurate.

5.14.1.4.3 The calculation of ratios must be accurate.

5.14.1.4.4 If the data are averaged, the time period considered and averaging method must be appropriate.

5.14.1.4.5 All calculations must be done in the same way for both the similar businesses and the subject business.

5.14.1.4.6 The price data used in the ratio must be valid as of the valuation date.

5.14.1.4.7 Where appropriate, adjustments may need to be made to render the similar businesses and the subject business more comparable.

5.14.1.4.8 Adjustments may need to be made for unusual, non-recurring, and non-operating items.

5.14.1.4.9 The selected ratios must be appropriate given the differences in risk and expectations of the similar businesses and the subject business.

5.14.1.4.10 Several value indications may be derived since several valuation multiples may be selected and applied to the subject business.

5.14.1.4.11 Appropriate adjustments for differences in the subject ownership interest and interests in the similar businesses with regard to control or lack of control, or marketability or lack of marketability, must be made, if applicable.

5.14.1.5 When prior transactions in the subject business are used to provide valuation guidance, adjustments may need to be made for the passage of time and for changed circumstances in the economy, the industry, and the business.

5.14.1.6 Anecdotal valuation rules, or rules of thumb, may be useful in the valuation of a business, business ownership interest, or security. However, value indications derived from the use of such rules should not be given substantial weight unless it can be shown that buyers and sellers place significant reliance on them.

5.14.2 *Income capitalisation approach* **to business valuation**

5.14.2.1 The *income capitalisation approach* **estimates the value of a business, business ownership interest or security by calculating the present value of anticipated benefits. The two most common income approach methods are capitalisation of income and** *discounted cash flow analysis* **or** *dividends method.*

5.14.2.1.1 In (direct) capitalisation of income, a representative income level is divided by a capitalisation rate or multiplied by

an income multiple to convert the income into value. In theory, income can be a variety of definitions of income and cash flow. In practice, the income measured is usually either pre-tax income or post-tax income. The capitalisation rate must be appropriate for the definition of income used.

5.14.2.1.2 In *discounted cash flow analysis* **and/or** *dividends method*, **cash receipts are estimated for each of several future periods. These receipts are converted to value by the application of a discount rate using present value techniques.** Many definitions of cash flow could be used. In practice, net cash flow (cash flow that could be distributed to shareholders), or actual dividends (particularly in the case of minority shareholders) are normally used. The discount rate must be appropriate for the definition of cash flow used.

5.14.2.1.3 Capitalisation rates and discount rates are derived from the market and are expressed as a price multiple (derived from data on publicly traded businesses or transactions) or an interest rate (derived from data on alternative investments).

5.14.2.2 Anticipated income or benefits are converted to value using calculations that consider the expected growth and timing of the benefits, the risk associated with the benefits stream, and the time value of money.

5.14.2.2.1 Anticipated income or benefits should be estimated considering the capital structure and historical performance of the business, expected outlook for the business, and industry and economic factors.

5.14.2.2.2 The *income approach* **requires the estimation of a capitalisation rate, when capitalising income to arrive at value, or a discount rate, when discounting cash flow.** In estimating the appropriate rate, the Valuer should consider such factors as the level of interest rates, rates of return expected by investors on similar investments, and the risk inherent in the anticipated benefit stream.

5.14.2.2.3 In capitalisation methods that employ discounting, expected growth is explicitly considered in the estimate of the future benefit stream.

5.14.2.2.4 In capitalisation methods that do not employ discounting, expected growth is included in the capitalisation rate. The relationship, stated as a formula, is discount rate minus long-term growth rate equals capitalisation rate (R =Y − Δa where R is the capitalisation rate; Y is the discount, or yield, rate; and Δa is the annualised change in value).

5.14.2.2.5 The capitalisation rate or discount rate should be consistent with the type of anticipated benefits used. For example, pre-tax rates should be used with pre-tax benefits; net after-income-tax rates should be used with net after-income-tax benefit streams; and net cash flow rates should be used with net cash flow benefits.

5.14.2.2.6 When the forecast income is expressed in nominal terms (current prices), nominal rates must be used, and when the forecast income is expressed in real terms (level prices), real rates must be used. Similarly, the expected long-term growth rate of income should be documented and clearly expressed in nominal or real terms.

5.14.3 *Asset-based business valuation* **approach**

5.14.3.1 In business valuation the *asset-based appro*ach **may be similar to the cost approach used by Valuers of different types of assets.**

5.14.3.2 The *asset-based approach* is founded on the principle of substitution, i.e., an asset is worth no more than it would cost to replace all of its constituent parts.

5.14.3.3 In the execution of the *asset-based approach*, the cost basis balance sheet is replaced with **a balance sheet that reports all assets, tangible and intangible, and all liabilities at** *Market Value* **or some other appropriate current value.** Taxes may need to be considered. If market or liquidation values apply, costs of sale and other expenses may need to be considered.

5.14.3.4 The *asset-based approach* **should be considered in valuations of controlling interests in business entities that involve one or more of the following:**

5.14.3.4.1 An investment or holding business, such as a property business or a farming business

5.14.3.4.2 A business valued on a basis other than as a going concern

5.14.3.5 The *asset-based approach* **should not be the sole valuation approach used in assignments relating to operating businesses appraised as going concerns unless it is customarily used by sellers and buyers.** In such cases, the Valuer must support the selection of this approach.

5.14.3.6 If the valuation of an operating business is not on a going concern basis, the assets should be valued on a *Market Value* basis or on a basis that assumes a shortened time period for exposure in the market, if that is appropriate. All costs related to the sale of the assets or the closing of the business need to be taken into account in this type of valuation. Intangible assets such as goodwill may not have value under these circumstances, although other intangible assets such patents, trademarks, or brands may retain their value.

5.14.3.7 If the holding business simply holds property and receives investment income from the property, *Market Values* should be obtained for each property.

5.14.3.8 If an investment holding business is to be valued, the securities (both quoted and unquoted), the liquidity of the interest, and the size of the interest may be relevant and **may lead to a deviation from the quoted price.**

5.15 Reconciliation processes

5.15.1 The value conclusion shall be based upon

5.15.1.1 the definition of value;

5.15.1.2 the purpose and intended use of the valuation; and

5.15.1.3 all relevant information as of the valuation date necessary in view of the scope of the assignment.

5.15.2 The value conclusion shall also be based on value estimates from the valuation methods performed.

5.15.2.1 The selection of and reliance on the appropriate approaches, methods and procedures depends on the judgment of the Valuer.

5.15.2.2 The Valuer must use judgment when estimating the relative weight to be given to each of the value estimates reached during the Valuation Process. The Valuer should provide the rationale and justification for the valuation methods used and for the weighting of the methods relied on in reaching the reconciled value.

6.0 Effective Date

6.1 This International Valuation Guidance Note became effective 31 July 2007.

International Valuation Guidance Note No. 7

Consideration of Hazardous and Toxic Substances In Valuation

1.0 Introduction

1.1 The objective of this Guidance Note (GN) is to assist Valuers in preparing valuations when specific hazardous or toxic substances may influence property values.

1.2 Hazardous and toxic substances are included among a number of possible environmental factors that, when appropriate, are specifically considered by Valuers. This GN is limited to consideration of hazardous and toxic substances because other environmental factors that may be encountered in valuations typically have less involvement with scientific and associated technical issues, including related law.

1.3 This GN addresses general concepts, principles, and considerations that guide Valuers in preparing valuations when hazardous or toxic materials that may influence property values are present. It also discusses concepts that must be understood by accountants, regulatory authorities, and other users of valuation services.

1.4 Valuers rarely have special qualifications in legal, scientific, or other technical areas that involve evaluating risks associated with hazardous or toxic substances. When considering the market effects of such risks in property valuations, Valuers commonly rely upon other experts' advice. As specified in the IVSC Code of Conduct, paras. 5.2 and 6.6, significant reliance upon other experts' advice must be disclosed and explained in the context of the property addressed in the Valuation Report.

1.5 Fundamental to the application of this GN are the Valuer's adherence to market-based valuations, objectivity, and full disclosure of relevant matters. Similarly, Valuers are obliged to write Valuation Reports that may be reasonably understood by clients and others. The obligation for clarity and full disclosure is particularly important when scientific, technical, and legal issues are involved.

1.6 This GN also provides for proper treatment and disclosure of hazardous and toxic substance issues when valuing specialised properties and in other situations, which preclude the application of *Market Value* concepts.

2.0 Scope

2.1 This GN applies to all valuations of property including plant and equipment. Special provisions of the GN should be observed when hazardous or toxic substances that may influence the property's *Market Value* or other defined value are known or reasonably believed to be present.

3.0 Definitions

3.1 *Hazardous or toxic substances* within the context of this GN involve specific materials that, by their presence or proximity, may have adverse effect on property value because of their potential to cause harm to life forms. Such materials may be incorporated into improvements to or on the site, or they may be found in or on the land. They may also be offsite, but nearby. In some instances they may be airborne.

3.1.1 In a more general use beyond this GN, environmental factors may be characterized as influences external to the property being valued which may have positive effect, negative effect, or no effect at all on the property's value. Hazardous or toxic substances may be found either on or off the site of the property valued.

3.2 *Hazardous substance* within the context of a valuation is any material within, around, or near the property being valued that has sufficient form, quantity, and bio-availability to create a negative impact on the property's *Market Value*.

3.3 *Toxic* describes the status of a material, whether gas, liquid, or solid, that in its form, quantity, and location at the date of valuation has capacity to cause harm to life-forms. *Toxicity* refers to the degree or extent of such capacity.

4.0 Relationship to Accounting Standards

4.1 While the expressions *Market Value* and *Fair Value* may not always be synonymous (see International Valuation Standards 1 and 2 [IVSs 1 and

2] and International Valuation Application 1 [IVA 1]), each type of value reflects market behaviour under conditions contained within the respective definitions. To the extent that property values reported under either type of value may be affected by hazardous or toxic substances, proper disclosure and the application of proper valuation procedures to the circumstances are necessary in making and reporting valuations.

4.2 This GN is applicable to all circumstances involving public disclosure of property values, whether reported individually or in the aggregate, when hazardous or toxic substances may have adverse effect on such values. In addition to the possible effect of such considerations on the properties valued, it is possible that there are other accompanying issues such as curative or restoration costs, maintenance or monitoring costs, third-party or regulatory liabilities, and the like. Thus, proper disclosure and handling are essential in valuations used for preparation of financial statements and related accounts.

4.3 In the ordinary course of conducting an asset valuation, the Valuer will be instructed by the Directors of the entity as provided in IVA 1. Any special instructions to the Valuer concerning the handling of hazardous or toxic substance issues that may have negative impact upon property value are, under IVA 1, important disclosures to be discussed by the Valuer in the Valuation Report. Such disclosures shall be accompanied by the Valuer's explanation of how the issues are handled in the Valuation Process; any assumptions that are made; and the effect, if any, such considerations have upon the value reported.

4.4 Although the value effects of hazardous or toxic substances are derived from the market in a *Market Value* assignment, such effects may not be as readily discerned when valuing property for which a *Depreciated Replacement Cost* method is appropriate. To comply with IVA 1 when applying the DRC method, Valuers should apply the principles of this GN to the extent possible and should fully disclose the extent of their analysis and the basis for their conclusions.

4.5 The accounting definition of *impairment loss* is the amount by which the carrying amount of an asset or a cash-generating unit exceeds its recoverable amount (IAS 36, para. 6). The negative impact of hazardous or toxic materials that are present in a property may contribute to its impairment. The impairment loss incurred by a property where such substances are present may include the adverse effect of those substances upon property value. (See para.5.4 below.)

5.0 Guidance

5.1 In dealing with a client or prospective client in matters pertaining to the valuation of property when known or reasonably discoverable environmental conditions that may have adverse influence on property values are present, the Valuer should disclose to the client the extent of his or her knowledge, experience, and competency to deal with the situation.

> 5.1.1 If the environmental factors are known or are suspected to exist at the time the Valuer and prospective client are discussing the potential engagement, the Valuer should satisfy himself or herself that the client understands the Valuer's competency and disclosure obligations and that undertaking the engagement will in no way compromise these obligations.

> 5.1.2 If the environmental factors are discovered after commencing the engagement, the Valuer should make known to the client the knowledge, experience, and competency disclosures specified by this Guidance, and should then comply with all other IVSs disclosure requirements.

5.2 Recognising that many environmental situations will require advice on physical, legal, scientific, and other technical issues, if the engagement is otherwise acceptable to both the client and the Valuer, the Valuer should take the necessary steps to complete the assignment competently. These steps may include appropriate personal study; association with another Valuer who has the requisite knowledge, experience, and competency; or obtaining the professional assistance of others who possess the requisite knowledge, experience, and competency.

5.3 Disclosure of the existence of any hazardous or toxic substance that may have adverse effect upon a property's value is included among the general reporting requirements of IVSs 1, 2, and 3. Also required is the Valuer's disclosure regarding how that factor has been dealt with in the engagement. If the engagement calls for valuation of the property as though no such environmental factor existed, full disclosure must be made of the limiting assumption, and reporting must comply with the statements above. (See paras. 5.1 and 5.2.) **The requirements for valuation reports are addressed in the Code of Conduct and IVS 3, Valuation Reporting.**

5.4 Where impairment is present in a property, the Valuer should estimate the value of the property as if the impairment had been removed. Where possible, the Valuer should identify the cost of remediation; but if this is not possible, the Valuer should disclose the fact that the property is impaired.

5.5 If a property is valued as if unaffected by hazardous substances, and such substances are known or suspected to exist, the Valuation Report should contain a qualification that clearly limits the scope of the valuation, an appropriate statement of purpose, properly qualified conclusions, and a restriction against use of the valuation conclusion without accompanying disclosure of the qualification and its explanation.

5.6 The names and nature of expert assistance of others who contributed specific information concerning effects of environmental factors on the property valued should be acknowledged in the Valuation Report.

5.7 When there are no known environmental factors that may have adverse effect on property value, the Valuer should, as a matter of routine practice, include within the Valuation Report a contingent and limiting condition or other disclaimer affirming that the valuation was made on the assumption that no such factors were known to exist at the date of valuation, but if such factors did exist they could well have an adverse effect on value.

5.8 There is growing worldwide concern about the effects of hazardous and toxic substances upon lives and property. Many potential hazards have been recently identified, and others are likely to be added over time as new and additional discoveries are made and subsequent controls are invoked by governments or are required by the market.

5.9 Some hazardous or toxic substances can have material effect on property values. However, **as Valuers normally deal with *Market Values*, it is the market's reaction to these substances that is at issue in *Market Value* engagements.** Over time, substances once believed to have no adverse effect on property value may be determined to have such an effect. Conversely, materials once believed to have substantial effect may be found to have little or no property value effect, or to have such effect only under certain market conditions.

5.10 The handling of physical, legal, scientific, and technical issues involved with hazardous or toxic substances is frequently beyond the skill of the Valuer. However, **the Valuer's role in consideration of such factors will be facilitated if**

5.10.1 situations involving environmentally sensitive substances are recognised and dealt with in accordance with this Guidance, whether they are encountered prior to undertaking an engagement or subsequent to its commencement;

5.10.2 proper reliance is placed upon the professional advice and assistance of others when special skills, knowledge, training, and experience are required, and any such assistance is acknowledged and explained in the Valuation Report;

5.10.3 proper treatment is given to the influence of hazardous or toxic substances in the Valuation Process, or alternatively, if the Valuation Process is to exclude consideration of such matters, proper disclosure is made of any assumptions made, the purpose of the analysis, and the likely effect of the assumptions on the defined value;

5.10.4 reasonable effort is made to ensure that reports and the value estimates they contain are not misleading and can be reasonably used only for the purpose for which they are intended.

5.11 Valuers are expected to correctly apply those recognised methods and techniques that are necessary to comply with this Guidance. When valuing property subject to some hazardous or toxic substance that adversely influences property value, the Valuer should apply those processes necessary to adequately reflect any such value losses, taking care to neither over- or understate the value effects. **In a *Market Value* engagement, it is the Valuer's responsibility to reflect the market effect of the particular condition or circumstance.**

5.12 Valuers are cautioned that there can be considerable controversy among legal, scientific, and other technical experts upon whose advice the Valuer may need to rely. Particular differences may be found in the methods experts use to determine the extent of clean-up, maintenance, or monitoring that may be associated with hazardous or toxic substances and the costs required to accomplish such clean-up, maintenance, or monitoring.

5.12.1 Engagements may require valuation of the affected property under an assumption that any value effect of the hazardous or toxic substances is excluded from the reported value. Such engagements are acceptable, provided that the resulting valuation is not misleading, that the client is informed of and agrees to this limiting assumption, and that the Valuation Report clearly sets forth the limitation and the reasons therefore.

5.12.2 Because of technical issues frequently involved in environmental matters, it is common for Valuers, directly or through the client, to seek the counsel of and rely upon the opinions of those who hold appropriate qualifications to evaluate problems involving hazardous or toxic substances. **Valuers should disclose the level and nature of reliance placed upon such opinions.**

5.13 Valuers and users of valuation services should recognise that the effect of a particular hazardous or toxic substance may vary widely with differences in properties, locations, and markets. Adverse value effects may range from none to those that are more than costs of cure and remediation. The latter may occur, for example, where *highest and best use* of the property affected is changed by the condition and where marketability or other usefulness of the property is altered. In any case, **it is the role of the Valuer to research and reflect the effects of the environmental factor on a particular property in its market.**

5.14 In the typical valuation engagement, the Valuer will not have the skills to make legal, scientific, or technical findings regarding hazardous or toxic substances, or other environmental factors that may have adverse effect on value. **It is important** to the credibility and usefulness of the reported value **that if any such conditions exist, they be properly considered and reported.**

5.14.1 When the Valuer knows that a hazardous or toxic substance is present in the property specified in a valuation engagement, the Valuer should follow all requirements of this Guidance. Normally, any technical experts upon whose advice the Valuer may rely will be engaged by the client or by others.

5.14.2 When the Valuer has some reason to believe that a potentially adverse hazardous or toxic substance may be present, the Valuer

should immediately make the client aware of the concern and request that the client take steps to resolve pertinent questions. By handling this concern on a private, confidential basis, the Valuer keeps information confidential that in itself could affect the property involved.

5.15 Guidelines for Valuers' responsibilities to observe, locate, and identify hazardous or toxic substances or circumstances may vary from time to time within and among jurisdictions. In general, determination of the nature, extent, and physical effects of environmental conditions is beyond the scope of service of Valuers.

5.16 In dealing with hazardous or toxic substances, the Valuer should research all related issues in a confidential manner so as not to raise undue speculation concerning the property.

5.17 It is not uncommon for individuals unfamiliar with hazardous or toxic substances issues to assume that if there is a physical effect of such substances, there must be an adverse economic reaction. Market experience shows there can be, and frequently are, important differences between general public perceptions and actual market effects of the presence of such substances. **The Valuer's role is to avoid such generally held but possibly erroneous assumptions and to carefully consider all significant factors, perform competent market research, and reflect relevant market attitudes towards the situation in Valuation Reports.**

6.0 Effective Date

6.1 This International Valuation Guidance Note became effective 31 January 2005.

International Valuation Guidance Note No. 8

The Cost Approach for Financial Reporting-(DRC) (Revised 2007)

1.0 Introduction

1.1 The purpose of this Guidance Note (GN) is to assist users and preparers of Valuation Reports in the interpretation of the meaning and application of *depreciated replacement cost* for financial reporting purposes.

1.2 *Depreciated replacement cost* is an application of the cost approach that may be used in arriving at the value of specialised assets for financial reporting purposes. *Depreciated replacement cost* may be the more applicable approach when comparable sales data is insufficient but sufficient market data exists concerning costs and accrued depreciation. As an application of the cost approach, it is based on the principle of substitution.

2.0 Scope

2.1 This GN provides background to the use of *depreciated replacement cost* in connection with International Valuation Application 1 (IVA 1), Valuation for Financial Reporting.

2.2 The *depreciated replacement cost* approach is also discussed in GN3 (Valuation of Plant and Equipment) and IVA 3 (Valuation of Public Sector Assets for Financial Reporting).

3.0 Definitions

3.1 *Depreciated Replacement Cost.* The current cost of replacing an asset with its modern equivalent asset less deductions for physical deterioration and all relevant forms of obsolescence and optimisation.

3.2 *Improvements.* Buildings, structures, or some modifications to land, of a permanent nature, involving expenditures of labour and capital, and intended to enhance the value or utility of the property. Improvements may have differing patterns of use and economic lives

3.3 *Modern Equivalent Asset.* An asset which has a similar function and equivalent productive capacity to the asset being valued, but of a current design and constructed or made using current materials and techniques.

3.4 *Optimisation.* The process by which a least cost replacement option is determined for the remaining service potential of an asset. It is a process of adjusting the replacement cost to reflect that an asset may be technically obsolete or over-engineered, or the asset may have a greater capacity than that required. Hence optimisation minimises, rather than maximises, a resulting valuation where alternative lower cost replacement options are available.

3.5 *Plant and Equipment.* Tangible assets, other than *realty*, that:

(a) are held by an entity for use in the production or supply of goods or services, for rental by others, or for administrative purposes; and

(b) are expected to be used over a period of time

The categories of plant and equipment are:

Plant. Assets that are inextricably combined with others and that may include specialised buildings, machinery, and equipment.

Machinery. Individual machines or a collection of machines. A machine is an apparatus used for a specific process in connection with the operation of the entity.

Equipment. Other assets that are used to assist the operation of the enterprise or entity.

3.6 *Service Potential.* The capacity of an asset to continue to provide goods and services in accordance with the entity's objectives.

3.7 *Specialised Property.* A *property* that is rarely, if ever, sold in the market, except by way of a sale of the business or entity of which it is part, due to uniqueness arising from its specialised nature and design, its configuration, size, location, or otherwise.

4.0 Relationship to Accounting Standards

4.1 *Depreciated replacement c*ost is used where there is insufficient market data to arrive at Market Value by means of market-based evidence.

4.1.1 International Accounting Standard (IAS) 16, Property, Plant and Equipment, paragraph 33, provides that in the absence of market-based evidence an entity may need to estimate the fair value of a specialised asset using an income or a depreciated replacement cost approach.

4.1.2 International Public Sector Accounting Standard (IPSAS) 17, Property, Plant and Equipment, paragraphs 42 and 43, prescribe the use of *depreciated replacement cost* for valuing *specialised buildings* and *other man-made structures* as well as *items of plant and equipment of a specialised nature.*

4.2 The application of *Fair Value* under accounting standards is discussed in IVA 1. In accounting standards, *Fair Value* is normally equated to *Market Value.*

5.0 Guidance

5.1 The classification of an asset as specialised should not automatically lead to the conclusion that a *depreciated replacement c*ost valuation must be adopted. **Even though an asset may be specialised, it may be possible if sufficient direct market evidence exists to undertake a valuation of the specialised property using the sales comparison approach and/or the income capitalisation approach.**

5.2 **In the absence of sufficient direct market evidence,** *depreciated replacement c*ost **is regarded as an acceptable method of arriving at the value of specialised assets but must incorporate market observations by the Valuer with regard to current costs and depreciation rates.** The method is based on the same theoretical transaction between rational informed parties as the Market Value concept.

5.3 **The Valuer estimates the cost of a** *modern equivalent asset* **at the relevant valuation date.** This may involve estimating the cost of having a suitable asset commissioned to order. The replacement cost needs to reflect all incidental costs that would be incurred, for example for design, delivery, installation and commissioning. In the case of *specialised property*, the cost of acquiring land suitable for the development of an equivalent specialised facility in the market should be included, together with the cost of all *improvements* that would be required to the land.

5.4 The Valuer then estimates depreciation by comparing the *modern equivalent asset* with the asset being valued. Depreciation rates may be all-encompassing or analysed separately for:

• **Physical deterioration**

• **Functional obsolescence**

• **External obsolescence**

5.4.1 In estimating the physical deterioration of the actual asset resulting from wear and tear over time, including any lack of maintenance, different valuation methods may be used for estimating the amount required to rectify the physical condition of the improvements. Estimates of specific elements of depreciation and contractors' charges can be used or direct unit value comparisons between properties in similar condition.

5.4.2 Functional obsolescence can be caused by advances in technology that result in new assets being capable of a more efficient delivery of goods and services. Modern production methods may render previously existing assets fully or partially obsolete in terms of current cost equivalency. The application of the optimisation process will account for many elements of functional obsolescence.

5.4.3 Obsolescence resulting from external influences may affect the value of the asset. External factors include changed economic conditions, which affect the supply of and demand for goods and services produced by the asset or the costs of its operation. External factors also include the cost and reasonable availability of raw materials, utilities, and labour.

5.4.4 When valuing *specialised property* it is not appropriate to depreciate the cost of replacing the land element.

5.5 In the application of depreciated replacement cost, the Valuer shall ensure that the key elements of a market transaction have been considered. These include:

5.5.1 **an understanding of the asset, its function, and its environment;**

5.5.2 **research and analysis to determine the remaining physical life (to estimate physical deterioration) and economic life of the asset;**

5.5.3 **knowledge of changes in preferences, technical innovations, and/or market standards that may affect the asset (to estimate functional obsolescence);**

5.5.4 **an analysis of potential external changes that may affect the asset (to estimate external obsolescence);**

5.5.5 **familiarity with the class of property through access to available market data;**

5.5.6 **knowledge of construction techniques and materials (to estimate the cost of a *modern equivalent asset*);** and

5.5.7 **sufficient knowledge to determine the impact of external obsolescence on the value of the improvements.**

5.6 **Depreciation rates and estimates of future economic life are influenced by market trends and/or the entity's intentions.** Valuers should identify these trends and intentions and be capable of using them to support the depreciation rates applied. The application of depreciated replacement cost should replicate the deductive process of a potential buyer with a limited market for reference.

5.7 In the final stage of the process Valuers should consider if the actual asset has any additional features not reflected in the cost of the *modern equivalent asset* and make any appropriate further adjustments. An example would be a *specialised property* where there is the possibility of a more valuable use in future when the *improvements* have reached the end of their economic life.

5. 8 **If it is clear that the result based on the depreciated replacement cost method is materially lower than a readily identifiable alternative use that is both financially and legally feasible at the date of valuation, the *Market Value* based on that alternative use shall be reported. This should include a statement that the value for the alternative use takes**

no account of matters such as business closure or disruption and any associated costs that would be incurred. The alternative use value will be evident from sales comparison and its valuation is not part of the depreciated replacement cost application but a separate valuation.

5.9 **If the Valuer considers that the value of the asset would be materially different if it ceases to be part of the going concern, a statement to this effect should be included in the report.**

5.10 **Where the value of a specialised asset is estimated by the** *depreciated replacement cost* **method, a statement should be made that it is subject to a test of adequate profitability in relation to the whole of the assets held by a for-profit entity or the cash generating unit.** The reasons why this statement is necessary are explained in Addendum A.

5.11 **For not-for-profit public sector entities, the reference to a test of adequate profitability is replaced by a test of adequate** *service potential,* which should be justifiable by the entity. Governments place particular emphasis on the test of adequate service potential in asset reporting as many agencies utilise public sector assets in the context of a service obligation to the general public. (The application of *depreciated replacement cost* to the valuation of public sector assets and the test of adequate service potential are discussed at greater length in IVA 3, Valuation of Public Sector Assets for Financial Reporting in paragraphs 5.4, 6.1, 6.5 and 6.8.4.)

5.12 **The valuation conclusion shall be reported in accordance with IVS 3, Valuation Reporting**.

5.12.1 **The Valuer reports the result as Market Value subject to the test of adequate profitability or justified service potential, a test which is the responsibility of the entity**.

5.12.2 **In reporting the value the Valuer shall identify the valuation method as depreciated replacement cost noting that the value can only be adopted in the accounts of the entity if the relevant test of either adequate profitability or service potential is applied and met**.

6.0 Effective Date

6.1 This International Valuation Guidance Note became effective 31 July 2007.

Addendum A: Profitability Test When Reporting DRC

1 Accounting standards require entities to periodically review their assets for "impairment", which is a permanent loss in the value of the asset to the entity. The appropriate figure to be included in the balance sheet for an asset following an "impairment review" is the higher of either its "Value in Use" or its "Fair Value" less costs to sell. In simple terms this means that the amount in the balance sheet should be written down to the higher of either the current value of the future benefits that will be derived by the entity from the continued use of the asset or the proceeds it would derive from the asset's immediate retirement and disposal.

2 The Market Value of an asset derived by reference to the sales of similar assets will usually approximate to the sum that the entity could obtain from the retirement and sale of the asset. If the Value in Use of the asset is lower than a Market Value based on sales comparisons, the latter figure can safely be relied upon as the base figure for inclusion in the accounts; it is an amount recoverable by the entity regardless of whether it continues to use or retire the asset.

3 In contrast, DRC is used to value assets, which are rarely, if ever, sold except as part of a sale of the entire operation of which they form part. The assumption that there will be demand for the use for which the asset is currently employed is an inherent feature of the approach. As a consequence, a Market Value derived using this approach will often not equate to the figure that would be obtained if the asset were retired and sold. If the Value in Use is lower than a Market Value arrived at using a DRC approach, the latter figure cannot be relied upon as the base figure, as it may not bear any relation to the amount that would be received following a cessation of operations.

4 Although the possibility that a valuation derived using a DRC approach would be materially affected by a cessation of operations is covered by the disclosure requirement in 5.9, the requirement in 5.12.1 to indicate additionally that the valuation is subject to "adequate profitability" emphasises to the entity that even if the Value in Use of the asset is lower than the reported Market Value, it may still be higher than the Net Realisable Value on cessation. It may therefore be necessary to write the reported Market Value down to the Value in Use in an impairment review.

5 The need to consider impairment is also a requirement of public sector accounting. However, in the public sector, assets are held for service delivery rather than profit. A valuation of a public sector asset using the cost approach has to be reported to be subject to a continuing requirement to use the asset for the provision of the service in question, i.e. that it has adequate service potential. This requirement may arise from political or social considerations rather than purely economic criteria. Combined with any appropriate disclosure under 5.9, this emphasises to users that the valuation cannot be relied upon as an indication of the amount that could be recovered if the service was discontinued and the asset retired.

International Valuation Guidance Note No. 9

Discounted Cash Flow Analysis for Market Valuations and Investment Analyses (Revised 2007)

1.0 Introduction

1.1 *Discounted cash flow (DCF) analysis* is a financial modelling technique based on explicit assumptions regarding the prospective income and expenses of a property or business. Such assumptions pertain to the quantity, quality, variability, timing, and duration of inflows and outflows that are discounted to present value. DCF analysis, with appropriate and supportable data and discount rates, is one of the accepted methodologies within the *income capitalization approach* to valuation. DCF analysis has gained widespread application due in part to the advancement of computer technology. DCF analysis is applied in valuations of real property, businesses and intangible assets; in investment analyses; and as an accounting procedure to estimate value in use. The use of DCF analysis has increased substantially in institutional, investment property and business valuation sectors and is frequently required by clients, underwriters, financial advisers and administrators, and portfolio managers.

1.2 DCF valuations, as with other income-based valuations, are established on analysis of historical data and assumptions about future market conditions affecting supply, demand, income, expenses, and the potential for risk. These assumptions determine the earning capability of a property or business upon which the pattern of its income and expenditures/outgoings is projected.

1.3 The objective of this Guidance Note (GN) is to prescribe Generally Accepted Valuation Principles (GAVP), best practice, and due diligence measures for Valuers to follow in performing DCF analysis for market and non-market based valuations and to distinguish between applications of DCF analysis in these two different types of valuation assignments.

2.0 Scope

2.1 This GN applies to market and non-market valuations developed by means of DCF analysis. It discusses the structure and components of DCF models and the reporting requirements for valuations based on DCF analysis.

2.2 The scope of this GN extends to the reasonableness and supportability of the assumptions upon which the DCF analyses are based. Assumptions made in any valuation directly affect the value conclusion. In accordance with the IVSC Code of Conduct, all assumptions underlying a valuation should be likely, reasonable, and supportable.

3.0 Definitions

3.1 *Discount Rate.* A rate of return used to convert a monetary sum, payable or receivable in the future, into present value. Theoretically it should reflect the opportunity cost of capital, i.e., the rate of return the capital can earn if put to other uses having similar risk.

3.2 *Discounted Cash Flow Analysis (DCF).* A financial modelling technique based on explicit assumptions regarding the prospective cash flow to a property or business. As an accepted methodology within the *income approach* to valuation, DCF analysis involves the projection of a series of periodic cash flows either to an operating property, a development property, or a business. To this projected cash flow series, an appropriate, market-derived discount rate is applied to establish an indication of the present value of the income stream associated with the property or business. In the case of operating real properties, periodic cash flow is typically estimated as gross income less vacancy and collection losses and less operating expenses/outgoings. The series of periodic net operating incomes, along with an estimate of the reversion/terminal value/exit value, anticipated at the end of the projection period, is then discounted. In the case of development properties, estimates of capital outlays, development costs, and anticipated sales income are estimated to arrive at a series of net cash flows that are then discounted over the projected development and marketing periods. In the case of a business, estimates of periodic cash flows and the value of the business at the end of the projection period are discounted. The most widely used applications of DCF analysis are the Present Value (PV), or Net Present Value (NPR) and the Internal Rate of Return (IRR) of cash flows.

3.3 *Financial Modelling.* The projection of a business' or property's periodic income or cash flow pattern from which measures of financial return can be calculated. Income or cash flow projections are generated through the use of a financial model that takes into account historical relationships between income, expense, and capital amounts as well as projections of those variables. Financial modelling may also be used as a management tool to test expectations for property performance, to gauge the integrity and stability of the DCF model or as a method to replicate the steps taken by investors in making decisions involving the purchase, sale, or holding of a property or business.

3.4 *Internal Rate of Return (IRR)*. The discount rate that equates the present value of the net cash flows of a project with the present value of the capital investment. It is the rate at which the Net Present Value (NPV) equals zero. The IRR reflects both the return on the invested capital and the return of the original investment, which are basic considerations of potential investors. Therefore, deriving the IRR from analysis of market transactions of similar properties having comparable income patterns is a proper method for developing market discount rates for use in valuations to arrive at *Market Value*.

3.5 *Investment Analysis*. A study undertaken for the purposes of development and investment, the evaluation of investment performance, or the analysis of a transaction involving investment properties. Investment analyses are variously called (economic) feasibility studies, market or marketability analyses, or financial projection studies.

3.6 *Net Present Value (NPV)*. The measure of the difference between the discounted revenues, or inflows, and the costs, or outflows, in a discounted cash flow analysis.

There is little real distinction between NPV and Present Value (PV). NPV is normally used to describe the difference between all discounted inflows and outflows while PV is often used where the initial outlay or price is not included in the cash flow. In a valuation that is done to arrive at *Market Value*, where discounted cash flows and the discount rate are market derived, the resulting NPV should be indicative of the *Market Value* and is often termed PV rather than NPV.

4.0 Relationship to Accounting Standards

4.1 Discounting is a standard procedure employed by accountants in considering the time value of money.

4.2 The International Financial Reporting Standards (IFRSs) prescribe a discounting procedure to estimate the value in use of an asset. An estimate of the value in use involves a) estimating the future cash inflows and outflows to be derived from the continuing use of the asset and from its ultimate disposal and b) applying the appropriate discount rate to these future cash flows. (IAS 36, para. 31)

4.3 IAS 36, para.55 states that "the discount rate (rates) shall be a pre-tax rate (rates) that reflect(s) current market assessments of: (a) the time value of money; and (b) the risks specific to the asset for which the future cash flow estimates have not been adjusted". It is also true that other measures of income or cash flow may be used so long as the discount rate(s) are appropriately matched with the income flow(s).

5.0 Guidance

5.1 Discounted cash flow models are structured upon a specified term, or duration. In real property analysis, although events such as rent reviews, lease renewal/reletting, redevelopment, or refurbishment can affect the analysis term, this term is typically driven by market behaviour that is characteristic of the class of property and its market sector. For example, the analysis term for investment properties typically runs between five and ten years. The Valuer, however, should be fully aware of the implications of different holding periods, e.g., a short holding period makes the appraisal conclusion more dependent upon the estimate of the terminal value at the expense of the periodic cash flow.

The frequency of inflows and outflows (monthly, quarterly, annually) should also be market derived. As with other accepted methodologies, inflows and outflows should be appropriate and reasonably supported. The correct discount rate needs to be applied to the cash flow. If the frequency of the time points selected for the cash flow are, for example, quarterly, the discount rate must be the effective quarterly rate and not a nominal rate. As each time period within a cash flow is in fact set off by time points, the Valuer must seek to place the various cash flows at the correct point in time within the cash flow. Often the frequency of the cash flow is decided by the time points at which rent is collected. If other events take place at more frequent times, the Valuer must decide whether to include them at the time point before or after they actually occur. Expenses/outgoings may be placed at the accounting point in time rather than the point of time at which they are carried out. The obvious best solution is to have a cash flow frequency that matches the timing of the most frequent aspect of the periodic cash flow.

The initial period (time interval) of a real property cash flow study is described as period 0 and this period is not discounted. Any inflows or outflows that are expected to occur within this time period should be included in period 0. Net income or expenses can be placed in period 0 and should be incorporated in this period if the cash receipts or payments take place during this period. For example, many investment properties receive net income monthly. Therefore, if annual intervals are used, the net income receivable in the initial year must be placed in period 0, regardless of whether a beginning or end period calculation is adopted.

Selection of the method for calculating the reversion/terminal value/exit value depends upon practices in the subject market as normally, it represents an estimate of the *Market Value* of the property at the termination date. Valuers should mirror those market practices and fully disclose the chosen method(s) and its(their) application. *Market Value* is understood as the present value of the future benefits of ownership. Thus, for an investment property, this normally means that cash flows/values at the time point of the terminal valuation (or depending on the method adopted, beyond the terminal valuation date) should be used rather than those in the period up to that date. A reversion/terminal value/exit value can be based on a projection of the net income for the year following the last year of the DCF analysis.

As with all other components of DCF analysis, the discount rate should also reflect market data, i.e., other market derived discount rates. Discount rates should be selected from comparable properties or businesses in the market. In order for these properties to be comparable, the revenue, expenses, risk, inflation, real rates of return, and income projections for the properties must be similar to those of the subject property.

5.1.1 Present value calculations of cash flows are most often calculated using appropriate discount rates for each class of cash flows. When non-annual time interval studies, such as monthly or daily intervals, are used, the annual discount rate must be adjusted to an effective and equivalent discount rate for the selected time interval. A reversion/terminal value/exit value is capitalised at a terminal capitalisation rate, or reversion yield, and discounted to present value at an appropriate discount rate. In many instances, a single discount rate is used for all cash flows.

5.1.2 The cash flows and sale prices of comparable properties may be analysed to derive market discount rates or internal rates of return (IRR).

5.1.3 DCF model cash flow can be developed both gross or net of tax and gross or net of debt financing, and in real (inflation or cost-index deflated) or nominal terms. The discount rate will therefore be based on the assumptions of the cash flow, gross or net of tax and gross or net of debt financing, and in real or nominal terms. Analyses of the market evidence to determine discount rate or cash flows must be based on the same assumptions.

5.2 In keeping with the IVSC Code of Conduct, it is incumbent on the Valuer to identify the components of DCF analysis, including the following:

5.2.1 a projection period wherein the commencement date of cash flow and the number and term of periods are specified;

5.2.2 the components of cash inflow and cash outflow grouped by category and the reason behind their selection;

5.2.2.1 For real property valuation, cash inflow includes income from rents and tenant services adjusted for collection, incentives and vacancy loss in the case of completed or built properties, and for income from sales, adjusted for cost of sales, in the case of development properties.

5.2.2.2 For real property valuation, cash outflow includes fixed and variable expenses, replacement allowance/renewal fund, and capital expenditures, where applicable; for development properties, the hard and soft costs should be identified.

5.2.2.3 For business valuation, the cash flow most often includes all cash inflows and outflows, of both an operating nature and a capital nature. The discounted cash flow then represents the money that an investor could remove from the business while leaving adequate cash to fund its operation and growth.

5.2.3 debt finance or debt service (payment of interest and principal) per period and the annual effective rate at which periodic interest is calculated, if applicable;

5.2.4 net cash flows per period (the sum of inflows less the sum of outflows);

5.2.5 the discount rate or rates that are applied to the net cash flows and the reasoning behind and support for their selection;

5.2.6 the terminal capitalisation rate/reversion yield that is applied to calculate the reversion/terminal value/exit value and the reasoning behind its selection; and

5.2.7 a list of all assumptions underlying the analysis.

5.3 DCF analysis makes use of available market evidence and typically reflects the thought processes, expectations, and perceptions of investors and other market participants. As a forecasting technique, DCF analysis should not be judged on the basis of whether or not the specific DCF forecast was ultimately realised but rather on the degree of market support for the DCF forecast at that time it was made.

5.3.1 When DCF is used to develop a *Market Value* estimate, the valuation should meet all criteria for *Market Value* estimates as set forth in IVS 1.

5.4 Where a client provides the Valuer with specific requirements that do not correspond to those for *Market Value* estimates as to holding period, financing terms, taxation, or discount rate, the resultant value estimate is to be considered *Non-Market Value*. The result is an estimate of investment value/worth specific to the assumptions provided rather than an estimate of *Market Value*.

5.5 DCF analysis may also be used to test the validity of conventional views by analysis of varying assumptions. The result of this type of sensitivity analysis is investment value/worth.

If DCF is used in this way, the results should be identified as a value other than *Market Value*, and the valuation should meet all criteria for non-market based valuations as set forth in IVS 2.

5.6 A Valuer should carry out sufficient research to ensure that cash flow projections and the assumptions that are the basis for the DCF model are appropriate and reasonable for the subject market.

5.6.1 As an example, the lease-by-lease analysis to support the cash flow projection for a multitenanted property should address contract/passing rent and market rent, lease expiration and lease review dates, rent escalations/stepped rents, operating expenses/outgoings, expense pass-throughs/ recoverable costs, lease incentives, leasing costs, vacancy allowances, capital expenditures, and any other specific provisions that apply.

5.6.2 Assumptions of growth or decline in income must be premised on analysis of economic and market conditions. Changes in operating expenses/outgoings should reflect all expense trends and specific trends for significant expense items.

5.6.3 The results of a DCF analysis should be tested and checked for errors and reasonableness.

5.7 To derive discount and terminal capitalisation rates, a Valuer makes use of various sources of data and information on real estate and capital markets. In addition to data on the income streams and resale prices of comparable properties or businesses, surveys of investor opinion and rates of return are useful in selecting discount rates provided that the market for the subject property is consistent with the market for the property acquired by the investors consulted in the survey.

5.8 It is the responsibility of the Valuer to ensure that the controlling input is consistent with market evidence and the prevailing market outlook. Further, the Valuer who supervises the construction of the DCF model or selection of a proprietary model is responsible for the integrity of that model in terms of theoretical and mathematical correctness, the magnitude of the cash flows, and the appropriateness of all inputs. A Valuer must have suitable experience and market knowledge to structure cash flow and provide other inputs to the model.

5.9 In reporting the results of a DCF analysis, a Valuer shall follow the requirements of the IVSC Code of Conduct and IVS 3, Valuation Reporting.

5.9.1 Disclosure must be made under those circumstances described in IVS 3, paragraphs 5.1.10, 7.0, and 8.2.3.

5.9.2 Inherent in DCF analysis are the explicit assumptions that are used as inputs for the analysis. To provide users of valuation services the ability to replicate the results, the Valuer must disclose the assumptions and support for their use in developing the DCF model. Using real property examples, these include but are not limited to

5.9.2.1 the commencement date, term, and frequency employed in the model;

5.9.2.2 the projected rent and other income and the rate at which income is projected to change;

5.9.2.3 the projected operating expenses and the rate at which expenses are projected to change;

5.9.2.4 the treatment of lease expirations/break costs, vacancies, and collection losses; and

5.9.2.5 the discount rate and terminal capitalization rate or reversion yield.

5.9.3 The Valuer must

5.9.3.1 indicate the annual effective rate at which periodic interest is calculated, where finance debt or debt service (payment of interest and principal) is a component of the projected periodic cash flow;

5.9.3.2 specify the rate(s) of taxation used, where applicable;

5.9.3.3 explain the reasoning behind any provision for lease incentives, where applicable;

5.9.3.4 explain the treatment of any capital expenditures incurred in the acquisition or improvement of property or business assets;

5.9.3.5 explain the basis for the adopted terminal capitalisation rate/reversion yield and the adopted discount rate or the effective, equivalent rate (if appropriate); and

5.9.3.6 identify the cash flow model by name of the developer or, if proprietary software, by product name and version; describe the methods and assumptions inherent in the model; and specify the dates on which the model was developed and employed.

6.0 Effective Date

6.1 This International Valuation Guidance Note became effective 31 July 2007.

International Valuation Guidance Note No. 10

Valuation of Agricultural Properties (Revised 2007)

1.0 Introduction

1.1 In many regions of the world, lands devoted to the production of agricultural commodities are the major economic asset and, frequently, the sole economic base of a region.

1.2 Lands devoted to agricultural use are thus a principal subject of valuation services for a multitude of reasons including private and public transfer of ownership, taxation, determination of collateral for financing, and economic, land-use, and investment studies. Reliable valuations of agricultural lands are essential to ensure the availability of capital necessary to support the continuity of the economic base, to promote the productive use of the land, to maintain the confidence of capital markets, and to meet the needs for general financial reporting.

1.3 Providing reliable and accurate valuation service for agricultural properties requires that the Valuer have a sound knowledge and understanding of the physical and economic elements that affect the productive capacity of agricultural lands and the value of the commodities produced thereon.

1.4 The physical and economic characteristics of agricultural lands differ from those of non-agricultural or urban environments in degree of importance.

> 1.4.1 Soils in an urban environment must be suitable for bearing the improvements that stand upon them. In agricultural properties, the soil is the principal agent in production, varying in its capacity to support a given amount of a particular commodity or class of commodities.

> 1.4.2 In urban environments, the economic use of a property and/or the amenities it provides may remain unchanged over a period of years and may even be guaranteed by contractual arrangements. While for some

agricultural properties, the same use may extend over a long duration (e.g., forests harvested after 25 years), for others, the economic benefits can vary from year to year, depending on the commodities the property is capable of producing.

1.4.3 The income stream associated with agricultural property will vary from year to year, depending on the type of agriculture for which it is used, the commodities produced, and the cyclical nature of the commodity markets.

2.0 Scope

2.1 This GN encompasses

1.2.1 Those characteristics of value associated with agricultural properties, and

1.2.2 The basic requirements of the Valuation Standards and Applications as they apply to the valuation of agricultural properties.

3.0 Definitions

The agricultural uses of properties may be classified in several broad groups, definitions of which follow.

3.1 *Crop(ping) Farms.* Agricultural properties used for growing commodities that are typically planted and harvested within a twelve-month cycle. Properties used for annual crop production may grow more than one type of annual crop over the same period and may or may not make use of irrigation to produce the crops. Some commodities are *annual crops* that may be left in the ground beyond a twelve-month cycle, per contract provisions or in circumstances where market conditions are unfavorable. These crops will last for more than one year after harvest but are considered less than permanent. Also see *irrigated land, perennial plantings.*

3.2 *Dairy Farms.* Agricultural properties used for the production of milk from cows or for other dairy products. These properties usually have extensive structural improvements (barns, milking parlours, silos) and equipment (feed bins, milking machines). Feed may be produced on the property, imported, or supplied by both sources.

3.3 *Forestry/Timberland.* Agricultural property used for the growing of non-orchard trees that are periodically harvested over extended growing periods (10 to 20 or more years). Considered to be agricultural properties because they produce a *crop*, i.e., wood, even though that crop requires a long-term growing period. Also see perennial plantings.

3.4 *Irrigated Land.* Lands used to produce crops or forage for livestock and which require the application of water other than that from natural rainfall, are called *irrigated crop(ping) farms* or *irrigated grazing land.* Properties that lack a water source other than natural rainfall are referred to as *dry land agricultural properties.*

3.5 *Livestock Ranches/Stations.* Agricultural properties used to raise and feed animals such as cattle, sheep, pigs, goats, horses, or combinations thereof. The actual use of these properties can take many forms. The animals may be bred, raised, and sold within the operation of the property. Young animals may be acquired from outside the property and then raised within the property. The animals may be raised for consumptive use or for breeding stock. Feed for the animals may be produced on the property, imported, or supplied by both sources. Properties used for the production and feeding of livestock have significant capital investment in the structural improvements (pens, livestock shelters, sheds, division fencing) and the livestock, which may or may not be depreciable depending on the laws and regulations of the local jurisdiction.

3.6 *Perennial Plantings.* Crops grown from plantings that have a life extending beyond one year or one-crop cycle. Examples are vineyards and orchards. These types of properties can have significant capital investment in the plantings, which represent a depreciable asset. Also see *forestry/timberland.*

3.7 *Specialised Livestock Facilities.* See *dairy farms, livestock ranches/stations.*

3.8 *Specialised, or Special Purpose Properties.* Agricultural properties that do not typically produce a crop but are used for the handling, processing, or storage of crops following harvest. These properties frequently have a small land base that is extensively developed with structural improvements (grain elevators) and equipment (lifting machinery). Properties may also be classified as *special purpose* by the nature of the commodity produced. Examples are truck farms, poultry farms, farms that produce certified crop seeds or fresh cut flowers, and racehorse breeding or training stables.

Other definitions

3.9 *Agricultural Activity.* Management by an entity of the biological trans-formation of biological assets for sale, into agricultural produce, or into additional biological assets. (See International Accounting Standard 41 [IAS 41], Agriculture., para. 5)

3.10 *Biological Asset.* A living animal or plant. (IAS 41, para. 5)

3.11 *Integrated Unit.* An agricultural entity that has common ownership of all or part of the processes involving the production and marketing of its products and/or commodities.

4.0 Relationship to Accounting Standards

4.1 International Accounting Standards 16 (Property, Plant and Equipment), 40 (Investment Property), and 41(Agriculture) apply to the valuation of agricultural property. An entity follows IAS 16 or IAS 40, depending on which standard is appropriate in the circumstances. IAS 16 requires that land be measured either at its cost less any accumulated depreciation and accumulated impairment losses or at a revalued amount. IAS 40 requires land that is investment property to be measured at its fair value, or cost less any accumulated depreciation and accumulated impairment losses. IAS 41, which establishes no new principles for land related to agricultural activity, requires that biological assets physically attached to land (e.g., trees in a plantation forest) be measured at their fair value less estimated point-of-sale costs, separately from the land.

4.2 IAS 41 acknowledges that there may be no separate market for biologi-cal assets attached to the land but that an active market may exist for the combined assets, i.e., the biological assets, raw land, and land improvements, as a package. An entity may, therefore, use information regarding the com-bined assets to determine fair value for the biological assets. The fair value of raw land and land improvements may be deducted from the fair value of the combined assets to arrive at the fair value of the biological assets. (See IAS 41, para. 25.) IAS 41 also gives guidance on how to determine fair value for a biological asset or agricultural produce where an active market exists as well as in the absence of an active market.

4.3 Agricultural property assets can be classified as:

- Land

- Structural improvements

- Plant and machinery (attached to the land)

- Plant and machinery (not attached to the land)

- Biological assets (attached to the land)

- Biological assets (not attached to the land)

The *Fair Value/Market Value* of biological assets is the contributory, or added, value they give to the land. IAS 41 requires that biological assets be measured upon initial recognition and at each balance sheet date.

4.4 IAS 16 recommends frequent revaluations, stating that every three to five years may be sufficient. IAS 40 requires revaluation on an annual basis.

5.0 Guidance

5.1 Diverse forms of commodity production and methods of operation are characteristic of agricultural properties. These properties may also represent various combinations of land, buildings, equipment, and crop plantings. Generally accepted valuation principles (GAVP) are as applicable to agricultural properties as they are to the valuation of other forms of real property.

5.1.1 The Valuer must have competence in valuing the various assets that comprise the property. (See IVSC Code of Conduct, section 5, Competence.)

5.2 *Market Value* must be recognised as the fundamental basis of valuation (IVS 1).

5.2.1 The Valuer shall arrive at the *Market Value* for the agricultural property, ensuring that the valuation is market-derived.

5.2.2 For financial reporting, the Valuer shall apportion the *Market Value* in accordance with the requirements of the IAS. For guidance, the reader is referred to IVA 1.

5.3 Where other bases of valuation are used, they must be distinguished from the *Market Value* basis.

5.3.1 When estimating values other than *Market Value* as required for financial reporting, depreciation schedules, or tax purposes, the Valuer must ensure that the distinction is clearly defined and noted.

5.4 Non-Realty Elements

5.4.1 When the valuation is made of an agricultural property that may include *non-realty elements* such as livestock, stored crops, and equipment, the Valuer needs to understand when a crop or other commodity is real property and when it may become personal property. Timber for example, is part of the real property while growing but becomes personal property when it is removed from the land.

5.5 The Valuer must understand the unique nature of agricultural productive factors, commodity markets, production practices, and cycles in the market region.

5.5.1 In the valuation of agricultural properties, the physical and environmental aspects of the property assume special importance. These include features such as climate, soil types and their productive capability, the availability or absence of water for irrigation, and the feeding/carrying capacity for livestock. External factors to be considered include the availability and adequacy of support facilities required for storage, processing, and transportation. The relative importance of these factors will vary depending upon the type of agriculture for which the property is suited or used. The Valuer needs to consider both internal and external factors in making a determination of which class of agricultural use the property is best suited for.

5.5.2 In keeping with the definition of *Market Value,* a *highest and best use* analysis of the property should always be conducted in order 1) to warrant that an agricultural use is to be continued, especially when it appears that another land use, e.g., subdivision development occasioned by encroaching urban/suburban expansion, might be more appropriate, and 2) to determine whether the specific agricultural use is to be continued.

5.5.3 Where the Valuer is specifically instructed to ignore uses other than the current agricultural use, the resulting valuation will not necessarily indicate the *Market Value* of the property, and this should be fully disclosed.

5.6 The estimate of stabilised income to the agricultural property must be based on the crop patterns and cycles in the market area.

5.6.1 The cash flow to agricultural properties is a function of both the production cycle followed on the property and cyclical forces such as commodity markets. The Valuer should understand the impact of these cycles on cash flows. The valuation of the property must be based on the stabilised pattern of income that is consistent with the production cycles commonly practiced in the region in which the property is located.

5.7 The Valuer of agricultural property that has more than one physical component or class of agricultural use must clearly state whether the value of each component or use is its value contribution as part of the whole property or its value as a separate, free-standing component.

5.7.1 The various components of a whole property may have value as separate parts which is greater or lesser than their value as part of the whole. The Valuer must determine whether each component is to be valued individually or as part of the whole property.

5.7.2 Agricultural properties may be managed to simultaneously produce more than one class of commodity based on different physical conditions within the property or on management decisions. In the valuation of agricultural properties on which crops of more than one agricultural classification are cultivated and harvested at different times, the value of each agricultural classification must be based on its contribution to total property value and not its stand-alone value.

5.7.3 The agricultural use of the property may require extensive building improvements, e.g., barns, silos, dairy machinery. Such improvements, while requisite to the proper operation of the property, are frequently secondary to the principal land asset. Their value must be based on their contribution to the total value of the property regardless of their cost or other measure.

Typically, such improvements have a value in use, i.e., their contributory value to the enterprise/entity. On those occasions where an allocation of value between the assets may be required, such an allocation is not to be taken as an indication of the individual value of the improvements as separate assets.

5.8 The requirements for valuation reports are addressed in the IVSC Code of Conduct and IVS 3, Valuation Reporting.

6.0 Effective Date

6.1 This International Valuation Guidance note became effective 31 July 2007.

International Valuation Guidance Note No. 11

Reviewing Valuations (Revised 2007)

1.0 Introduction

1.1 A valuation review is a review of a Valuer's work undertaken by another Valuer exercising impartial judgment.

1.2 Because of the need to ensure the accuracy, appropriateness, and quality of Valuation Reports, valuation reviews have become an integral part of professional practice. In a valuation review, the correctness, consistency, reasonableness, and completeness of the valuation are considered.

   1.2.1 A valuation review may call for input from experts with specialist knowledge of construction costs, property income, legal and tax matters, or environmental problems.

   1.2.2 A valuation review provides a credibility check on the valuation under review, and tests its strength by focusing upon

      1.2.2.1 the apparent adequacy and relevance of the data used and enquiries made;

      1.2.2.2 the appropriateness of the methods and techniques employed;

      1.2.2.3 whether the analysis, opinions, and conclusions are appropriate and reasonable; and

      1.2.2.4 whether the overall product presented meets or exceeds Generally Accepted Valuation Principles (GAVP).

1.3 Valuations reviews are performed for a variety of reasons, including:

   1.3.1 Due diligence required of financial reporting and asset management;

   1.3.2 Expert testimony in legal proceedings and circumstances;

1.3.3 A basis for business decisions; and

1.3.4 Determination of whether a report complies with regulatory requirements, where

1.3.4.1 Valuations are used as part of the mortgage lending process, especially mortgages insured or regulated by the government, and

1.3.4.2 It is necessary to test whether Valuers have met regulatory standards and requirements within their jurisdiction.

2.0 Scope

2.1 The requirements in this GN apply to the development and reporting of valuation reviews.

2.2 Compliance with this GN is incumbent upon any Valuer who, in a supervisory or managerial capacity, signs a valuation review, thereby accepting responsibility for the contents of that review.

3.0 Definitions

3.1 *Administrative (Compliance) Review.* A valuation review performed by a client or user of valuation services as an exercise in due diligence when the valuation is to be used for purposes of decision-making such as underwriting, purchasing, or selling the property. A Valuer may, on occasion, perform an administrative review to assist a client with these functions. An administrative review is also undertaken to ensure that a valuation meets or exceeds the compliance requirements or guidelines of the specific market and, at a minimum, conforms to Generally Accepted Valuation Principles (GAVP).

3.2 *Desk Review.* A valuation review that is limited to the data presented in the report, which may or may not be independently confirmed. Generally performed using a checklist of items. The reviewer checks for the accuracy of calculations, the reasonableness of data, the appropriateness of methodology, and compliance with client guidelines, regulatory requirements, and professional standards. Also see *field review.*

3.3 *Field Review.* A valuation review that includes inspection of the exterior and sometimes the interior of the subject property and possibly inspection of the comparable properties to confirm the data provided in the report. Generally performed using a checklist that covers the items examined in a desk review and may also include confirmation of market data, research to gather additional data, and verification of the software used in preparing the report. Also see *desk review.*

3.4 *Technical Review.* A valuation review performed by a Valuer to form an opinion as to whether the analyses, opinions, and conclusions in the report under review are appropriate, reasonable, and supportable.

3.5 *Valuation Review.* A valuation assignment that covers a range of types and purposes. The principal characteristic all valuation reviews have in common is that one Valuer exercises impartial judgment in considering the work of another Valuer. A valuation review may support the same value conclusion in the valuation under review or it may result in disagreement with that value conclusion. Valuation reviews provide a credibility check on the valuation as well as a check on the strength of the work of the Valuer who developed it, as regards the Valuer's knowledge, experience, and independence.

In some States a valuation review may also be an update done by a Valuer of the same valuation firm that carried out the original valuation.

Valuation organisations around the world distinguish between various types of reviews, e.g., *administrative (compliance) reviews, technical reviews, desk reviews, field reviews,* reviews to ensure that a valuation has been carried out in accordance with professional standards (where the bases of valuation used in the valuation under review are accepted), reviews that muster general market information to support or contest the value conclusion, and reviews that examine the specific data in the valuation under review with comparable data from a sample group.

4.0 Relationship to Accounting Standards

4.1 The relationship between accounting standards and valuation practice is discussed in IVA 1.

5.0 Guidance

5.1 In developing a valuation review, the Review Valuer shall

5.1.1 identify the client and intended users of the Valuation Review, the intended use of the Review Valuer's opinions and conclusions, and the purpose of the assignment;

5.1.2 identify the subject property, the date of the valuation review, the property and ownership interest valued in the report under review, the date of the report under review, the effective date of the opinion in the report under review, and the Valuer(s) who completed the report under review;

5.1.3 identify the scope of the review process to be performed;

5.1.4 identify all assumptions and limiting conditions in the valuation review;

5.1.5 develop an opinion as to the completeness of the report under review within the scope of work applicable to the assignment;

5.1.6 develop an opinion as to the apparent adequacy and relevance of the data and any adjustments;

5.1.7 develop an opinion as to the appropriateness of the methods and techniques used and develop the reasons for agreement or any disagreement with the report under review; and

5.1.8 develop an opinion as to whether the analyses, opinions, and conclusions in the work under review are appropriate, reasonable, and supportable.

5.2 In reporting the results of a valuation review, the Review Valuer shall

5.2.1 state the identity of the client and intended users, the intended use of the assignment results, and the purpose of the assignment;

5.2.2 state the information that must be identified in accordance with paragraphs 5.1.1-5.1.4 above;

5.2.3 state the nature, extent, and detail of the review process undertaken;

5.2.4 state the opinions, reasons, and conclusions required in paragraphs 5.1.5-5.1.8 above;

5.2.5 indicate whether all known pertinent information is included; and

5.2.6 include a signed Compliance Statement in the review report.

5.3 The Review Valuer shall not consider events affecting the property or market that occurred subsequent to a valuation, but only information that was readily available in the market at the time of the valuation.

5.4 Reasons for agreement or disagreement with the conclusions of a valuation report should be fully explained by the Review Valuer.

5.4.1 Where the Review Valuer agrees with the conclusions of a valuation report, reasons for such agreement should be fully explained and disclosed.

5.4.2 Where the Review Valuer does not agree with the conclusions of a valuation report, the reasons for such disagreement should be fully explained and disclosed.

5.4.3 Where the Review Valuer is not in possession of all the facts and information on which the Valuer relied, the Review Valuer must disclose the limitations of his or her conclusions.

5.5 Where the scope of the work undertaken is sufficient to constitute a new valuation, such valuation must conform to the requirements of the International Valuation Standards and IVSC Code of Conduct.

6.0 Effective Date

6.1 This International Valuation Guidance Note became effective 31 July 2007.

International Valuation Guidance Note No. 12

Valuation of Trade Related Property (Revised 2007)

1.0 Introduction

1.1 Trade Related Properties (TRPs) are individual properties, such as hotels, fuel stations, and restaurants that usually change hands in the marketplace while remaining operational. These assets include not only land and buildings, but also fixtures and fittings (furniture, fixtures and equipment) and a business component made up of intangible assets, including transferable goodwill.

1.2 This Guidance Note provides direction on the valuation of TRPs as operating assets as well as the allocation of TRP value into its main components. Component values are usually required for depreciation and tax purposes. This Guidance Note should also be read in conjunction with the Guidance Notes cited in para. 2.1 below.

1.3 Some concepts involved in the valuation of a business not classed as a TRP (see GN 6, Business Valuation) must be distinguished from those involved in the valuation of *Trade Related Property*. (Also see paras. 5.6 and 5.7.2 below.)

2.0 Scope

2.1 This Guidance Note focuses on TRP valuation. For further insight into the application of valuation principles, the following IVSs Guidance Notes should be consulted:

2.1.1 GN 1, Real Property Valuation,

2.1.2 GN 3, Valuation of Plant and Equipment,

2.1.3 GN 4, Valuation of Intangible Assets,

2.1.4 GN 5, Valuation of Personal Property,

2.1.5 GN 6, Business Valuation,

2.1.6 GN 10, Discounted Cash Flow Analysis for Market Valuations and Investment Analyses.

3.0 Definitions

3.1 *Capitalisation.* At a given date the conversion into the equivalent capital value of net income or a series of net receipts, actual or estimated, over a period.

3.2 *Discounted Cash Flow.* A financial modeling technique based on explicit assumptions regarding the prospective cash flow to a property or business. The most widely used applications of DCF analysis are the Internal Rate of Return (IRR) and Net Present Value (NPV).

3.3 *Goodwill.*

> 3.3.1 Future economic benefits arising from assets that are not capable of being individually identified and separately recognised. (IFRS 3, Appendix A)

> 3.3.2 *Personal Goodwill.* The value of profit generated over and above market expectations, which would be extinguished upon sale of the trade related property, together with those financial factors related specifically to the current operator of the business, such as taxation, depreciation policy, borrowing costs and the capital invested in the business.

> 3.3.3 *Transferable Goodwill.* That *intangible asset* that arises as a result of property-specific name and reputation, customer patronage, location, products and similar factors, which generate economic benefits. It is inherent to the trade related property, and will transfer to a new owner on sale.

3.4 *Reasonably Efficient Operator,* or *Average Competent Management.* A market based concept whereby a potential purchaser, and thus the Valuer, estimates the maintainable level of trade and future profitability that can be achieved by a competent operator of a business conducted on the premises, acting in an efficient manner. The concept involves the trading potential rather than the actual level of trade under the existing ownership so it excludes personal goodwill.

3.5 *Trade Related Property. Certain classes of real property, which are designed for a specific type of business and that are normally bought and sold in the market, having regard to their trading potential.*

4.0 Relationship to Accounting Standards

4.1 Under International Financial Reporting Standards (IFRSs), like other types of real property, a TRP may be carried on an entity's balance sheet at either cost or at fair value (see IVA 1). It may be necessary to allocate the value of a TRP between its different components for depreciation purposes.

5.0 Guidance

5.1 This Guidance Note describes that category of property referred to as TRPs and explains how **TRPs are valued in accordance with International Valuation Standard 1, Market Value Basis of Valuation.**

5.2 When performing a TRP valuation, the Valuer may also find **relevant guidance in the six Guidance Notes cited in para. 2.1 above. If the valuation is for inclusion in a Financial Statement, the Valuer should refer to IVA 1, Valuation for Financial Reporting.**

5.3 **TRPs are considered as individual trading concerns and typically are valued on the basis of their potential Earnings Before Interest, Taxes, Depreciation and Amortisation (EBITDA), as adjusted to reflect the trading of a reasonably efficient operator and often on the basis of either DCF methodology or by use of a capitalisation rate applied to the EBITDA.**

5.4 **Valuations of TRPs are usually based on assumptions that there will be a continuation of trading by a Reasonably Efficient Operator, with the benefit of existing licences, trade inventory, fixtures, fittings and equipment, and with adequate working capital. The value of the property including transferable goodwill is derived from an estimated maintainable level of trade. If the valuation is required on any other assumption, the Valuer should make such assumption explicit through disclosure. While the actual trading performance may be the starting point for the assessment of the fair maintainable level of trade, adjustments should be made for atypical revenues or costs so as to reflect the trade of a reasonably efficient operator.**

5.5 Profit generated, in excess of market expectations that may be attributed to the manager is not included. The manager's particular tax position, depreciation policy, borrowing costs and capital invested in the business are not considered for the purpose of establishing a common basis to compare different properties under different managers.

5.6 Although the concepts and techniques are similar to those often used in the valuation of a large-scale business, to the extent that the valuation of a TRP does not usually consider tax, depreciation, borrowing costs and capital invested in the business, the valuation is based on different inputs from those of a valuation of a sizable business.

5.7 The valuation conclusion may need to be broken down between the different asset components for the purposes of financial reporting, for property taxation or, when required, for property lending purposes.

5.7.1 The components of TRP entity value are typically:

5.7.1.1 land;

5.7.1.2 building(s);

5.7.1.3 fixtures and fittings (furniture, fixtures and equipment), including software;

5.7.1.4 inventory, which may or may not be included (this should be disclosed);

5.7.1.5 intangible assets, including transferable goodwill; and

5.7.1.6 any licences and permits required to trade.

5.7.2 Items such as working capital and debt are considered in valuing equity for businesses, but equity is not valued for TRPs. TRPs may, however, comprise part of a business.

5.7.3 An estimation of the individual values of the components can only represent an apportionment, unless direct market evidence is available for one or more of these components to isolate component value from the overall TRP value.

5.8 TRPs are by their nature, specialist assets that are usually designed for a specific use. **Changes in market circumstances, whether structural to the industry or due to the local competition or another reason, can have a material impact on value.**

5.9 It is necessary to distinguish between the asset value of a Trade Related Property and the ownership value of the business. In order to undertake a valuation of a TRP, **a Valuer will require sufficient knowledge of the specific market sector so as to be able to judge the trading potential achievable by a Reasonably Efficient Operator, as well as knowledge of the value of the individual component elements.**

6.0 Effective Date

6.1 This International Valuation Guidance Note became effective 31 July 2007.

International Valuation Guidance Note No. 13

Mass Appraisal For Property Taxation

1.0 Introduction

1.1 The objective of this Guidance Note is to provide a framework for the performance of *Mass Appraisal* assignments for *Ad Valorem Property Taxation* throughout IVSC Member States. The Guidance Note provides assistance in understanding recognised Mass Appraisal methods, the design and implementation of property taxation systems and the relationship of Mass Appraisal to International Valuation Standards.

1.2 The *Mass Appraisal Process* may be utilised as a methodology for *Ad Valorem Property Taxation,* or statistical and economic studies under government administrative programs. The appraisal outputs facilitate revenue raising, revenue equalisation, and the distribution of financial benefits or grants to government authorities. In this Guidance Note, reference to Mass Appraisal implies Mass Appraisal for the above purposes.

1.3 For a property taxation system to be effective, the following elements must be in place:

(a)   a legal system and legal infrastructure that define, support and protect property rights;

(b)   a recording and inventory system for all parcels of land, which represents the basis of taxation;

(c)   sufficient market data from which valuations may be determined;

(d)   sufficient resources and trained personnel to implement the system;

(e)   continued maintenance of the inventory and databases to ensure more refined data, more accurate valuations, and more equitable taxation; and

(f)   a process for sampling and testing developed models to ensure consistency in methodology and application.

1.4 The Mass Appraisal process includes:

(a)   identifying properties to be appraised;

(b)   defining the market area in terms of consistent behaviour on the part of property owners and would-be purchasers;

(c)   identifying characteristics of supply and demand that affect the creation of value in the defined market area;

(d)   developing a model structure that reflects the relationship among the characteristics affecting value in the market area;

(e)   calibrating the model structure to determine, among other attributes, the contribution of the individual property features affecting value;

(f)   applying the conclusions reflected in the model to the characteristics of the property(ies) being appraised;

(g)   validating the adopted mass appraisal process, model, measurements or other readings including the performance measures, on an ongoing basis and/or at discrete stages throughout the process;

(h)   reviewing and reconciling the Mass Appraisal results.

1.5 The valuation basis for Mass Appraisal is *Market Value* as defined in *IVS 1, Section 3,* subject to any modification of the concept as specified under relevant instructions or legislation. If such instructions or legislation stipulate a valuation basis other than Market Value as defined above, Valuers should apply appropriate valuation methods to accomplish the objectives of IVSC Standards under these circumstances. See *IVS 2, Section 5,* and also para. 5.5.1 (e) below under Disclosure in Mass Appraisal Assignment Reports.

1.6 Mass Appraisals can be prepared with or without computer assistance. While computerised methodology has made the Mass Appraisal process more efficient and more widespread, it has not altered that process. Data banks and computerised applications are used in data storage, mapping, data analysis, and testing of the results.

1.7 The development of Mass Appraisal systems for Property Taxation should follow recognised scientific standards in statistical applications.

1.8 While local legal requirements will take precedence, observance of the *IVSC Code of Conduct* is, nonetheless, incumbent upon assessment personnel, who carry out Mass Appraisals. The concept of Market Value is recognised as the assessment basis in most jurisdictions. The requirements of the *IVSC Code of Conduct* necessarily supplement those of local law. Requirements under the *Code of Conduct* apply to:

(a)   the mass valuation process itself; and

(b)   the use of computers and computer-generated models in the mass appraisal process.

2.0 Scope

2.1 The professional responsibility of Valuers is, in most instances, pre-scribed by statute or regulations affecting Mass Appraisal assignments. It is the professional duty of the Valuer to be familiar with, adhere to, and administer the provisions of the law established in the Ad Valorem property taxing jurisdiction.

2.2 The various outputs from Mass Appraisal programs have financial im-plications in government administration. For purposes of revenue raising, revenue equalisation, or the distribution of benefits or grants, any departure from an accurate basis of assessment will result in inequities. Local stat-utes prescribe the basis and definitions of values to be returned (i.e., the assessments and/or indices developed in Mass Appraisal assignments), the administrative procedures for the collection and delivery of valuation data, the time-frames between undertaking Mass Appraisals, and the processes for appeal of assessments or indices.

2.3 The scope of the completed assignment shall be consistent with:

(a)   the expectations of participants in the market for the same or similar valuation services; and

(b)   the requirements of IVSC Standards, Guidance Notes and Applica-tions for the same or a similar assignment.

3.0 Definitions

3.1 *Ad Valorem Property Taxation.* A revenue-raising procedure, based on the assessed value of property related to a scale of charges defined by statute within a specified time-frame.

3.2 *Calibration.* The process of analysing sets of property and market data to determine the specific parameters operating upon a model.

3.3 *Mass Appraisal.* The practice of appraising multiple properties as of a given date by a systematic and uniform application of appraisal methods and techniques that allow for statistical review and analysis of results.

3.4 *Mass Appraisal Process.* The procedures applied in mass appraisal assignments for arriving at assessments and/or indices. This process includes the eight steps, identified in para. 1.4 above.

4.0 Relationship to Accounting Standards

4.1 Mass Appraisal does not fall under the governance of national or international accounting standards.

4.2 Valuers should be aware that revaluation procedures for financial reporting purposes are unrelated to Mass Appraisal procedures for Ad Valorem Property Taxation.

4.3 Legislative requirements and standards of appraisal level and uniformity in valuations for Ad Valorem Property Taxation are likely to produce variations in property values from those determined for financial reporting purposes.

5.0 Guidance

5.1 Data Collection and System Recording

5.1.1 A robust data collection system must be available to the Valuer. The recording of data has evolved from the use of manual methods to the creation of sophisticated data banks that facilitate computer-assisted appraisal, often incorporating geographic information systems (GIS). Property data may be quantitative (e.g., land areas, dimensions, building specifications) and/or qualitative (assessment

of the physical condition, character, or market desirability of the improvements).

5.1.1.1 Appraisal data banks are built around land tenure records, e.g., title deeds, transfer documents, and sales information, in national, federal, state or local government jurisdictions that define property ownership or interests in land.

5.1.2 Characteristics of the market that are relevant to the purpose and intended use of the Mass Appraisal shall be recorded in the system including:

(a)   location of the defined market area;

(b)   physical, legal, and economic attributes of the properties;

(c)   time-frame of market activity; and

(d)   property interests reflected in the market.

5.2 The Development and Maintenance of Assessment Lists

5.2.1 Assessment Lists will contain information on property owner-ship, value definitions, details of the assessment, date of the assessment, and date on which the assessment comes into force.

5.2.2 Assessment Lists must allow for periodic adjustments or alterations to ensure the currency and consistency of assessed values.

5.3 Mass Appraisal Value Definitions

5.3.1 Where mass appraisal is undertaken for the purpose of Ad Valorem Property Taxation, value definitions are generally mandated by local statute. Specific valuation methodologies may be required under different value definitions.

5.4 Standards of Appraisal Level and Uniformity

5.4.1 In the interests of assessment equity, standards of appraisal level (the proximity between assessments and actual prices) and uniformity (the statistical measure of valuation consistency) must be observed in the application of mass appraisal systems.

5.5 Disclosure in Mass Appraisal Assignment Reports

5.5.1 Valuers undertaking Mass Appraisal assignments are subject to the provisions of *IVS 3, Valuation Reporting*. The Valuer shall disclose the following essential data that is specific to Mass Appraisal reporting:

(a)   the client and other intended users;

(b)   the purpose and intended use of the appraisal;

(c)   the scope of work necessary to complete the assignment, including any special limiting conditions;

(d)   any extraordinary assumptions and hypothetical conditions needed to carry out the assignment, provided these are reasonable and result in a credible analysis;

(e)   the relevant basis of valuation if, under reasonable terms and conditions, the value opinion to be developed is other than Market Value;

(f)   the characteristics of the properties that are relevant to the purpose and intended use of the Mass Appraisal;

(g)   a reference to each individual property in the Assessment List or grouping, indicating where information is stored in the property record relating to its identity;

(h)   the characteristics of the market that are relevant to the purpose and intended use of the Mass Appraisal (see para. 5.1.2).

5.6 Departure

5.6.1 Departure from the instructions in this Guidance Note should only result from required compliance with statutory provisions, administrative instructions, or the agreed or amended terms of appraisal contracts.

5.6.2 Further discussion on Departure provisions is set out in section 6.8 of the *IVSC Code of Conduct* and section 8.2 of *International Valuation Standard 3*.

6.0 Effective Date

6.1 This International Valuation Guidance Note became effective on 1 January 2005.

International Valuation Guidance Note No. 14

Valuation of Properties in the Extractive Industries

1.0 Introduction

1.1 The purpose of this Guidance Note (GN) is to provide clarification and guidance on the valuation of assets or property interests (rights) held by entities involved in the Extractive Industries. It distinguishes among the various property interests that must be recognised, and discusses concepts that should be understood by financial reporting and regulatory authorities, courts, financiers, investors, participants in natural resource transactions, and other users of valuation services for property involved in the Extractive Industries.

1.2 Reliable valuations of Extractive Industries assets, including interests (rights) in natural resource properties, are essential to ensure the availability of capital necessary to support the continuity of the Extractive Industries component of the world's economic base, to promote the productive use of Mineral and Petroleum natural resources, and to maintain the confidence of capital markets.

1.3 Extractive Industries comprise the Minerals Industry and the Petroleum Industry, but do not include activities focused on the extraction of water from the earth.

1.4 The Minerals and Petroleum Industries are characterised by the extraction from the earth of natural resources, which may pass through a series of ownership, processing and measurement stages. It is important to Valuers and the users of valuation services that distinctions are made among real property, personal property, and business interests involved in these stages. Financial reporting requires the recognition of various asset classifications into which these interests may fall. Additionally, clear and precise understanding of these distinctions is necessary for valuations to be performed and used in the public interest, regardless of the application.

1.5 Valuations in the Extractive Industries often must rely heavily on information provided by (a) Technical Expert(s) or other accredited specialist(s) specific to the industry.

1.6 A typical characteristic of the Extractive Industries that sets them apart from other industries or economic sectors is the depletion or wasting of natural resources, that can be replaced in their original state by natural actions following extraction only in special cases. Special cases of natural replacement may occur for water transported minerals and geothermal fluid. The means of production is extraction from the earth of natural resources that form part of the Real Estate.

> 1.6.1 The ultimate quantity and quality of material of economic interest that might be extracted from an Extractive Industry natural resource property is often not known at the Effective Date of Valuation.

1.7 Examples of depleting or wasting natural resources include, but are not limited to:

> 1.7.1 metallic Mineral deposits containing metals such as copper, aluminium, gold, iron, manganese, nickel, cobalt, zinc, lead, silver, tin, tungsten, uranium, and platinum group metals;

> 1.7.2 non-metallic Mineral deposits such as coal, potash, phosphates, sulphur, magnesium, limestone, salt, mineral sands, diamonds and other gemstones;

> 1.7.3 construction materials such as sand, gravel, crushed stone, and dimension stone;

> 1.7.4 Petroleum deposits including oil, natural gas, natural gas liquids, other gases, heavy oil, and oil sands.

1.8 There are contrasts between the production and transportation phases of the Minerals and Petroleum Industries that must be understood:

> 1.8.1 Items 1.7.1, 1.7.2 and 1.7.3 above include products of the Minerals Industry, which extracts valuable mineralization, generally by mining in a surface mine (open pit, open-cast, open-cut, or strip mine; a quarry used to produce construction material is also considered a surface mine), or an underground mine. Some extraction is undertaken through wells, for example, sulphur extraction, and in situ leaching (solution mining) of various salts and uranium minerals. Some extraction is also done by dredging the floors of bodies of water, such as for gravel, mineral sands, diamonds, and alluvial gold. Extraction of mineral products from water,

such as halite (common salt) and magnesium, is also part of the Minerals Industry.

1.8.2 The Minerals Industry generally has a planned extraction phase, though this phase is often extended through Mineral Reserve additions. Once extraction is completed, no more known economically recoverable asset remains in place at that time.

1.8.3 The raw materials cited in para.1.7.4 above are produced by the Petroleum Industry, which extracts valuable product generally through wells drilled into the earth's crust. Some extraction is also undertaken using mining methods, for example, open pit mining of oil sand and oil shale. The extraction of a solid asset is more labour intensive than the extraction of a fluid asset. A single person may operate oil and gas extraction by pumps or valves, with the occasional need for well maintenance or well work-over crews.

1.8.4 The Petroleum Industry frequently has more than one economical extraction phase for crude oil. At the conclusion of the initial (primary) extraction phase, much of the initial Petroleum Reserve of crude oil may remain. Secondary and/or enhanced recovery methods are often applied to recover more oil and natural gas. Generally, a large percent of the initial oil in place remains in place at the conclusion of production operations.

1.8.5 Another significant difference between the Minerals and Petroleum Industries relates to land surface requirements for processing plant and infrastructure. Relatively little surface area is required for oil or gas well operations. A mining operation often requires a larger land area for stockpiles and disposal of waste material, as well as an open pit if applicable.

1.8.6 Crude oil, natural gas, and refined Petroleum products are more often than not transported to market or port by pipeline. In contrast, a mined product is generally transported to market or port by rail or truck, resulting in differing start-up costs and environmental impacts.

1.9 The Minerals and Petroleum Industries are both major industries throughout the world. Their products are essential in all modern economies by provision of raw and refined materials for other downstream industries, such as energy generation, construction, manufacturing, transport and communications.

1.10 Exploration of Minerals and Petroleum properties is a high-risk activity. Considerable work and study must be undertaken to determine the technical and economic viability of production. The large majority of Mineral and Petroleum properties do not reach the production stage.

1.11 The projected net earnings derived or potentially derived from an Extractive Industry natural resource property is its main source of value. The net earnings may vary from year to year, depending on the type of natural resource commodity, the cyclical nature of the commodity markets and prices, and variations in production rate and costs.

1.12 Mineral and Petroleum natural resource properties are valued primarily based on the presence of Mineral or Petroleum Reserves, and Mineral or Petroleum Resources, or the potential for discovery of Resources. The quantity and quality of such Reserves/Resources may vary over time due to changing economic and technical advances, as well as exploration success. Nevertheless, they are ultimately finite and will deplete over time.

1.13 The fixed assets and specialised plant and equipment (see Glossary for definitions) used in the extraction and processing of raw products of the Extractive Industries, may retain relatively little or no value when separated from production at the site.

1.14 Exploration Properties have asset value derived from their potential for the existence and discovery of economically viable Mineral or Petroleum deposits contained within. Exploration Property interests are bought and sold in the market. Many of these transactions involve partial interest arrangements, such as farm-in, option or joint venture arrangements.

1.14.1 The value of an Exploration Property is largely dependent upon surface and subsurface geological and related information, and its interpretation. Little may be known about the characteristics of a deposit that may be contained within the property until the deposit is discovered and explored.

1.14.2 Extractive Industries deposits are often located in remote areas and are generally substantially or completely buried below the land surface, and sometimes below the floor of bodies of water or under the sea.

1.15 The residual value of the real property interest, plant and equipment as well as environmental reclamation requirements (as liabilities and property improvements), are pertinent factors in the valuation process for Extractive Industries properties.

2.0 Scope

2.1 This Guidance Note provides specific guidance for valuation of assets and interests of the Extractive Industries. It provides supplemental guidance for application of the International Valuation Standards (IVSs 1, 2 and 3), International Valuation Applications (IVAs 1, 2 and 3) and Guidance Notes (GNs). In doing so, it specifically supplements the following GNs for their application to the Extractive Industries;

GN 1 Real Property Valuation;

GN 2 Valuation of Lease Interests;

GN 3 Valuation of Plant and Equipment;

GN 4 Valuation of Intangible Assets;

GN 6 Business Valuation;

GN 8 The Cost Approach for Financial Reporting-(DRC); and

GN 9 Discounted Cash Flow Analysis for Market Valuations and Investment Analyses.

2.2 The ownership of, or rights to, an industrial water supply and water storage system, can form an important component in the valuation of Properties in the Extractive Industries. Water rights may attach to land or may be obtained elsewhere. Adequate rights and facilities for transportation and storage of off-site water may be required for a reliable water supply. Valuation of the contribution of such rights poses special problems that must be addressed by the Valuer. However, this GN does not provide specific guidance for valuation of water ownership, rights, transportation and storage.

2.3 Where mark-to-market financial reporting procedures apply or are contemplated, Valuers should observe the provisions of IVA 1, *Valuation for Financial Reporting,* in conjunction with this GN. In some States, securities exchanges and administrations may have specific reporting requirements for the Minerals and Petroleum Industries that override IVSs provisions.

2.4 While providing supplemental guidance for the conduct and reporting of valuations of Extractive Industries property and interests in accordance with para. 2.1 above, the provisions of this GN do not replace provisions elsewhere in the current edition of the International Valuation Standards.

3.0 Definitions

3.1 *Extractive Industries.* Those industries involved in the finding, extracting and associated processing of natural resources located on, in or near the earth's crust. They are composed of the Minerals Industry and the Petroleum Industry. They do not include the industry sector focused on extraction of water from the earth, but they do include extraction of geothermal fluid for its energy content.

3.2 *Exploration Property* or *Area.* A Mineral or Petroleum real property interest that is being actively explored for Mineral deposits or Petroleum accumulations, but for which economic viability has not been demonstrated.

3.3 *Feasibility Study in the Extractive Industries.* A comprehensive study of a Mineral deposit or Petroleum accumulation, in which all geological, engineering, operating, economic, marketing, environmental, regulatory and other relevant factors are considered in sufficient detail. The study could reasonably serve as the basis for a final decision by a proponent or financial institution to proceed with, or finance, the development of the prospective property for Mineral or Petroleum production. See also *Prefeasibility Study.*

3.4 *Mineral.* Any naturally occurring material useful to, and/or having a value placed on it by humankind, and found in or on the earth's crust. For the purposes of this GN, Minerals include metallic minerals, industrial minerals, aggregates, precious stones and fuel minerals; but Minerals do not include Petroleum, which is defined separately.

3.5 Mineral Reserve. As defined by the Combined [Mineral] Reserves International Reporting Standard Committee (CRIRSCO): "the economically mineable part of a Measured and/or Indicated Mineral Resource. It includes diluting materials and allowances for losses, which may occur when the material is mined. Appropriate assessments that may include Feasibility Studies, have been carried out, and include consideration of, and modification by, realistically assumed mining, metallurgical, economic, marketing, legal, environmental, social and governmental factors. These assessments demonstrate at the time of reporting that extraction is justified. Mineral Reserves are subdivided in order of increasing confidence into Probable Mineral Reserves and Proved Mineral Reserves."

The United Nations Framework Classification (UNFC) similarly defines a Mineral Reserve and its subdivisions, applying the UNFC coding system. Entities electing to adopt the UNFC or other definitions of Mineral Reserve for public financial reporting purposes must reconcile the Mineral Reserves to the CRIRSCO Proved and Probable Mineral Reserve categories for valuation purposes.

3.6 *Mineral Resource*. As defined by CRIRSCO: "a concentration or occurrence of material of intrinsic economic interest in or on the earth's crust (a deposit) in such form and quantity that there are reasonable prospects for eventual economic extraction. The location, quantity, grade, geological characteristics and continuity of a Mineral Resource are known, estimated or interpreted from specific geological evidence and knowledge. Mineral Resources are subdivided, in order of increasing geological confidence, into Inferred, Indicated and Measured categories. Portions of a deposit that do not have reasonable prospects for eventual economic extraction must not be included in a Mineral Resource."

The United Nations Framework Classification (UNFC) similarly defines a Mineral Resource and its subdivisions, applying the UNFC coding system. For the purposes of this GN, mineralisation classified into the UNFC's G4 ("Reconnaissance Study") category, is excluded from a Mineral Resource. Entities electing to adopt the UNFC or other definitions of Mineral Resources for public financial reporting purposes must reconcile the Mineral Resources to the CRIRSCO Inferred, Indicated and Measured Mineral Resource categories for valuation purposes.

3.7 *Minerals Industry.* Entities involved in exploration for Minerals, and the mining, processing and marketing of Minerals. This GN is not designed to cover assets downstream from the metals refineries or minerals processing plants, such as assets involved in the distribution of refined metals to metals fabricators, or mineral products to retailers or the final market.

3.8 *Petroleum.* Any naturally occurring hydrocarbon, whether in a gaseous, liquid or solid state. Raw Petroleum products are primarily crude oil and natural gas.

3.9 *Petroleum Industry.* Entities involved in exploration for Petroleum, and the extraction, processing, refining and marketing of crude Petroleum and associated gases. This GN is not designed to cover assets downstream from the petroleum refineries and natural gas processing plants, such as assets involved in the distribution of refined petroleum products to retailers.

3.10 *Petroleum Reserves.* As defined by the Society of Petroleum Engineers (SPE) and the World Petroleum Congress (WPC): "those quantities of Petroleum, which are anticipated to be commercially recovered from known accumulations from a given date forward. All (Petroleum) Reserve estimates involve some degree of uncertainty. The uncertainty depends chiefly on the amount of reliable geologic and engineering data available at the time of the estimate and the interpretation of these data. The relative degree of uncertainty may be conveyed by placing reserves into one of two principal classifications, either Proved or Unproved. Unproved Reserves are less certain to be recovered than Proved Reserves and may be further sub-classified as Probable and Possible Reserves to denote progressively increasing uncertainty in their recoverability." Proved Reserves can be categorised as Developed or Undeveloped.

The United Nations Framework Classification (UNFC) similarly defines Petroleum Reserves and their subdivisions, applying the UNFC coding system.

3.11 *Petroleum Resources.* For the purpose of this GN, petroleum resources comprise only Petroleum Reserves and Contingent Resources. Contingent Resources as defined by the Society of Petroleum Engineers (SPE)/World Petroleum Congress (WPC), in conjunction with the American Association of Petroleum Geologists (AAPG), are "those quantities of petroleum, which are estimated, on a given date, to be potentially recoverable from known accumulations, but which are not currently considered to be commercially recoverable."

The United Nations Framework Classification (UNFC) similarly defines Petroleum Resources and subdivisions, applying the UNFC coding system. For the purpose of this GN, petroleum accumulations classified into the UNFC's G4 ("Potential Geological Conditions") category are excluded from Petroleum Resources.

3.12 *Prefeasibility Study in the Extractive Industries.* A study of a Mineral or Petroleum deposit, in which all geological, engineering, operating, economic, environmental and other relevant factors, are considered in sufficient detail to serve as the reasonable basis for a decision to proceed to a Feasibility Study.

3.13 *Royalty* or *"Royalty Interest"* in the *Extractive Industries*. The landowner's or lessor's share of production, in money or product, free of charge for expenses of production. An *"Overriding Royalty"* is a share of mineral or petroleum produced, free of the expense of production, paid to someone other than the lessor, over and above any lessor's Royalty.

3.14 *Technical Expert in the Extractive Industries* (called *Technical Expert* elsewhere in this GN). A person, who is responsible for all or part of the *Technical Assessment* that supports an Extractive Industry Valuation. A Technical Expert must have appropriate experience relevant to the subject matter, and in States where required by statute or regulation, must be a member or license-holder in good standing of a professional organisation that has the authority to sanction members or licensees. An accredited specialist may not take responsibility for all or part of a *Technical Assessment* without also being a Technical Expert.

3.15 *Technical Assessment in the Extractive Industries*. A technical document, prepared by (a) Technical Expert(s) that supports the Extractive Industry Valuation and is appended to, or forms part of, a Valuation Report.

4.0 Relationship to Accounting Standards

4.1 Amongst national GAAPs there are currently several approaches to the measurement of "Upstream Activities" that include exploration for, discovery of, and acquisition or development of, Mineral or Petroleum Resources up to when the Reserves are first capable of being sold or used. The extreme high-risk element in expenditure on these activities has led to two main approaches to Historical Cost accounting for the Extractive Industries, those being:

(a)   all "exploration and evaluation costs" to be written off unless such costs are expected to be recouped, or the activities have not yet established whether the costs are economically recoverable (i.e., adaptations of a "successful efforts" approach). In applications of this approach, there are variations as to which types of cost are permitted to be capitalised and the treatment of costs prior to the determination of "success", or otherwise, of the exploration and evaluation activities; and

(b)   all expenditures incurred in finding and developing Mineral and Petroleum Reserves to be capitalised and treated as a part of the cost of whatever Reserves may have been found (i.e., a "full cost" approach).

4.2 In December 2004, the International Accounting Standards Board (IASB) released IFRS 6 *Exploration for and Evaluation of Mineral Resources*. Under the provisions of the Standard, entities are permitted to recognise their exploration and evaluation expenditures as "exploration and evaluation assets". The Standard requires such assets to be measured at cost at initial recognition. After initial recognition, an entity may choose to apply a cost or revaluation model (as outlined in either IAS 16 *Property, Plant and Equipment*, or IAS 38 *Intangible Assets*) to measure their exploration and evaluation assets.

4.2.1 The concept of exploration and evaluation assets, and the costs that make up those assets, apply equally to the cost and revaluation models described above.

4.3. IFRS 6 states at paragraph 9 that: "An entity shall determine a policy for which expenditures are recognised as *exploration and evaluation assets* and apply the policy consistently. In making this determination, an entity considers the degree to which the expenditure can be associated with finding specific mineral resources. The following are examples of expenditures that might be included in the initial measurement of *exploration and evaluation assets* (the list is not exhaustive):

- acquisition of rights to explore;

- topographical, geological, geochemical and geophysical studies;

- exploratory drilling;

- trenching;

- sampling; and

- activities in relation to evaluating technical feasibility and commercial viability of extracting a mineral resource."

4.3.1 IFRS 6, paragraph 5(a), excludes "activities that precede the exploration for and evaluation of mineral resources" from the scope of the Standard.

4.3.2 IFRS 6, paragraph 10, additionally states that: "Once the technical feasibility and commercial viability of extracting a mineral resource are demonstrable, expenditures related to the development of that mineral resource shall not be recognised as *exploration and evaluation assets.* The *Framework* and IAS 38 *Intangible Assets* provide guidance on the recognition of assets arising from development (or the development phase of an internal project)."

4.3.3 When facts and circumstances stated in paragraph 20 of the Standard suggest that the carrying amount of exploration and evaluation assets may exceed their recoverable amount, entities are required to measure and disclose any resulting impairment loss. The level at which such assets are assessed for impairment may comprise one or more cash-generating units, which is a higher level of aggregation than that otherwise allowed under IAS 36.

4.3.4 In the context of the IFRS 6, a minerals resource includes minerals, oil, natural gas and similar non-regenerative resources (see the Defined Terms in Appendix A to IFRS 6) and also in paragraphs 3.6 and 3.11 above.

4.4 IASB Standards that require value determinations to be provided under the provisions of this GN include:

- IAS 36 *Impairment of Assets* – for determining the recoverable amount of an asset (including assets that incorporate reserves and resources) in order to ascertain whether the asset is impaired. This process requires determination of "fair value less costs to sell" and/or "value in use" as defined in the Standard.

- IFRS 3 *Business Combinations* – for determining the carrying amount of assets that were acquired in the acquisition of a business (including assets that incorporate reserves and resources); and

- IAS 16 *Property, Plant and Equipment* – for the revaluation (if chosen) of property, plant and equipment that relates to extractive operations.

4.5 This Guidance Note recognises that the Historical Cost of finding and developing Mineral and Petroleum Reserves is usually not indicative of the realisable value of such Reserves once they have become established.

5.0 Guidance

5.1 Valuation Concepts

5.1.1 The provisions of this GN are designed to assure application of Generally Accepted Valuation Principles (GAVP) to Extractive Industries Valuations, in accordance with the valuation fundamentals expressed in the IVSs *Concepts Fundamental to Generally Accepted Valuation Principles.*

5.1.2 The standard of value is Market Value defined in IVS 1, *Market Value Basis of Valuation.* **If some other type of value is to be determined in accordance with IVS 2,** *Bases Other Than Market Value,* **a clear definition of that value should be provided by the Valuer and highlighted in the Valuation Report as prescribed in IVS 3, and a clear and conspicuous explanation provided.**

5.1.3 The property type(s) involved in valuation of Minerals and Petroleum Industry property must be correctly identified in order to correctly select the applicable IVSC Standards and GNs. Naturally occurring *in situ* **Minerals and Petroleum are a part of physical land and Real Estate. The ownership of such** *in situ* **Minerals and Petroleum, an interest in such natural resources, and the right to explore and extract such natural resources, are Real Property, except where otherwise defined by statute. Minerals and Petroleum are Personal Property during transportation and processing. The operation of a mine, quarry or petroleum well is a business activity, as is the transportation and processing of Minerals and Petroleum. Such business activity is generally conducted by an Extractive Industries business enterprise that owns real property and personal property assets, and the activity contributes to the Going Concern Value of the enterprise.**

5.1.4 A key aspect of the valuation of an Extractive Industry natural resource property is that the property interests and related rights being valued must be properly identified.

5.1.5 A Market Valuation of an Extractive Industry property as Real Property must be based on the Highest and Best Use (HABU) of the property. This requires consideration of non-Minerals or non-Petroleum uses for the property, if such uses are possible. Consideration must also be given to a change in exploration, development or operating strategy, or potential for leasing the property, in order to maximise its economic benefit.

5.1.6 In determining the HABU, the Valuer should determine the most probable use that is physically possible, appropriately justified, legally permissible, financially feasible, and which results in the highest value of the property being valued.

5.1.7 In conducting a Market Valuation, the three Valuation Approaches are generally available for consideration:

(a) Sales Comparison Approach (termed Market Approach for Business Valuations), generally by indirect means (see para. 5.3.1 below);

(b) Income (Capitalisation) Approach, including market-related discounted cash flow;

(c) Cost Approach (termed Asset-Based Approach for Business Valuations), including depreciated replacement cost and equivalent cost analysis.

5.1.8 Where one or more of the above Valuation Approaches has been applied in preference to others, the reason must be stated.

5.1.9 As applied to Mineral and Petroleum natural resource property interests, the appropriate Valuation Methods employed depend upon the stage of exploration or development of the property. For convenience, such Mineral and Petroleum properties can be categorised as four main types, though the categorisation is sometimes the subject of the opinion of a Valuer or Technical Expert.

- Exploration properties;

- Resource properties;

- Development properties;

- Production properties.

5.1.10 Exploration Properties are defined at para. 3.2.

5.1.11 Resource properties contain a Mineral Resource or Petroleum Resource but have not been demonstrated by a Prefeasibility Study or a Feasibility Study to be economically viable.

5.1.12 Development properties, in general, have been demonstrated by a Feasibility Study to be economically viable but are not yet in production.

5.1.13 Production properties contain a Mineral or Petroleum producing operation active at the time of Valuation.

5.1.14 The different stages of exploration and development carry different levels of risk. The risk pertains to the likelihood of eventual or continued Mineral or Petroleum production. As an Exploration Property is advanced to a Resource property, to a Development property, and to a Production property, more technical information is collected, enabling technical analysis, including Prefeasibility and Feasibility Studies, to be carried out, and thereby reducing the risk factor, as the amount of capital investment at risk rapidly increases.

5.1.15 The results from the Valuation Approaches and Methods employed must be weighed and reconciled into a concluding opinion of value. The reasons for giving a higher weighting to one Approach or Method over another must be stated.

5.2 Competence and Impartiality

5.2.1 Valuations prepared under this Guidance Note shall comply with all provisions of the IVSC Code of Conduct.

5.2.2 To develop a Valuation of an Extractive Industry asset or interest, the Valuer must have competence relevant to the subject asset or interest, or retain the services of (an) appropriately skilled Technical Expert(s).

5.2.3 Providing a reliable and accurate valuation typically requires the Valuer to have specialised training, or assistance from (a) Technical

Expert(s) or other accredited specialists(s), in geology, Resource and Reserve estimation, engineering, and economic and environmental aspects relevant to the subject natural resource type and geographic setting. The defined term Technical Expert includes "Competent Person", "Independent Valuer", and similar requirements that may apply in some States, if the intended use of the Valuation Report is related to public financial reporting or other regulatory purpose.

5.2.4 The Valuer is responsible for the decision to rely on a Technical Assessment, data, or opinion provided by other experts or specialists. This includes responsibility for conducting reasonable verification that those persons are appropriately qualified and competent and that their work is credible.

5.3 Special Considerations of Extractive Industries Valuations

5.3.1 Each Mineral deposit, Petroleum accumulation and Exploration Property is unique. Therefore, direct comparison of Mineral or Petroleum natural resource property transactions is often difficult or inappropriate. However, sales analysis is an important valuation tool. Sales adjustments or ratio analysis can frequently be applied for indirect sales comparison purposes. Sales analysis and other market analysis can often yield market factors such as a market discount rate, a risk factor or uncertainty factor that may be used in the Income Approach.

5.3.2 For a Valuation Report to provide an estimate of Market Value, the valuation analysis must be based on market evidence and current expectations and perceptions of market participants for the property valued, and such market evidence must be consistently applied in the Valuer's analysis.

5.3.3 The method most commonly used by businesses for investment decision-making within the Extractive Industries is net present value analysis/discounted cash flow analysis (NPV analysis/DCF analysis). The Valuer is cautioned that this and other methods, such as those based on option theory, will yield other than Market Value estimates of Investment Value or Value in Use, unless great care is taken to assure that a Market Value estimate is obtained. For the Valuer to report a Market Value estimate resulting from such an analysis, all inputs and assumptions must reflect available market-based evidence and current expectations and perceptions of market participants, in accordance with GN 9. Any departure from the requirements and analysis protocol of GN 9 must be specified.

5.3.4 The Market Value of Extractive Industries' natural resource properties and businesses are usually more or less than the value of the sum of their parts or component values. For example, the Market Value of a real estate tract owned in fee simple, that contains a Mineral deposit, is rarely the sum of the independent values of the Minerals, land surface, and plant and equipment. Similar situations may often occur in the Petroleum Industry.

5.3.5 For a producing Mineral or Petroleum Industry natural resource property, there may be separate ownership rights over component parts utilized by the enterprise, such as the Reserve, Royalties, and plant and equipment. It is important for a Valuer of the enterprise to correctly recognise these. There may also be a requirement to provide valuations of the separate ownership interests.

5.3.6 Material data relied on in developing the value estimate should be verified for accuracy whenever reasonable to do so. This may include selective review of drill hole information and samples and related analytical data for a subject natural resource property, and confirmation of published information pertaining to transactions of similar properties.

5.3.7 If there is more than one estimate of the quantity and quality of Resources and Reserves for a subject natural resource property, the Valuer shall decide which estimates it is appropriate to disclose and discuss, and which estimate to use as the basis in the Valuation process, and shall state the reasons. A critique of alternative estimates may be submitted with the Valuation Report.

5.3.8 The Valuer shall take account of, and make reference to other matters that have a material impact on the Valuation. Dependent on the property type and rights being valued, these may include:

- the status of tenements, rights and other interests;

- all Mineral or Petroleum deposits within the boundaries of the tenements or rights;

- access to markets and the quality and quantity of product that can be sold;

- services and infrastructure, and any toll arrangements, fees or liabilities related thereto;

- environmental assessments and rehabilitation liabilities;

- any Native Title aspects;

- capital and operating costs;

- timing and completion of capital projects;

- residual value estimates;

- material agreements and statutory/legal requirements;

- taxation and Royalties;

- liabilities and financial exposures;

- site rehabilitation, reclamation and closure costs;

- any other aspect that has a material bearing on the Valuation.

5.4 Disclosure in Extractive Industries Valuation Reports

5.4.1 The Valuation Report shall properly identify the property type(s), specific property interest(s) and related rights being valued as specified in IVS 3.

5.4.2 The Valuation Report shall disclose the name, professional qualifications and relevant industry experience of the Valuer, and other Technical Expert(s) whose Technical Assessment has been relied upon to support the Valuation.

5.4.3 The Valuation Report should be supported by disclosure of relevant Extractive Industries Codes, Standards or Rules of Practice applicable to the Valuation and supporting Technical Assessment. All estimates of a Mineral or Petroleum Resource or Reserve disclosed in the valuation report or supporting Technical Assessment shall abide by the definitions provided in Section 3 above, and the classification

systems referenced in those definitions, unless jurisdictional or other reasonable cause is disclosed.

5.4.4 Maps, geological sections, diagrams and photographs shall be included in the Valuation Report, if appropriate and possible, to aid the communication of information. Relevant technical information supporting the Valuation of a subject natural resource property(ies), including estimates of Resources and Reserves being valued, shall be disclosed and discussed in a Technical Assessment.

5.4.5 The Valuation Report shall disclose whether or not the entity employing/retaining the Valuer, or the owner of the subject asset or its operating management, has provided the Valuer with a statement that all available data and information requested by the Valuer or otherwise relevant to the Valuation have been supplied to the Valuer.

6.0 Effective Date

6.1 This International Valuation Guidance Note became effective on 31 July 2007.

International Valuation Guidance Note No. 15

The Valuation of Historic Property

1.0 Introduction

1.1 Historic properties are assets that embody a cultural, historic, and/or architectural heritage.

1.2 Historic properties may have legal or statutory protection because of their cultural and economic importance. Many governments have enacted measures to safeguard specific historic properties or to protect whole areas of special architectural or historic interest.

1.3 Private organisations play a significant role in promoting historic preservation and education about historic properties. In some cases, historic properties also bring economic benefits through increased tourism in the communities where they are located.

1.4 The valuation of historic properties requires consideration of a variety of factors that are associated with the importance of these properties, including the legal and statutory protections to which they are subject; the various restraints upon their use, alteration and disposal; and possible financial grants or rate/tax exemptions to the owners of such properties in some jurisdictions.

1.5 The costs to restore and maintain historic properties may be considerable and these costs, in turn, affect the value of the properties.

1.6 The assessment of the highest and best use of historic properties will depend on the specific restrictions that apply to them. In some situations, the use of historic properties is limited to restoration for non-commercial use whilst in others, adaptation to some other use, including commercial use, is permissible.

2.0 Scope

2.1 This Guidance Note covers real property that has cultural and historic significance, specifically focusing upon historic buildings and sites. It does not address either natural heritage assets or heritage assets that are personal property, e.g., works of art. (Guidance Note 5 offers direction on the valuation of personal property.)

2.2 This Guidance Note applies to the valuation of historic properties in both public and private sectors. Historic properties owned either by public sector or private sector entities are distinguished by similar cultural characteristics, and share common problems in regard to restoration and/or adaptation. But the specific legal and statutory protections that apply to private and public historic properties and other restraints upon their use, alteration and disposal may differ.

2.3 Historic property is a broad term, encompassing many property types. Some historic properties have been restored to their original condition; some have been partially restored (e.g., the building façade); and others have not been restored. Historic property also includes properties partially adapted to current standards (e.g., the interior space), and properties that have been extensively modernised. All historic properties (buildings and/or sites) have some degree of historic character. This Guidance Note addresses properties having historic character to some degree or other.

3.0 Definitions

International Valuation Standards Definitions

3.1 *Historic House Owner Associations.* Not-for-profit membership associations that promote the preservation of historic properties and provide their owner-members with advice on matters such as the management, repair, maintenance, taxation and insurance of historic properties.

3.2 *Historic Property.* Real property publicly recognised or officially designated by a government-chartered body as having cultural or historic importance because of its association with an historic event or period, with an architectural style, or with the nation's heritage. Four characteristics are commonly associated with historic properties: 1) their historic, architectural and/or cultural importance; 2) the statutory or legal protection to which they may be subject; 3) restraints and limitations placed upon their use, alteration and disposal; and 4) the frequent obligation in some jurisdictions that they be accessible to the public. The terms, historic property and heritage asset, often overlap but are not in all cases equivalent. See also *Heritage Asset, Publicly Designated Historic Properties.*

3.3 *Listing of (Heritage) Buildings* or *Historic Properties Register.* A recording of officially designated historic properties. Not all historic properties are necessarily listed in registers. Many properties publicly recognised as having cultural and historic importance also qualify as historic properties.

3.4 *Preservation Incentives.* Incentives to the owners of historic properties, primarily fiscal in nature, to promote the restoration and maintenance of such properties. Examples may include exemptions on inheritance taxes for conservation properties gifted to heritage trusts, government subsidies, exemptions in municipal rates/taxes, investment tax credits to owners of historic properties, transferable development rights and deductions taken on conservation easements donated to nonprofit organisations.

3.5 *Publicly Designated Historic Properties.* Those properties, the historic status of which is officially recognised by government-chartered bodies to identify historic properties and to promote historic preservation. Such bodies may be established by national/federal, state/provincial, or county/municipal governments. Local non-governmental historical societies may also designate historic properties and maintain *private historic property lists* or *registers* that confer many of the same benefits whilst remaining exempt from government restrictions. See also *Listing of (Heritage) Buildings* or *Historic Register.*

International Public Sector Accounting Standards Definition

3.6 *Heritage Asset.* An asset having some cultural, environmental, or historical significance. Heritage assets may include historical buildings and monuments, archeological sites, conservation areas and nature reserves, and works of art. Heritage assets often display the following characteristics (although these characteristics are not necessarily limited to heritage assets):

(a)   Their economic benefit in cultural, educational and historic terms is unlikely to be fully reflected in a financial value based purely on market price;

(b)   Legal and/or statutory obligations may impose prohibitions or severe restrictions on disposal by sale;

(c)   They are often irreplaceable and their economic benefit may increase over time even if their physical condition deteriorates; and

(d)   It may be difficult to estimate their useful lives, which in some cases could be hundreds of years.

The above definition is consistent with the description of heritage and conservation assets in IPSAS 17.9 (n.b., IPSAS 17 does not currently contain a formal definition of heritage assets).

Definitions from the UNESCO Glossary of World Heritage Terms

3.7 *Cultural Heritage*. Three groups of assets are recognised:

1. Monuments: architectural works, works of monumental sculpture and painting, elements or structures of an archaeological nature, inscriptions, cave dwellings and combinations of features, which are of outstanding universal value from the point of view of history, art or science;

2. Groups of buildings: groups of separate or connected buildings which, because of their architecture, their homogeneity or their place in the landscape, are of outstanding universal value from the point of view of history, art or science; and

3. Sites: works of man or the combined works of nature and man, and areas including archaeological sites, which are of outstanding universal value from the historical, aesthetic, ethnological or anthropological point of view.

World Heritage Convention, Article I, UNESCO, 1972.

3.8 *Cultural Property*. Property inscribed in the *World Heritage List* after having met at least one of the *cultural heritage criteria* and the *test of authenticity*. (World Heritage Convention, Article II, UNESCO, 1972)

4.0 Relationship to Accounting Standards

4.1 International Public Sector Accounting Standard 17 (Property, Plant and Equipment) does not require an entity to recognise heritage assets that would otherwise meet the definition of, and recognition criteria for, property, plant and equipment. If an entity does recognise heritage assets, it must apply the disclosure requirements of IPSAS 17 and may, but is not required to, apply the measurement requirements of IPSAS 17 (paras. 2 and 8). The IPSAS Discussion Paper on Heritage Assets (January 2006) requires the valuation of heritage assets where this is practicable. However, where valuation is impracticable, an entity would be required to make relevant disclosures, including reasons why valuation is not practicable.

4.2 This Guidance Note considers historic structures as a category of heritage and conservation assets.

5.0 Guidance

5.1 The valuation of historic properties involves special considerations dealing with the nature of older construction methods and materials, the current efficiency and performance of such properties in terms of modern equivalent assets, the appropriateness of methods used to repair, restore, refurbish, or rehabilitate the properties, and the character and extent of legal and statutory protections affecting the properties.

5.2 The sales comparison, cost and income capitalisation approaches may be employed in the valuation of historic properties. The selection of the approach or approaches to be used depends on the availability of data required to apply that or those approaches.

5.2.1 In applying the sales comparison approach, the historic nature of the property may change the order of priority normally given to attributes of comparable properties. It is especially important that the Valuer find comparable properties with historic features similar to those of the subject. Criteria for the selection of comparable properties include similarity in location (i.e., in zoning, permissible use, legal protection, and concentration of historic properties), architectural style, property size, and the specific cultural or historic associations of the subject property. A variety of adjustments may have to be made to the comparable sales. These involve differences in location, costs of restoration or rehabilitation, or specific encumbrances. Adjustments are made in the following situations:

5.2.1.1 when costs must be incurred to restore or rehabilitate the subject property, but not the comparable sales; and

5.2.1.2 where the specific encumbrances upon the subject, e.g., restrictive covenants or preservation easements, differ from those upon the comparable properties.

5.2.2 Historic properties having a commercial use are often valued by means of the income capitalisation approach. Where the distinctive architecture and ambiance of an historic property contribute to its drawing power under an income-producing use and that income-producing use is considered to be the highest and best use of the historic property, the valuation will address the following:

5.2.2.1 All work proposed to restore, adapt or rehabilitate the historic property must meet existing zoning requirements and covenant obligations.

5.2.2.2 Where listed building consents or a zoning variance and/or building code exemptions are required, the projected timeframe to obtain such authorisation needs to be taken into consideration.

5.2.2.3 The income capitalisation approach should consider the cost effectiveness of an income-producing historic property in terms of the rental and/or commercial income the property is able to generate. In particular, it should address the additional costs involved in maintaining the property, especially those costs incurred due to functional obsolescence or reserves set aside for any required sinking fund.

5.2.3 When applying the cost approach to historic property, the Valier needs to consider whether the historic features of a building would be of intrinsic value in the market for that property. Some historic buildings will be of value simply because of their symbolic status, for example a famous art gallery where the building is as, or more, important than the function it fulfils. In other words, the service potential of such a building is inseparable from its historic features. The modern equivalent of such properties would need to reflect either the cost of reproducing a replica, or if this is not possible because the original materials or techniques are no longer available, the cost of the modern building with a similarly distinctive and high specification.

In many cases the historic features will add no value, or be viewed as an encumbrance by a purchaser in the market, for example a hospital operating in an historic building. In such cases the modern equivalent would reflect the cost of a new building constructed to a conventional modern specification.

In all cases the adjustments for physical deterioration and functional obsolescence will need to reflect factors such as the higher cost of maintenance associated with historic property and the loss of flexibility for adapting the building to the changing needs of an occupier.

The land or site, upon which an historic property stands may be subject to constraints upon its use. In turn, any such constraints will affect land and overall property value.

5.3 Historic, or heritage assets, for which there is no reliable or relevant sales evidence, which have no potential for generating income, and which would or could not be replaced may be incapable of reliable valuation. An example could be a partially ruined building with no income generating potential. Where a reliable assessment of value is not possible, the Valuer must disclose the reasons for this conclusion in the report.

5.4 Legal measures to safeguard historic properties may limit or restrict the use, intensity of use, or alteration of an historic property. Examples include restrictive covenants that run with the land regardless of the owner; preservation easements that prohibit certain physical changes, usually based on the condition of the property at the time the easement was acquired or immediately after proposed restoration of the property; and conservation easements that limit the future use of a property so as to protect open space, natural features, or wildlife habitat.

5.4.1 Restrictive covenants and preservation easements, whether existing or proposed, may have a major influence on the highest and best use of an historic property, and thereby have a significant effect on property value. Preservation easements can be donated, purchased, or obtained by compulsory acquisition/eminent domain.

5.5 The valuation conclusion shall be reported in accordance with IVS 3, Valuation Reporting.

6.0 Effective Date

6.1 This International Valuation Guidance Note became effective on 31 July 2007.

Glossary of Terms for International Valuation Standards

International Valuation Standards Committee

Glossary of Terms for International Valuation Standards

The eighth edition of the International Valuation Standards comprises

- Introduction

- Concepts Fundamental to Generally Accepted Valuation Principles

- Code of Conduct

- Property Types

- International Valuation Standards:
  Introduction to International Valuation Standards
  IVS 1: Market Value Basis of Valuation
  IVS 2: Bases other than Market Value
  IVS 3: Valuation Reporting

- International Valuation Applications:
  IVA 1: Valuation for Financial Reporting
  IVA 2: Valuation for Secured Lending Purposes
  IVA 3: Valuation of Public Sector Assets for Financial Reporting

- Guidance Notes, of which there are fifteen
  GN 1: Real Property Valuation
  GN 2: Valuation of Lease Interests
  GN 3: Valuation of Plant and Equipment
  GN 4: Valuation of Intangible Assets
  GN 5: Valuation of Personal Property
  GN 6: Business Valuation
  GN 7: Consideration of Hazardous and Toxic Substances in Valuation
  GN 8: Cost Approach for Financial Reporting-(DRC)
  GN 9: Discounted Cash Flow Analysis for Market Valuations and Investment Analyses
  GN 10: Valuation of Agricultural Properties
  GN 11: Reviewing Valuations
  GN 12: Valuation of Trade Related Property
  GN 13: Mass Appraisal for Property Taxation

GN 14: Valuation of Properties in the Extractive Industries
GN 15: Valuation of Historic Property

- Glossary

International Financial Reporting Standards and International Accounting Standards referred to in the Glossary are

- Framework for the Preparation and Presentation of Financial Statements
- IFRS 3, Business Combinations
- IFRS 5, Non-current Assets Held for Sale and Discontinued Operations
- IFRS 6, Exploration for and Evaluation of Mineral Resources
- IAS 1, Presentation of Financial Statements
- IAS 2, Inventories
- IAS 16, Property, Plant and Equipment
- IAS 17, Leases
- IAS 27, Consolidated and Separate Financial Statements
- IAS 31, Interests in Joint Ventures
- IAS 32, Financial Instruments: Disclosure and Presentation
- IAS 36, Impairment of Assets
- IAS 38, Intangible Assets
- IAS 39, Financial Instruments: Recognition and Measurement
- IAS 40, Investment Property
- IAS 41, Agriculture

International Public Sector Accounting Standards referred to in the Glossary include

- IPSAS 16, Investment Property
- IPSAS 17, Property, Plant and Equipment
- IPSAS 21, Impairment of Non-Cash-Generating Assets

The UNESCO document referred to in the Glossary

World Heritage Convention, Articles I and II

Adjusted Book Value	The book value that results when one or more asset or liability amounts are added, deleted, or changed from the reported book amounts.	GN 6, 3.1
Administrative (Compliance) Review	A valuation review performed by a client or user of valuation services as an exercise in due diligence when the valuation is to be used for purposes of decision-making such as underwriting, purchasing, or selling the property. A Valuer may, on occasion, perform an administrative review to assist a client with these functions. An administrative review is also undertaken to ensure that a valuation meets or exceeds the compliance requirements or guidelines of the specific market and, at a minimum, conforms to Generally Accepted Valuation Principles (GAVP).	GN 11, 3.2
Ad Valorem Property Taxation	A revenue-raising procedure, based on the assessed value of property related to a scale of charges defined by statute within a specified time-frame. See also Assessed, Rateable, or Taxable Value.	GN 13, 3.1

Agricultural Activity	Management by an entity of the biological transformation of biological assets for sale, into agricultural produce, or into additional biological assets.	IAS 41, 5
All Risks Yield (ARY)	See capitalisation rate.	
Appraiser	See Professional Property Valuer.	
Annuity	A series of payments made or received at intervals either for life or for a fixed number of periods.	
Arm's-Length Transaction	A transaction between parties who do not have a particular or special relationship (for example, parent and subsidiary companies or landlord and tenant) that may make the price level uncharacteristic of the market or inflated because of an element of Special Value. The Market Value transaction is presumed to be between unrelated parties, each acting independently.	IVS 1, 3.2.6
Assessed, Rateable, or Taxable Value	A value which is based upon definitions contained within applicable laws relating to the assessment, rating, and/or taxation of property. Although some jurisdictions may cite market value as the assessment basis, required valuation methodology may produce results, which differ from market value as defined herein.	

The term, assessed value, is North American usage; rateable value is Commonwealth usage.

See also Ad Valorem Property Taxation.

Asset	i) A resource owned or controlled by an entity as a result of past events and from which some future economic benefit(s) can be expected to flow to the entity. Ownership of an asset is itself an intangible. However, the asset owned may be either tangible or intangible.	Concepts Fundamental to Generally Accepted Valuation Principles, 3.4
	ii) A resource controlled by an entity as a result of past events, and from which future economic benefits are expected to flow to the entity.	IAS Framework 49(a); IAS 38, 8

iii) An item of property, plant and equipment should be recognised as an asset when:

    a) it is probable that future economic benefits associated with the asset will flow to the entity; and

    b) the cost of the asset to the entity can be measured reliably.

The term is used to denote real and personal property, both tangible and intangible. Ownership of an asset is itself an intangible.

See also Current Assets, Fixed or Long-term Assets, Investment Asset, Operational Asset, Specialised Asset, Surplus Asset.

Asset-Based Approach	A means of estimating the value of a business and/or equity interest using methods based on the Market Value of individual business assets less liabilities.	GN 6, 3.2
	An approach to value that examines the balance sheet of the business that reports all assets, tangible and intangible, and all liabilities at Market Value, or some other appropriate current value. The asset-based approach should not be the sole valuation approach used in assignments involving operating businesses appraised as going concerns unless it is customarily used by sellers and buyers.	GN 6, 5.14.3.3, 5.14.3.5
Assumptions	Suppositions taken to be true. Assumptions involve facts, conditions, or situations affecting the subject of, or approach to, a valuation but which may not be capable or worthy of verification. They are matters that, once declared, are to be accepted in understanding the valuation. All assumptions underlying a valuation should be reasonable.	Code of Conduct, 3.1
	See also Special, Unusual, or Extraordinary Assumptions	

Auction Price	The price that is the final accepted bid at a public auction; may or may not include any fees or commissions.	GN 5, 3.1
	See also Hammer Price, Private Treaty Sale.	
Average Competent Management	See Reasonably Efficient Operator.	
Basis of Value	A statement of the fundamental measurement principles of a valuation on a specified date.	IVS 2, 3.1
Biological Asset	A living animal or plant.	IAS 41, 5
Book Value	With respect to assets, the capitalised cost of an asset less accumulated depreciation, depletion or amortisation as it appears on the account books of the business.	GN 4, 3.1.1; GN 6, 3.3.1
	With respect to a business entity, the difference between total assets (net of depreciation, depletion and amortisation) and total liabilities of a business as they appear on the balance sheet. It is synonymous with net book value, net worth and shareholder's equity.	GN 4, 3.1.2; GN 6, 3.3.2
	See also Adjusted Book Value.	

Business Entity	A commercial, industrial, service or investment entity pursuing an economic activity; generally, a profit-making entity. A business entity may be unincorporated (sole proprietorships, partnerships) or incorporated (closely-held or publicly held), or take the form of trust arrangements or multiple entities. The ownership interest in a business may be undivided, divided among shareholders, and/or involve a majority interest and minority interest. See also Going Concern, Holding Company or Investment Business, Operating Company, Trade Related Property.	Property Types, 4.1, 4.2, 4.7, 4.8; GN 6, 3.4
Business Valuation	The act or process of arriving at an opinion or estimation of the value of a business or entity or an interest therein.	GN 6, 3.5
Business Valuer	A person, who by education, training and experience is qualified to perform a valuation of a business, business ownership interest, security and/or intangible assets.	GN 6, 3.6
Calibration	The process of analysing sets of property and market data to determine the specific parameters operating upon a model.	GN 13, 3.2

Capitalisa-tion	i) At a given date, the conversion into the equivalent capital value of net income or a series of net receipts, actual or estimated, over a period.	GN 4, 3.3; GN 6, 3.7; GN 12, 3.1
	ii) In business valuation, the term refers to the capital structure of a business entity.	
	iii) In business valuation, this term also refers to the recognition of an expenditure as a capital asset rather than a periodic expense.	
	Method of arriving at the value of a property by reference to net returns and an expected percentage yield or return. In some States, capitalisation refers to the conversion of a stream of income into capital value using a single conversion factor.	
Capitalisa-tion Factor	Any multiple or divisor used to convert income into capital value.	GN 4, 3.4; GN 6, 3.8
	See also Capitalisation Rate, Income Multiplier, Valuation Ratio.	

Capitalisa-tion Rate (All Risks Yield)	Any divisor (usually expressed as a percentage) that is used to convert income into capital value. The interest rate or yield at which the annual net income from an investment is capitalised to ascertain its capital value at a given date. The term, overall capitalisation rate, is North American usage; all risks yield is Commonwealth usage. See also Terminal Capitalisation Rate.	GN 4, 3.5; GN 6, 3.9
Capital Structure	The composition of invested capital.	GN 6, 3.10
Carrying Amount	The amount at which an asset is recognised after deducting any accumulated depreciation (amortisation) and accumulated impairment losses thereon.	IAS 16, 6; IAS 36, 6; IAS 38, 8
	The amount at which an asset is recognized in the statement of financial position.	IPSAS 16, 6
	See also net carrying amount.	
Cash Generating Assets	Assets held to generate a commercial return.	IPSAS 21.14

Cash Flow	The actual or estimated, periodic net income produced by the revenues and expenditures/outgoings in the operation and ultimate resale of an income-producing property.	
	Gross Cash Flow: Net income after taxes, plus non-cash items such as depreciation and amortisation.	GN 4, 3.6.1; GN 6, 3.11.1
	Net Cash Flow: During an operating period, that amount of cash that remains after all cash needs of the business have been satisfied. Net cash flow is typically defined as being cash available to equity or invested capital.	GN 4, 3.6.2; GN 6, 3.11.2
	Equity Net Cash Flow: Net income after taxes, plus depreciation and other non-cash charges, less increases in working capital, less capital expenditures, less decreases in invested capital debt principal, plus increases in invested capital debt principal.	GN 4, 3.6.3; GN 6, 3.11.3
	Invested Capital Net Cash Flow: Equity net cash flow, plus interest payments net of tax adjustment, less net increases in debt principal.	GN 4, 3.6.4; GN 6, 3.11.4
Cash Generating Unit	The smallest identifiable group of assets that generates cash inflows that are largely independent of the cash inflows from other assets or groups of assets.	IAS 36, 6

Certifica-tion of Value	The statement of a valuation in a proscribed format to meet statutory or regulatory requirements. See also Compliance Statement, Valuation Report.	
Collectibles	Broad descriptive term for objects collected because of the interest they arouse owing to their rarity, novelty, or uniqueness. In some States, the term may be applied to fine art, antiques, gems and jewelry, musical instruments, numismatic and philatelic collections, rare books, and archival materials, among others. Elsewhere the term is normally used for these and a wide variety of other items not found in any other category.	GN 5, 3.2
Comparable Data	Data generally used in a valuation analysis to develop value estimates; comparable data relate to properties that have characteristics similar to those of the property being valued (the subject property). Such data include sale prices, rents, income and expenses, and market-derived capi-talisation and yield/discount rates.	GN 1, 3.2
Comparable Sales Meth-od (Market or Direct Market Comparison Method)	See Sales Comparison Approach.	

Compliance Review	See Administrative Review	
Compliance Statement	An affirmative statement attesting to the fact that the Valuer has followed the ethical and professional requirements of the IVSC Code of Conduct in performing the assignment. IVS 3, 5.1.10 and 5.1.10.1 deal with the contents of a compliance statement.	IVS 3, 3.1
Component Value	The value of those components, created by the separation of property interests. See also Marriage Value.	Property Types, 2.6.1
Compulsory Acquisition/ Purchase	In accordance with statutory procedures and practices, the government's taking of private property for public use upon the payment of compensation as provided for by statute. The term, compulsory acquisition/ purchase, is Commonwealth usage. The terms, condemnation and damages, are used in North America. See also Condemnation.	

Condemnation	The act or process of enforcing the right of eminent domain. In condemnation, the loss in value to the remainder, resulting from a partial taking, is known as damages.	
	The terms, condemnation and damages, are North American usage.	
	See also Compulsory Acquisition/ Purchase.	
Conservation Assets	See Heritage and Conservation Assets.	
Contract Rent or Passing Rent	The rent specified by a given lease arrangement; although a given contract rent may equate to the Market Rent, in practice they may differ substantially, particularly for older leases with fixed rental terms.	GN 2, 3.1.10.2
	The term, contract rent is North American usage; passing rent is Commonwealth usage.	
Contractor's Method	See Cost Approach.	
Control	The power to direct the management and policies of a business.	GN 6, 3.12
Control Premium	The additional value inherent in the control interest that reflects its power of control, as contrasted to a minority interest. See also Discount for Lack of Control.	GN 6, 3.13

Cost	i) The price paid for goods or services becomes its cost to the buyer ii) The amount required to create or produce the good or service. Cost is a production-related concept, distinct from exchange. Once the good is completed or the service is rendered, its cost becomes an historic fact. The total cost of a property includes all direct and indirect costs of its production. See also Price, Value	Concepts Fundamental to Generally Accepted Valuation Principles, 4.3, 4.10; Introduction to IVSs 1, 2 and 3, 3.2
Cost Approach	One of the approaches to value commonly applied in Market Value estimates and many other valuation situations.	GN 1, 3.11
	A comparative approach to the value of property or another asset, that considers as a substitute for the purchase of a given property, the possibility of constructing another property that is an equivalent to the original or one that could furnish equal utility with no undue cost resulting from delay. The Valuer's estimate is based on the reproduction or replacement cost of the subject property or asset, less total (accrued) depreciation.	GN 5, 3.3
	The cost approach establishes the value of a real property by estimating the cost of acquiring land and building a new property with equal	Property Types, 2.7.3

utility or adapting an old property to the same use with no undue cost due to delay. An estimate of entrepreneurial incentive or developer's profit/loss is commonly added to land and construction costs. For older properties, the cost approach develops an estimate of depreciation including items of physical deterioration and functional obsolescence.

See also Depreciated Replacement Cost, Depreciation, Replacement Cost, Reproduction Cost.

Cost Approach for Valuing Fine Art	A comparative approach to the value of fine art that considers as a substitute for the purchase of a given work of fine art the possibility of creating another work of fine art that replaces the original. The Valuer's estimate is based on the reproduction or replacement cost of the subject work of fine art, and the nature of the replacement, i.e., whether it be new for old, indemnity basis, a replica, or a facsimile.	GN 5, 3.4

"New for old" refers to the cost of purchasing the same item or, if unavailable, an item similar in nature and condition in the retail market for new works of fine art.

"Indemnity basis" refers to the cost of replacing an item with a similar item in similar condition in the second-hand retail market for art and antiques.

A "replica" is a copy of the original item, as near as possible to the original in terms of nature, quality, and age of materials but created by means of modern construction methods.

A "facsimile" is an exact copy of the original item, created with materials of a closely similar nature, quality, and age and using construction methods of the original period.

Cost Model   After recognition as an asset, an item of property, plant and equipment shall be carried at its cost less any accumulated depreciation and any accumulated impairment losses.   IAS 16, 30

See also Revaluation Model.

Crop(ping) Farms   Agricultural properties used for growing commodities that are typically planted and harvested within a twelve-month cycle. Properties used for annual crop production may grow more than one type of annual crop over the same period and may or may not make use of irrigation to produce the crops. Some commodities are annual crops that may be left in the ground beyond a twelve-month cycle, per contract provisions or in circumstances where market conditions are unfavorable. These crops will last for more than one year after harvest but are considered less than permanent.   GN 10, 3.1

See also Irrigated Land, Perennial Plantings.

| **Cultural Heritage** | Three groups of (cultural heritage) assets are recognised:

1. Monuments: architectural works, works of monumental sculpture and painting, elements or structures of an architectural nature, inscriptions, cave dwellings and combinations of features, which are of outstanding universal value from the point of view of history, art or science;

2. Groups of buildings: groups of separate or connected buildings which, because of their architecture, their homogeneity or their place in the landscape, are of outstanding universal value from the point of view of history, art or science; and

3. Sites: works of man or the combined works of nature and man, and areas including archeological sites, which are of outstanding universal value from the historical, aesthetic, ethnological or anthropological point of view. | World Heritage Convention, Article I, UNESCO |
| **Cultural Property** | Property inscribed in the World Heritage List after having met at least one of the cultural heritage criteria and the test of authenticity. | World Heritage Convention, Article II, UNESCO |

Current Assets	i) Assets not intended for use on a continuing basis in the activities of the entity such as stocks, obligations owed to the entity, short-term investments, and cash in bank and in hand. In certain circumstances real estate, normally treated as a fixed asset may be treated as a current asset. Examples include improved real estate held in inventory for sale.	Concepts Fundamental to Generally Accepted Valuation Principles, 3.5.1
	ii) An asset which satisfies any of the following criteria:	IAS 1, 57

ii) ...

a) it is expected to be realised in, or is held for sale or consumption in, the entity's normal operating cycle;

b) it is held primarily for the purpose of being traded;

c) it is expected to be realised within twelve months after the balance sheet date; or

d) it is cash or cash equivalent (as defined in IAS 7 Cash Flow Statements) unless it is restricted from being exchanged or used to settle a liability for at least twelve months after the balance sheet date.

All other assets shall be classified as non-current.

See also Non-Current Assets.

Dairy Farms	Agricultural properties used for the production of milk from cows or for other dairy products. These properties usually have extensive structural improvements (barns, milking parlours, silos) and equipment (feed bins, milking machines). Feed may be produced on the property, imported, or supplied by both sources.	GN 10, 3.2
Damages	See Condemnation.	
Debenture	Written acknowledgement or evidence of a debt, especially stock issued as security by a company for borrowed money.	
Deed Restrictions and Restrictive Covenants	Lawful limitations, which run with the land, and may affect the use, development, and conveyance of ownership.	Property Types, 2.2.4.1
Depreciable Amount	i) The cost of an asset, or other amount substituted for cost (in the financial statements), less its residual value.	IAS 16, 6; IAS 36, 6; IAS 38, 8; IPSAS 17, 13
	ii) That element of an asset that depreciates over its useful life. The depreciable amount represents the wasting element of the asset, the balance being the residual amount. However, leasehold land would also be depreciable.	

Depreciated Replacement Cost	An application of the cost approach used in assessing the value of specialised assets for financial reporting purposes, where direct market evidence is limited or unavailable.	Concepts Fundamental to Generally Accepted Valuation Principles, 9.4
	The current cost of replacing an asset with its modern equivalent asset less deductions for physical deterioration and all relevant forms of obsolescence and optimisation.	IVA 1, 3.1; IVA 3, 3.1; GN 8, 3.1
	See also Cost Approach.	
Depreciation	i) In the context of asset valuation, depreciation refers to the adjustments made to the cost of reproducing or replacing the asset to reflect physical deterioration and functional (technical) and economic (external) obsolescence in order to estimate the value of the asset in a hypothetical exchange in the market when there is no direct sales evidence available. In financial reporting, depreciation refers to the charge made against income to reflect the systematic allocation of the depreciable amount of an asset over its useful life to the entity. It is specific to the particular entity and its utilisation of the asst, and is not necessarily affected by the market.	Concepts Fundamental to Generally Accepted Valuation Principles, 3.7
	ii) The systematic allocation of the depreciable amount of an asset over its useful life.	IAS 16, 6; IAS 36, 6; IPSAS 17, 13; IPSAS 21.14

Desk Review	A valuation review that is limited to the data presented in the report, which may or may not be independently confirmed. Generally performed using a checklist of items. The reviewer checks for the accuracy of calculations, the reasonableness of data, the appropriateness of methodology, and compliance with client guidelines, regulatory requirements, and professional standards.	GN 11, 3.4

See also field review.

Develop	To carry out any building, engineering, mining or other operations in, on, over or under the land or the making of any material change in the use of any building or land.	

Discount for Lack of Control	An amount or percentage deducted from a pro-rata share of the value of 100 percent of an equity interest in a business, to reflect the absence of some or all of the powers of control.	GN 6, 3.14

See also Control Premium.

Discount Rate	A rate of return used to convert a monetary sum, payable or receivable in the future, into present value. Theoretically it should reflect the opportunity cost of capital, i.e., the rate of return the capital can earn if put to other uses having similar risk.	GN 9, 3.1

Discounted Cash Flow (DCF) Analysis	A financial modelling technique based on explicit assumptions regarding the prospective cash flow to a property or business. As an accepted methodology within the income approach to valuation, DCF analysis involves the projection of a series of periodic cash flows either to an operating property, a development property, or a business. To this projected cash flow series, an appropriate, market-derived discount rate is applied to establish an indication of the present value of the income stream associated with the property or business. In the case of operating real properties, periodic cash flow is typically estimated as gross income less vacancy and collection losses and less operating expenses/outgoings. The series of periodic net operating incomes, along with an estimate of the reversion/terminal value/exit value, anticipated at the end of the projection period, is then discounted. In the case of development properties, estimates of capital outlays, development costs, and anticipated sales income are estimated to arrive at a series of net cash flows that are then discounted over the projected development and marketing periods. In the case of a business, estimates of periodic cash flows and the value of the business at the end of the projection period are discounted. The most widely used applications of DCF analysis are the Present Value	GN 9, 3.2; GN 12, 3.2

(PV), or Net Present Value (NPV), and the internal rate of return (IRR) of cash flows.

Dividends Method	See Discounted Cash Flow Analysis	
Easement	Nonpossessory (incorporeal) interest in landed property conveying use, but not ownership, of a portion of that property. See also Rights of Way.	Property Types, 2.2.4.2
Economic Life	Either i) the period over which an asset is expected to be economically usable by one or more users; or ii) the number of production or similar units expected to be obtained from the asset by one or more users.	IAS 17, 4
Economic Obsolescence	See External Obsolescence.	
Economic Rent	See Market Rent.	

Elements of Comparison	Specific characteristics of properties and transactions that cause the prices paid for real estate to vary. Elements of comparison include, but are not limited to, the following: property rights conveyed, financing terms, conditions of sale, market conditions, location, and physical and economic characteristics.	GN 1, 3.3
Equipment	See Plant and Equipment.	
Equitable or Equity Interest	The interest of a beneficiary under a trust as opposed to the legal interest of the trustee(s).	Property Types, 2.2.5.2
	A beneficiary is said to hold equitable title while legal title is held by the trustee(s).	
Exploration Property or Area	A Mineral or Petroleum real property interest that is being actively explored for Mineral deposits or Petroleum accumulations, but for which economic viability has not been demonstrated.	GN 14, 3.2
External Obsolescence	A loss in value due to factors outside the subject asset.	
	External obsolescence is also called economic, environmental or locational obsolescence. Examples of external obsolescence are changes in competition or in surrounding land uses like an industrial plant near a residential area. It is deemed	

incurable as the expense to cure the problem is impractical.

External Valuer	A Valuer who, together with any associates, has no material links with the client, an agent acting on behalf of the client, or the subject of the assignment. See also Independent Valuer, Internal Valuer.	Code of Conduct, 3.5
Extractive Industries	Those industries involved in the finding, extracting and associated processing of natural resources located on, or near the earth's crust. They are composed of the Minerals Industry and the Petroleum Industry. They do not include the industry sector focused on extraction of water from the earth, but they do include extraction of geothermal fluid for its energy content.	GN 14, 3.1
Fair Value	The amount for which an asset could be exchanged between knowledgeable, willing parties in an arm's-length transaction.	IVS 2, 3.2; GN 3, 3.1
Fair Value Less Costs to Sell	The amount obtainable from the sale of an asset or cash-generating unit in an arm's length transaction between knowledgeable, willing parties, less the costs of disposal.	IAS 36, 6

Fair Value Model	See Revaluation Model.	
Feasibility Study in the Extractive Industries	A comprehensive study of a Mineral deposit or Petroleum accumulation, in which all geological, engineering, operating, economic, marketing, environmental, regulatory and other relevant factors are considered in sufficient detail. The study could reasonably serve as the basis for a final decision by a proponent or financial institution to proceed with, or finance, the development of the prospective property for Mineral or Petroleum production. See also Prefeasibility Study in the Extractive Industries.	GN 14, 3.3
Fee Simple (Estate)	Absolute ownership subject only to limitations imposed by the State; also called a freehold.	Property Types, 2.2.2
Field Review	A valuation review that includes inspection of the exterior and sometimes the interior of the subject property and possibly inspection of the comparable properties to confirm the data provided in the report. Generally performed using a checklist that covers the items examined in a desk review and may also include confirmation of market data, research to gather additional data, and verification of the software used in preparing the report. See also Desk Review.	GN 11, 3.5

Finance Lease	A lease that transfers substantially all the risks and rewards incident to ownership of an asset. Title may or may not eventually be transferred.	IAS 17, 4

See also Operating Lease.

Financial Asset	Any asset that is	IAS 32, 11

a) cash;

b) an equity instrument of another entity;

c) a contractual right:

    (i) to receive cash or another financial asset from another entity; or

    (ii) to exchange financial instruments with another entity under conditions that are potentially favorable to the entity; or

d) a contract that will or may be settled in the entity's own equity instruments and is:

    (i) a non-derivative for which the entity is or may be obliged to receive a variable number of the entity's own equity instruments; or

    (ii) a derivative that will or may be settled other than by the exchange of a fixed amount of cash or another financial asset for a fixed number of the entity's own equity instruments. For this purpose the entity's own equity instruments do not include instruments that are themselves contracts for the future receipt or delivery of the entity's own equity instruments.

Financial Instrument	Any contract that gives rise to a financial asset of one entity and a financial liability or equity instrument of another entity.	IAS 32, 11
Financial Interests	The interests created by mortgage pledges where the property is used as collateral to secure finance or a charge is taken over the property. An owner's equity position is considered a separate financial interest.	Property Types, 2.2.5.3
	Financial interests result from the legal division of ownership interests in businesses and real property (e.g., partnerships, syndications, corporations, cotenancies, joint ventures), from the contractual grant of an option to buy or sell property (e.g., realty. stocks, or other financial instruments) at a stated price within a specified period, or from the creation of investment instruments secured by pooled real estate assets.	Property Types, 5.1
Financial Liability	Any liability that is	IAS 32, 11
	(a) a contractual obligation	
	(i) to deliver cash or another financial asset to another entity; or	

(ii) to exchange financial assets or financial liabilities with another entity under conditions that are potentially unfavourable to the entity.

(b) a contract that will or may be settled in the entity's own equity instruments and is:

(i) a non-derivative for which the entity is or may be obliged to deliver a variable number of the entity's own equity instruments; or

(ii) a derivative that will or may be settled other than by the exchange of a fixed amount of cash or another financial asset for a fixed number of the entity's own equity instruments. For this purpose the entity's own equity instruments do not include instruments that are themselves contracts for the future receipt or delivery of the entity's own equity instruments.

Financial Modelling	The projection of a business' or property's periodic income or cash flow pattern from which measures of financial return can be calculated. Income or cash flow projections are generated through the use of a financial model that takes into account historical relationships between income, expense, and capital amounts as well as projec-	GN 9, 3.3

tions of those variables. Financial modelling may also be used as a management tool to test expectations for property performance, to gauge the integrity and stability of the DCF model, or as a method to replicate the steps taken by investors in making decisions involving the purchase, sale, or holding of a property or business.

See also Discounted Cash Flow Analysis.

Financial Statements

i) A complete set of financial statements (which) comprises:

IAS 1, 8

   a) balance sheet;

   b) income statement;

   c) a statement showing either:

      (i) all changes in equity; or

      (ii) changes in equity other than those arising from transactions with equity holders acting in their capacity as equity holders;

   d) a cash flow statement; and

   e) notes, comprising a summary of significant accounting policies and other explanatory notes.

ii) In accounting, these comprise the balance sheet and income and expenditure statement (Profit and Loss Account). They are written statements of the financial position of a person or company.

iii) Financial records of prescribed content and form for publication in the interests of common information needs of a wide range of third-party users who are not necessarily identifiable. There is a measure of public accountability associated with financial statements that are developed within a regulatory framework of accounting standards and the law. Financial statements are used to report the financial position and performance of an entity.

Fixed or Long-term Assets   See Non-Current Assets.

Fixtures and Fittings   The totality of improvements integral to a property, valued collectively.   GN 5, 3.5

See Trade Fixtures or Tenant's Fixtures.

Forced Sale   A circumstance where a seller is under compulsion to sell and/or a proper marketing period is not available. The price obtainable under these circumstances will not meet the definition of Market Value. Rather the price obtainable will depend on the nature of the pressure on the seller or the reasons why proper marketing cannot be undertaken. The price may also reflect the consequences for the seller of fail-   IVS 2, 6.11

ing to sell within a specified period. The price obtainable in a forced sales typically cannot be predicted, but will reflect the particular circumstances of the forced sale rather than a hypothetical exchange where the seller is acting without compulsion and/or the transaction occurs after a proper marketing period.

Forestry/ Timberland	Agricultural property used for the growing of non-orchard trees that are periodically harvested over extended growing periods (10 to 20 or more years). Considered to be agricultural properties because they produce a crop, i.e., wood, even though that crop requires a long-term growing period. Also see Perennial Plantings.	GN 10, 3.3
Fractional Interests	See Partial Interests.	
Freehold	Absolute ownership subject to limitations imposed by the state; also known as a fee simple estate. An estate held for perpetuity.	Property Types, 2.2.2
Freehold Interest	A fee simple estate, representing the perpetual ownership in land.	GN 2, 3.1.1

Freehold subject to Lease Interest/s	Has the same meaning as leased fee interest, representing the ownership interest of a lessor owning real estate that is subject to (a) lease(s) to others.	GN 2, 3.1.2
Functional Obsolescence	A loss in value within a structure due to changes in tastes, preferences, technical innovations, or market standards. Functional obsolescence includes excess capital costs and excess operating costs. It may be curable or incurable. Also called Technical Obsolescence.	
Furniture, Fixtures, and Equipment (FF&E)	Tangible personal property plus trade fixtures and leasehold improvements. See also Personal Property.	Property Types, 3.2.2.2; GN 5, 3.6
GAVP	Generally Accepted Valuation Principles; best practice in the Valuation profession.	Introduction/IVS Objectives and Scope
Going Concern	The entity is normally viewed as a going concern, that is, as continuing in operation for the foreseeable future. It is assumed that the entity has neither the intention nor the necessity of liquidation or of curtailing materially the scale of its operations. An operating business.	IAS Framework 23; IAS 1, 23-24 GN 4, 3.11; GN 6, 3.19.1

	Going concern also serves as a valuation premise, under which Valuers and accountants consider a business as an established entity that will continue in operation indefinitely. The premise of a going concern serves as an alternative to the premise of liquidation.	GN 6, 3.19.2, 5.7.1
Goods and Chattels Personal	In certain States, the term used for identifiable, portable, and tangible objects considered by the general public to be personal property.	Property Types, 3.2.1; GN 5, 3.7
	See also Personal Property.	
Goodwill	i) An intangible but marketable asset based on the probability that customers will continue to resort to the same premises where the business is carried on under a particular name, or where goods are sold or services provided under a trade name, with the continuing prospect of earning an acceptable profit being likely.	
	ii) Goodwill may include two distinct components: goodwill that is property-specific, or inherent within the property and transferable to a new owner on sale of the property, and personal goodwill that is associated with the proprietor or manager. (In such case, the goodwill element will be extinguished upon sale of the property.)	Property Types, 4.4.2.1

	iii) Future economic benefits arising from assets that are not capable of being individually identified and separately recognised.	IFRS 3, Appendix A
	See also Personal Goodwill, Transferable Goodwill.	
Government Business Enterprise (GBE)	An entity that has all of the following characteristics:	IPSAS 21.14
	a) is an entity with the power to contract in its own name;	
	b) has been assigned the financial and operational authority to carry on a business;	
	c) sells goods and services, in the normal course of its business, to other entities at a profit or full cost recovery;	
	d) is not reliant on continuing government funding to be a going concern (other than purchases of outputs at arm's length); and	
	e) is controlled by a public service entity.	
Ground Lease	Usually a long-term lease of land with the lessee permitted to improve or build on the land and to enjoy those benefits for the term of the lease.	GN 2, 3.1.3

Hammer Price	The accepted and announced bid, exclusive of any fees or commissions and, therefore, not necessarily the purchase price.	GN 5, 3.8
	See also Auction Price, Private Treaty Sale.	
Hazardous Substance	In the context of valuation, any material within, around, or near the property being valued that has sufficient form, quantity, and bio-availability to create a negative impact on the property's Market Value.	GN 7, 3.2
Headlease or Master Lease	A lease to a single entity that is intended to be the holder of subsequent leases to sublessees that will be the tenants in possession of the leased premises.	GN 2, 3.1.4
	Headlease is Commonwealth usage; master lease is North American usage.	
Headlease-hold Interest or Sandwich Lessor Interest	The holder of a headlease or master lease.	GN 2, 3.1.5
	Headleasehold interest is Commonwealth usage; sandwich lessor interest is North American usage.	
Heritage Asset	An asset having some cultural, environmental or historical significance. Heritage assets include historical buildings and monuments, archaeological sites, conservation areas and nature reserves, and works of art. Heritage assets often display the	

following characteristics (although these characteristics are not necessarily limited to heritage assets):

a) their economic benefit in cultural, educational and historic terms is unlikely to be fully reflected in a financial value based purely on market price;

b) legal and/or statutory obligations may impose prohibitions or severe restrictions on disposal by sale;

c) they are often irreplaceable and their economic benefit may increase over time even if their physical condition deteriorates; and

d) it may be difficult to estimate their useful lives, which in some cases could be hundreds of years.

This definition is consistent with the definition of heritage assets in IPSAS 17, 9.

Highest and Best Use	The most probable use of a property which is physically possible, appropriately justified, legally permissible, financially feasible, and which results in the highest value of the property being valued. See also Market Value.	Concepts Fundamental to Generally Accepted Valuation Principles, 6.3

Historic (Historical) Cost Convention (Accounting)	i) The traditional accounting convention for the compilation of financial statements on the basis of costs actually incurred by the current owner. The use of such accounting convention may not reflect the underlying value of the assets at the date of the annual accounts.	
	ii) Assets are recorded at the amount of cash or cash equivalents paid or the fair value of the consideration given to acquire them at the time of their acquisition. Liabilities are recorded at the amount of proceeds received in exchange for the obligation, or in some circumstances (for example, income taxes), at the amounts of cash or cash equivalents, expected to be paid to satisfy the liability in the normal course of business.	IAS Framework, 100(a)
	See also Current Cost Convention.	
Historic House Owner Associations	Not-for-profit membership associations that promote the preservation of historic properties, and provide their owner-members with advice on matters such as the management, repair, maintenance, taxation and insurance of historic properties.	GN 15, 3.1

Historic Property	Real property publicly recognised or officially designated by a government-chartered body as having cultural or historic importance because of its association with an historic event or period, with an architectural style, or with the nation's heritage. Four characteristics are commonly associated with historic properties: 1) their historic, architectural and/or cultural importance; 2) the statutory or legal protection to which they may be subject; 3) restraints and limitations placed upon their use, alteration and disposal; and 4) the frequent obligation in some jurisdictions that they be accessible to the public. The terms, historic property and heritage asset, often overlap but are not in all cases equivalent.	GN 15, 3.2
	See also Heritage Assets, Publicly Designated Historic Properties.	
Holding Company or Investment Business	An entity which maintains the controlling interest in subsidiary companies by virtue of ownership of stock in those companies.	Property Types 4.3.1
	A business which receives returns on its assets.	GN 6, 3.21
Impairment	A loss in the future economic benefits, or service potential of an asset, over and above the systematic recognition of the loss of the asset's future economic benefits or service potential through depreciation.	IPSAS 21.14

Impairment Loss	The amount by which the carrying amount of an asset or a cash-generating unit exceeds its recoverable amount.	IAS 36, 6
Improvements	Buildings, structures, or some modifications to land, of a permanent nature, involving expenditures of labour and capital, and intended to enhance the value or utility of the property. Improvements have differing patterns of use and economic lives. See also Land, Value of Improvements.	IVA 1, 3.2; GN 8, 3.2
Income Capitalisation Approach	A comparative approach to value that considers income and expense data relating to the property being valued and estimates value through a capitalisation process. Capitalisation relates income (usually net income) and a defined value type by converting an income amount into a value estimate. This process may consider direct relationships (whereby an overall capitalisation rate or all risks yield is applied to a single year's income), yield or discount rates (reflecting measures of return on investment) applied to a series of incomes over a projected period, or both. The income approach reflects the principles of substitution and anticipation.	Concepts Fundamental to Generally Accepted Valuation Principles, 9.2.1.2; Property Types, 2.7.2.1; GN 1, 5.12.1; GN 5, 3.9

Income Multiplier or Years' Purchase	The ratio between the sale price or value of a property and the average annual income or income expectancy; may be based on gross or net income. It is applied to income to arrive at capital value.	
	The term, income multiplier, is North American usage; years' purchase is Commonwealth usage.	
	See also Capitalisation Factor, Investment Method, Valuation Ratio.	
Independent Valuer	A Valuer who meets the specific requirements of independence, which may attach to many assignments, and are applied by regulation or by law with some clients and in certain States.	Code of Conduct, 3.6; IVA 2, 6.8.3
	See also External Valuer.	
Infrastructure Assets	Assets that usually display some or all of the following general characteristics:	
	a) they are part of a system or network;	
	b) they are specialised in nature and do not have alternative uses;	
	c) they are immovable; and	
	d) they may be subject to constraints at time of disposal.	
	The above definition is consistent with the definition of infrastructure assets in IPSAS 17, 21.	

Intangible Assets	Assets that manifest themselves by their economic properties; they do not have physical substance; they grant rights and privileges to their owner; and usually generate income for their owner. Intangible Assets can be categorised as arising from: Rights; Relationships; Grouped Intangibles; or Intellectual Property.	
	In general, the accounting profession limits the recognition of individual intangible assets to those that are: commonly recognisable; have a statutory or contractual remaining life; and/or must be individually transferable and separable from the business.	GN 4, 3.14, 3.14.5
	An identifiable non-monetary asset without physical substance.	IAS 38, 8
Intangible Property	The rights and privileges granted to the owner of intangible assets.	GN 4, 3.15
Integrated Unit	An agricultural entity that has common ownership of all or part of the processes involving the production and marketing of its products and/or commodities.	GN 10, 3.9

Internal Rate of Return (IRR)	The discount rate that equates the present value of the net cash flows of a project with the present value of the capital investment. It is the rate at which the Net Present Value (NPV) equals zero. The IRR reflects both the return on the invested capital and the return of the original investment, which are basic considerations of potential investors. Therefore, deriving the IRR from analysis of market transactions of similar properties having comparable income patterns is a proper method for developing market discount rates for use in valuations to arrive at Market Value.	GN 9, 3.4
	Used in discounted cash flow analysis to find the implied or expected rate of return of the project, the IRR is the rate of return which gives a zero net present value (NPV).	
Internal Valuer	A Valuer who is in the employ of either the entity that owns the assets or the accounting firm responsible for preparing the entity's financial records and/or reports. An Internal Valuer is generally capable of meeting all the requirements of independence and professional objectivity required under the Code of Conduct, but for reasons of public presentation and regulation may not always be acceptable to fill the role of Independent Valuer in certain types of assignments.	Code of Conduct, 3.4
	See also External Valuer.	

Intrinsic Value	The amount considered, on the basis of an evaluation of available facts, to be the "true" or "real" worth of an item. A long-term, Non-Market Value concept that smoothes short-term price fluctuations.	GN 5, 3.10
Invested Capital	The sum of the debt and equity in a business on a long-term basis.	GN 6, 3.23
Invested Cash Flow	See Cash Flow.	
Investment Analysis	A study undertaken for the purposes of development and investment, the evaluation of investment performance, or the analysis of a transaction involving investment properties. Investment analyses are variously called (economic) feasibility studies, market or marketability analyses, or financial projection studies.	GN 9, 3.5
Investment Asset	An asset owned by a corporation and considered extraneous to the operational requirements of the corporate owner.	Concepts Fundamental to Generally Accepted Valuation Principles, 3.5.3
	Land and/or buildings held to earn a present or future rental income and/or for the preservation or gain of capital value or both. It is not held for use in the production or supply of goods or services or for administrative purposes, or for sale in the ordinary course of business.	
	See also Operational Asset.	

Investment Method

A valuation procedure that capitalises expected future income or utility as a basis for estimating the Market Value of the subject asset.

The underlying assumption is that the investor will pay no more for the subject asset than would have to be paid for another asset with an income stream of comparable amount, duration, and certainty.

See also Income Capitalisation Approach.

Investment Property

i) Property (land or a building - or part of a building - or both) held (by the owner or by the lessee under a finance lease) to earn rentals or for capital appreciation or both, rather than for:

IAS 40, 5; IPSAS 16,6

a) use in the production or supply of goods or services or for administrative purposes, or

b) sale in the ordinary course of operations.

ii) In real estate, property owned for the purpose of leasing to a third party, for possible future occupation by the owner, or for future development to earn rental income or profit on resale.

Investment Value or Worth	The value of property to a particular investor, or a class of investors, for identified investment or operational objectives. This subjective concept relates specific property to a specific investor, group of investors, or entity with identifiable investment objectives and/or criteria.	IVS 3, 3.3
	The investment value, or worth, of a property asset may be higher or lower than the Market Value of the property asset. The term investment value, or worth, should not be confused with the Market Value of an investment property.	
	The term, investment value, is North American usage; worth is Commonwealth usage.	
Irrigated Land	Lands used to produce crops or forage for livestock and which require the application of water other than that from natural rainfall, are called irrigated crop(ping) farms or irrigated grazing land. Properties that lack a water source other than natural rainfall are referred to as dry land agricultural properties.	GN 10, 3.4

Joint Venture	A combination of two or more entities that join to undertake a specific project; differs from a partnership in that it is limited in duration and project-specific.	Property Types, 5.1.2.2
	A contractual arrangement whereby two or more parties undertake an economic activity which is subject to joint control.	IAS 31, 3
Land	Valuation of land as if vacant, and of land and improvements to or on the land, is an economic concept. Whether vacant or improved, land is also referred to as real estate.	Concepts Fundamental to Generally Accepted Valuation Principles, 2.1, 2.2
	The earth's surface, the space beneath which extends to the centre of the earth, and the space above which extends to the sky.	
	The ownership of land and the rights attached to the ownership are subject to the laws of a particular State.	
	See also Improvements, Property, Real Estate, Real Property.	

Lease	i) A contract arrangement in which rights of use and possession are conveyed from a property's title owner (called the landlord, or lessor) in return for a promise by another (called a tenant or lessee) to pay rents as prescribed by the lease. In practice the rights and the duties of the parties can be complex, and are dependent upon the specified terms of their contract.	GN 2, 3.1.6
	ii) An agreement whereby the lessor conveys to the lessee in return for a payment or series of payments the right to use an asset for an agreed period of time.	IAS 17, 4
Lease Interest	Also known as Lessee Interest, Tenant's Interest, or Leasehold Estate. The ownership interest that is created by the terms of a lease rather than the underlying rights of real estate ownership. The lease interest is subject to the terms of a specific lease arrangement, expires within a specified time, and may be capable of subdivision, or subleasing to other parties.	GN 2, 3.1.7
Leased Fee Estate	The ownership interest that the landlord or lessor maintains in a property under a lease with the rights of use and occupancy being conveyed or granted to a tenant or lessee.	Property Types, 2.2.3
	The ownership interest in a leased property.	
	Compare Leasehold Estate.	

Leasehold Estate	The interest which a tenant or lessee acquires under a lease including rights of use and occupancy for a stated term under certain conditions (e.g., the payment of a premium and/or rent).	Property Types, 2.2.3
	Leaseholds may be of various duration such as 25 years, 60 years and 99 years etc.	
Leasehold Improvements or Tenant's Improvements	Fixed improvements or additions to land or buildings, installed by and paid for by the tenant to meet the tenant's needs; typically removable by the tenant upon expiration of the lease; removal causes no material damage to the real estate.	Property Types, 3.2.2; GN 5, 3.11
	See also Personal Property, Trade Fixtures or Tenant's Fixtures.	
Leasehold Interest	See Lease Interest.	
Legal Estates	Rights or interests in real property derive from legal estates; legal estates are defined by the laws of the State in which they exist, and are usually subject to outside limitations imposed by the State, e.g., taxation, compulsory acquisition, regulation, or appropriation in cases of intestacy.	Property Types, 2.2.1

Legal Life	The life of the intangible asset allowed by law (i.e., the period of legal or contractual protection of the intangible asset).	GN 4, 3.16; 5.8.2.1.4.2
Lessee	A person to whom property is rented under a lease. The lessee is commonly called a tenant.	
Lessee Interest	See Lease Interest.	
Lessor	One who owns the rights to use an asset, which is transferred to another (lessee) under a lease agreement. The lessor is usually referred to as the landlord.	
Lessor Interest	The interest held by the lessor in any of the circumstances set out in (in the provisions of) a Freehold subject to Lease Interest/s, a Head-lease or Master Lease, or a Head-leasehold Interest.	GN 2, 3.1.8
Limiting Conditions	Constraints which are imposed on valuations by clients, the Valuer, or local statutory law.	Code of Conduct, 3.2

Liquidation Value	The value of assets estimated with regard to specific circumstances under which the assets are sold. Liquidation value describes a situation where a group of assets employed together in a business are offered for sale separately, usually following a closure of the business. Although associated with forced sale, these terms have distinct meanings. There is no reason why assets cannot be liquidated by an orderly sale following proper marketing.	IVS 2, 6.9.2
Listing of (Heritage) Buildings or Historic Properties Register	A recording of officially designated historic properties. Not all historic properties are necessarily listed in registers. Many historic properties publicly recognised as having cultural and historic importance also qualify as historic properties.	GN 15, 3.3
Livestock Ranches/ Stations	Agricultural properties used to raise and feed animals such as cattle, sheep, pigs, goats, horses, or combinations thereof. The actual use of these properties can take many forms. The animals may be bred, raised, and sold within the operation of the property. Young animals may be acquired from outside the property and then raised within the property. The animals may be raised for consumptive use or for breeding stock. Feed for the animals may be produced on the property, imported, or supplied by both sources. Properties used for the production and	GN 10, 3.5

feeding of livestock have significant capital investment in the structural improvements (pens, livestock shelters, sheds, division fencing) and the livestock, which may or may not be depreciable depending on the laws and regulations of the local jurisdiction.

Loan Security An asset which is legally nominated to be available to a lender for realisation and recovery of money owed following default by the borrower.

Machinery See Plant and Equipment.

Majority Control The degree of control provided by a majority position. GN 6, 3.24

Majority Interest Ownership position greater than 50% of the voting interest in a business. GN 6, 3.25

Market Rent The estimated amount for which a property, or space within a property, should lease on the date of valuation between a willing lessor and a willing lessee on appropriate terms in an arm's-length transaction, after proper marketing wherein the parties had each acted knowledgeably, prudently and without compulsion. Whenever Market Rent is provided, the "appropriate lease terms" which it reflects should also be stated. GN 2, 3.1.10.1

Market Value	The estimated amount for which a property should exchange on the date of valuation between a willing buyer and a willing seller in an arm's-length transaction after proper marketing wherein the parties had each acted knowledgeably, prudently, and without compulsion.	IVS 1, 3.1
	See also Highest and Best Use.	
Marketability Discount	An amount or percentage deducted from an equity interest to reflect lack of marketability.	GN 6, 3.28
Marriage Value	See Synergistic Value.	
Mass Appraisal	The practice of appraising multiple properties as of a given date by a systematic and uniform application of appraisal methods and techniques that allow for statistical review and analysis of results.	GN 13, 3.3
Master Lease	See Headlease.	

Mineral	Any naturally occurring material useful to, and/or having a value placed on it by humankind, and found in or on the erath's crust. For the purposes of GN 14, Minerals include metallic minerals, industrial minerals, aggregates, precious stones and fuel minerals, but Minerals do not include Petroleum, which is defined separately.	GN 14, 3.4
	See also Petroleum.	
Mineral Reserve	As defined by the Combined [Mineral] Reserves International Reporting Standard Committee (CRIRSCO): "the economically mineable part of a Measured and/or Indicated Mineral Resource. It includes diluting materials and allowances for losses, which may occur when the material is mined. Appropriate assessments that may include Feasibility Studies, have been carried out, and include consideration of, and modification by, realistically assumed mining, metallurgical, economic, marketing, legal, environmental, social and governmental factors. These assessments demonstrate at the time of reporting that extraction is justified. Mineral Reserves are subdivided in order of increasing confidence into Probable Mineral Reserves and Proved Mineral reserves".	GN 14, 3.5

Mineral Resource	As defined by CRIRSCO: "a concentration or occurrence of material of intrinsic economic interest in or on the earth's crust (a deposit) in such form and quantity that there are reasonable prospects for eventual economic extraction. The location, quality, grade, geological characteristics and continuity of a Mineral Resource are known, estimated or interpreted from specific geological evidence and knowledge. Mineral Resources are subdivided, in order of increasing geological confidence, into Inferred, Indicated and Measured categories. Portions of a deposit that do not have reasonable prospects for eventual economic extraction must not be included in a Mineral Resource.	GN 14, 3.6
Minerals Industry	Entities involved in the exploration for Minerals, and the mining, processing and marketing of Minerals. GN 14 is not designed to cover assets downstream from the metals refineries or minerals processing plants, such as assets involved in the distribution of refined metals to metal fabricators, or mineral products to retailers or the final market.	GN 14, 3.7
Minority Discount	A discount for lack of control applicable to a minority interest.	GN 6, 3.29

Minority Interest	Ownership position of less than 50% of the voting interest in a business.	GN 6, 3.30
	That portion of the profit and loss and net assets of a subsidiary attributable to equity interests that are not owned, directly or indirectly through subsidiaries, by the parent.	IAS 27, 4; IFRS 3, A
Modern Equivalent Asset (MEA)	An asset which has a similar function and equivalent productive capacity to the asset being valued, but of a current design and constructed or made using current materials and techniques.	GN 8, 3.3
	The term, modern equivalent asset, is Commonwealth usage.	
Mortgage	A pledge of an interest in property as security or collateral for repayment of a loan with provision for redemption on repayment. In the event the borrower (mortgagor) defaults, the lender (mortgagee) has the power to recover the property pledged.	IVA 2, 3.2
Mortgage Lending Value (MLV)	The value of the property as determined by a prudent assessment of the future marketability of the property taking into account long-term sustainable aspects of the property, the normal and local market conditions, and the current use and alternative appropriate uses of the property. Speculative elements shall not be taken into account in the assessment of mortgage lending value. The mortgage lending value	Directive 2006/48/EC of the European Parliament

shall be documented in a transparent and clear manner.

Net Present Value (NPV)	The measure of the differences between the discounted revenues, or inflows, and the costs, or outflows, in a discounted cash flow analysis.	GN 9, 3.6
Net Realisable Value	The estimated selling price of an asset in the ordinary course of business, less the estimated costs of completion and the estimated costs necessary to make the sale. Net realisable value refers to the net amount that an entity expects to realise from the sale of inventory in the ordinary course of business. Fair value reflects the amount for which the same inventory could be exchanged between knowledgeable and willing buyers and sellers in the marketplace. The former is an entity-specific value; the latter is not. Net realisable value for inventories may not equal fair value less costs to sell.	IAS 2, 6; 2, 7
Non-Cash-Generating Assets	Assets other than cash-generating assets.	IPSAS 21.14
Non-Current Assets	Tangible and intangible assets, which fall into two broad categories, namely property, plant and equipment, and other non-current assets. Also called fixed, or long-term assets.	Concepts Fundamental to Generally Accepted Valuation Principles, 3.5.2

Obsolescence	A loss in value due to a decrease in the usefulness of property caused by decay, changes in technology, people's behaviourial patterns and tastes, or environmental changes. Obsolescence is sometimes classified according to items of outmoded design and functionality, items with structural design unable to meet current code requirements, and factors arising outside the asset, such as changes in user demand.	IVA 3, 3.3
Operating Company	A business that performs an economic activity by making, selling, or trading a product or service.	GN 6, 3.33
Operating Lease	A lease other than a finance lease. See also Finance Lease	IAS 17, 4
Operational Asset	An asset considered requisite to the operations of a going concern or corporation. See also Investment Asset.	Concepts Fundamental to Generally Accepted Valuation Principles, 3.5.3
Optimisation	The process by which a least cost replacement option is determined for the remaining service potential of an asset. It is a process of adjusting the replacement cost to reflect that an asset may be technically obsolete or over-engineered, or the asset may have a greater capacity than that required. Hence optimisation minimises, rather than maximises, a resulting valuation where	IVA 3, 3.4; GN 8, 3.4

alternative lower cost replacement options are available.

Option	An agreement to keep open an offer to buy, sell, or lease real property for a specified period at a stated price. An option creates a contractual right, the exercise of which is generally contingent upon the fulfillment of specified conditions.	Property Types, 5.1.3
Oral Report	The results of a valuation, verbally communicated to a client or presented before a court either as expert testimony or by means of deposition. A report communicated orally to a client should be supported by a work file and at a minimum followed up by a written summary of the valuation. See also Written report.	IVS 3, 3.2
Owner-Occupied Property	Property held (by the owner or by the lessee under a finance lease) for use in the production or supply of goods or services or for administrative purposes.	IAS 40, 5; IPSAS 16, 6
Partial or Fractional Interest	Rights in real property created by legal divisions of the ownership interest. For example, real property is not only owned in sole proprietorships, but may also be held by corporations (shareholders), partnerships, joint tenancies, and tenancies in common.	Property Types, 2.2.5.1

Participa-tion Rent	See Turnover Rent.	
Partnership	An ownership interest in which two or more persons jointly own a business or property and share its profits and losses. Partnerships may be general or limited.	Property Types, 5.1.1
Passing Rent	See Contract Rent.	
Percentage Rent	See Turnover Rent.	
Perennial Plantings	Crops grown from plantings that have a life extending beyond one year or one crop cycle. Examples are vineyards and orchards. These types of properties can have significant capital investment in the plantings, which represent a depreciable asset. Also see forestry/timberland.	GN 10, 3.6
Personal Goodwill	The value of profit generated over and above market expectations, which would be extinguished upon sale of the trade related property, together with those financial factors related specifically to the current operator of the business, such as taxation, depreciation policy, borrowing costs and the capital invested in the business. See also Goodwill, Transferable Goodwill.	GN 4, 3.12.2; GN 6, 3.20.2; GN 12, 3.3.2

Personal Property	A legal concept referring to all rights, interests, and benefits related to ownership of items other than real estate. In certain States, items of personal property are legally designated as personalty in distinction to realty, which may either refer to real property or real estate. Items of personal property can be tangible, such as a chattel, or intangible, such as a debt or patent. Items of tangible personal property typically are not permanently affixed to real estate and are generally characterized by their moveability.	GN 5, 3.13
	Personal property includes interests in tangible and intangible items, which are not real estate.	Concepts Fundamental to Generally Accepted Valuation Principles, 2.4
Personalty	A legal term used in certain States to designate items of personal property in distinction to realty, which may either refer to real property or real estate. Personalty includes tangible and intangible items, which are not real estate.	GN 5, 3.14
	See also Personal Property, Realty.	
Petroleum	Any naturally occurring hydrocarbon, whether in a gaseous, liquid or solid state. Raw Petroleum products are primarily crude oil and natural gas.	GN 14, 3.8
	See also Extractive Industries.	

Petroleum Industry	Entities involved in exploration for Petroleum, and the extraction, processing and marketing of crude Petroleum and associated gases. GN 14 is not designed to cover assets downstream from the petroleum refineries and natural gas processing plants, such as assets involved in the distribution of refined petroleum products to retailers.	GN 14, 3.9
Petroleum Reserves	As defined by the Society of Petroleum Engineers (SPE) and the World Petroleum Congress (WPC): "those quantities of Petroleum, which are anticipated to be commercially recovered from known accumulations from a given date forward. All (Petroleum) Reserve estimates involve some degree of uncertainty. The uncertainty depends chiefly on the amount of reliable geologic and engineering data available at the time of the estimate and the interpretation of these data. The relative degree of uncertainty may be conveyed by placing reserves into one of two principal classifications, either Proved or Unproved. Unproved Reserves are less certain to be recovered than proved Reserves and may be further sub-classified as Probable and Possible Reserves to denote progressively increasing uncertainty in their recoverability. Proved Reserves can be categorised as Developed or Undeveloped".	GN 14, 3.10

Petroleum Resources	For the purpose of GN 14, petroleum resources comprise only Petroleum Reserves and Contingent Resources. Contingent Resources, as defined by the Society of Petroleum Engineers (SPE)/World Petroleum Congress (WPC), in conjunction with the American Association of Petroleum Geologists (AAPG), are "those quantities of petroleum, which are estimated, on a given date, to be potentially recoverable from known accumulations, but which are not currently considered to be commercially recoverable".	GN 14, 3.11
Plant	See Plant and Equipment.	
Plant and Equipment	Tangible assets, other than realty, that:	GN 3, 3.3; GN 5, 3.15; GN 8, 3.5

(a) are held by an entity for use in the production or supply of goods or services, for rental to others, or for administrative purposes; and

(b) are expected to be used over a period of time.

The categories of plant and equipment are:

Plant. Assets that are inextricably combined with others and that may include specialised buildings, machinery, and equipment.

Machinery. Individual machines or a collection of machines. A machine is an apparatus used for a specific process in connection with the operation of the entity.

Equipment. Other assets that are used to assist the operation of the enterprise or entity.

Tangible items that:　　　　　　IAS 16. 6

a) are held for use in the production or supply of goods and services, for rental to others, or for administrative purposes; and

b) are expected to be used during more than one (accounting) period.

See also Personal Property.

Plant and Machinery　　　See Plant and Equipment.

Portfolio　　　An assemblage of the various properties held or managed by a single entity.

Prefeasibility Study in the Extractive Industries　　　A study of a Mineral or Petroleum deposit, in which all geological, engineering, operating, economic, environmental and other relevant factors, are considered in sufficient detail to serve as the reasonable basis for a decision to proceed as a Feasibility Study.　　　GN 14, 3.12

See also Feasibility Study in the Extractive Industries.

Present Value	See Net Present Value.	
Preservation Incentives	Incentives to the owners of historic properties, primarily fiscal in nature, to promote the restoration and maintenance of such properties. Examples may include exemptions on inheritance taxes for conservation properties gifted to heritage trusts, government subsidies, exemptions in municipal rates/taxes, investment tax credits to owners of historic properties, transferable development rights and deductions taken on conservation easements donated to nonprofit organizations.	GN 15, 3.4
Price	An amount asked, offered, or paid for a good or service.	Concepts Fundamental to Generally Accepted Valuation Principles, 4.2
	The concept of price relates to the exchange of a commodity, good or service. Price is the amount asked, offered, or paid for the item. Once the exchange has been transacted, the price, whether disclosed or undisclosed, becomes an historic fact. The price paid represents the intersection of supply and demand.	Introduction to IVSs 1, 2 and 3, 3.1
	See also Cost, Value.	

Principle of Substitution	A prudent person will not pay more for a good or service than the cost of acquiring an equally satisfactory substitute good or service, in the absence of the complicating factors of time, greater risk, or inconvenience. The lowest cost of the best alternative, whether a substitute or the original, tends to establish Market Value.	Concepts Fundamental to Generally accepted Valuation Principles, 9.2
	This principle is fundamental to the three approaches to Market Value.	
Private Treaty Sale	A sale negotiated and transacted between persons rather than by public auction or another method. The sale price paid in a private treaty sale is generally not known except by the parties to the transaction.	GN 5, 3.16
	See also Auction Price, Hammer Price.	
Professional Property Valuer	A person who possesses necessary qualifications, ability, and experience to estimate property value for a diversity of purposes including transactions involving transfers of property ownership, property considered as collateral to secure loans and mortgages, property subject to litigation or pending settlement on taxes, and property treated as fixed assets in financial reporting. A Professional Property Valuer may also possess the specific expertise to perform valuations of other categories	Introduction/IVS Objectives and Scope; GN 5, 3.17

of property, i.e., personal property, businesses, and financial interests.

See also External Valuer, Independent Valuer, Internal Valuer, Valuer.

Property	A legal concept, encompassing all the interests, rights and benefits related to ownership. Property consists of the private rights of ownership, which entitle the owner to a specific interest or interests in what is owned. To distinguish between real estate, a physical entity, and its ownership, a legal concept, the ownership of real estate is called real property. Ownership of an interest in an item other than real estate is referred to as personal property.	Concepts Fundamental to Generally Accepted Valuation Principles, 2.3, 2.4
	The International Valuation Standards Committee recognises the following four property types: real property, personal property, businesses, and financial interests.	Property Types, 1.0
	See also Personal Property, Real Property.	
Property Company	A holding company in real property.	
Property, Plant and Equipment (PP&E)	i) Assets intended for use on a continuing basis in the activities of an entity including land and buildings; plant and equipment;	Concepts Fundamental to Generally Accepted Valuation Principles, 3.5.2.1

and other categories of assets, suitably identified; less accumulated depreciation. Property, plant, and equipment are tangible, or physical, assets.

ii) Tangible items that: a) are held for use in the production or supply of goods or services, for rental to others, or for administrative purposes; and b) are expected to be used during more than one period.	IAS 16, 6; IPSAS 17, 12

Property Rights	The rights that are related to the ownership of the real estate. These include the right to develop or not to develop the land, to lease it to others, to sell it, to give it away, to farm it, to mine it, to alter its topography, to subdivide it, to assemble it, to use it for waste disposal, or to choose to exercise none of these rights. The combination of property rights is sometimes referred to as the bundle of rights. Property rights are typically subject to public and private restrictions such as easements, rights of way, specified development density, zoning, and other restrictions that may encumber property.	GN 1, 3.7
Property with Trading Potential	See Trade Related Property.	

Public Building	A building that serves some community or social function and is held in public ownership. Examples include courthouses, municipal centres, schools, prisons, police stations, military facilities, libraries, hospitals, clinics, and social or public housing.	IVA 3, 3.5
Public Sector Asset	A property, owned and/or controlled by governmental or quasi-governmental entity, for the provision of some public service or good. Public sector assets comprise different asset types, including conventional assets as well as heritage and conservation assets, infrastructure assets, public utility plants, recreational assets, and public buildings (e.g., military facilities), each category of which constitutes property, plant and equipment within the meaning of IPSASs and IFRSs.	IVA 3, 3.6

Public sector assets typically include:

a) assets, which have atypical tenure, are irreplaceable, are non-cash-generating, or provide goods or services in the absence of any market competition;

b) land with restrictions on its sale or leasing; and

c) land, which is designated for a specialised use that is not necessarily its highest and best use.

See also Heritage Asset, Infrastructure Assets, Public Building, Public Utility, and Recreational Assets.

Public Utility	A property that a) produces a service or good for general public consumption; and b) is usually a monopoly or quasi-monopoly provider subject to some form of governmental control.	IVA 3, 3.7
Publicly Designated Historic Properties	Those properties, the historic status of which is officially recognised by government-chartered bodies to identify historic properties and to promote historic preservation. Such bodies may be established by national/federal, state/provincial, or county/municipal governments. Local non-governmental historical societies may also designate historic properties and maintain private historic property lists or registers that confer many of the same benefits whilst remaining exempt from governmental restrictions. See also Listing of (Heritage) Buildings or Historic Registers.	GN 15, 3.5
Rate of Return	An amount of income (loss) and/or change in value realised or anticipated on an investment, expressed as a percentage of that investment.	GN 4, 3.19; GN 6, 3.34

Real Estate	Land and all things that are a natural part of the land, e.g., trees and minerals, as well as things that are attached to the land by people, e.g., buildings and site improvements. All permanent building attachments such as plumbing, heating and cooling systems; electrical wiring; and built-in items like elevators, or lifts, are also a part of real estate. Real estate includes all attachments, both below and above the ground. See also Improvements, Land, Real Property.	GN 1, 3.8
Real Property	All the rights, interests, and benefits related to the ownership of real estate. Real property is a legal concept distinct from real estate, which is a physical asset. There may also be potential limitations upon ownership rights to real property. See also Property, Real Estate.	GN 1, 3.9
Realty	A term used to distinguish either real property or real estate from items of personal property, which in certain states are legally referred to as personalty. See also Personalty. The term, realty, is North American usage.	Property Types, 2.1.1

Reasonably Efficient Operator, or Average Competent Management	A market-based concept whereby a potential purchaser, and thus the Valuer, estimates the maintainable level of trade and future profitability that can be achieved by a competent operator of a business conducted on the premises, acting in an efficient manner. The concept involves the trading potential rather than the actual level of trade under the existing ownership, so that it excludes personal goodwill.	GN 12, 3.4
Recognition	The process of incorporating in the balance sheet or income statement an item that meets the definition of an element and satisfies the following criteria for recognition:	IAS Framework, 82, 83
	a) it is probable that any future economic benefit associated with the item will flow to or from the entity; and	
	b) the item has a cost or value that can be measured with reliability.	
Recoverable Amount	The recoverable amount of an asset or a cash-generating unit is the higher of its fair value less costs to sell and its value in use.	IAS 36, 6
Recoverable Costs	See Expense Pass-throughs.	

Recoverable Service Amount	The higher of a non-cash-generating asset's fair value less costs to sell and its value in use.	IPSAS 21.14
Recreational Assets	Properties held in public ownership that	IVA 3, 3.8

a) are managed by or on behalf of national, municipal or local government authorities; and

b) provide for recreational use by the general public.

Examples include parks; playgrounds; green belts; walks and trails; swimming pools; playing courts, fields and courses; and other properties equipped with recreational and athletic facilities.

Rent(al)	See Contract Rent, Market Rent, Turnover Rent.
Rent Escalations or Stepped Rents	Upward rental adjustments based on some external change or indexing, and specified in a lease clause.

Replacement Cost (New)	A replacement cost estimate envisions constructing a structure of comparable utility, employing the design and materials that are currently used in the market.	Concepts Fundamental to Generally Accepted Valuation Principles, 4.11
	The current cost of a similar new item having the nearest equivalent utility as the item being appraised.	GN 4, 3.20; GN 6, 3.35
	The cost of replacing an asset with an equally satisfactory substitute asset; normally derived from the current acquisition cost of a similar asset, new or used, or of an equivalent productive capacity or service potential. Replacement cost assumes the use of modern materials, techniques and designs.	
	See also Modern Equivalent Asset, Reproduction Cost.	
Report Date	The date of the valuation report. May be the same or different from the valuation date.	GN 4, 3.21; GN 6, 3.36
Reproduction Cost (New)	The cost to create a virtual replica of the existing structure, employing the same design and similar building materials.	Concepts Fundamental to Generally Accepted Valuation Principles, 4.11
	The current cost of an identical new item.	GN 4, 3.22; GN 6, 3.37
	In the market for fine art, reproduction cost is equivalent to the cost of creating a facsimile of the original item.	
	See also Cost Approach for Valuing Fine Art, Replacement Cost.	

Residual Value	The estimated amount that an entity would currently obtain from disposal of an asset, after deducting the estimated costs of disposal, if the asset were already of the age and in the condition expected at the end of its useful life.	IAS 16, 6
	The net amount which the entity expects to obtain for an asset at the end of its useful life after deducting the expected costs of disposal.	IPSAS 17, 12
	The remaining value of an asset at the end of a prescribed period of time (in this definition residual value is similar to scrap value).	
Revaluation Model	After recognition as an asset, an item of property, plant and equipment whose fair value can be measured reliably shall be carried at a revalued amount, being its fair value at the date of the revaluation less any subsequent accumulated depreciation and subsequent accumulated impairment loss. Revaluations shall be made with sufficient regularity to ensure that the carrying amount does not differ materially from that which would be determined using fair value at the balance sheet date.	IAS 16, 31
	See also Cost Model.	

Revalued Amount	The fair value of an asset at the date of a revaluation less any subsequent accumulated depreciation and subsequent accumulated impairment losses.	IAS 16, 31
	The value of property, plant and equipment as established by appraisal or valuation normally undertaken by professionally qualified Valuers.	
Reversion Yield	See Terminal Capitalisation Rate.	
Rights of Way	Rights or privileges, acquired through use or contract, to pass over a portion or strip of landed property owned by another.	Property Types, 2.2.4.2
Royalty or "Royalty Interest" in the Extractive Industries	The landowner's or lessor's share of production, in money or product, free of charge for expenses of production. An "Overriding Royalty" is a share of mineral or petroleum produced, free of the expense of production, paid to someone other than the lessor, over and above any lessor's Royalty.	GN 14, 3.13
Sale and Leaseback	A simultaneous sale of real estate and lease of the same property to the seller. The buyer becomes the lessor, or landlord, and the seller becomes the lessee, or tenant. Because there may be unique circumstances or relationships between the parties, sale and leaseback transactions may or may not involve typical market terms.	GN 2, 3.1.11

Sales Comparison Approach	A comparative approach to value that considers the sales of similar or substitute properties and related market data and establishes a value estimate by processes involving comparison. In general, a property being valued (a subject property) is compared with sales of similar properties that have been transacted in the open market. Listing and offerings may also be considered.	Concepts Fundamental to Generally Accepted Valuation Principles, 9.2.1.2
	A general way of estimating a value indication for personal property or an ownership interest in personal property, using one or more methods that compare the subject to similar properties or to ownership interests in similar properties. This approach to the valuation of personal property is dependent upon the Valuer's market knowledge and experience as well as recorded data on comparable items.	GN 5, 3.18
Salvage Value	The value of an assets estimated with regard to the specific circumstances under which the asset is sold. Salvage value describes the value of an asset that has reached the end of its economic life for the purpose it was made. The asset may still have value for an alternative use or for recycling.	IVS 2, 6.9.3
Sandwich Lessor Interest	See Headleasehold Interest.	

Securitised Investment Instruments	Instruments securing both debt and equity positions, representing an alternative to the direct ownership of property. Investors are able to own and trade shares of an interest in a property or pool of properties in the same way they would buy and sell shares of corporate stock. The market for such securities includes both a private, or institutional, sector and a public sector; examples include real estate investment trusts (REITs), collateralised mortgage obligations (CMOs), commercial mortgage-backed securities (CMBSs), real estate operating companies (REOCs) and separate and commingled funds.	Property Types, 5.1.4; 5.1.4.1; 5.1.4.2
Service Potential	The capacity of an asset to continue to provide goods and services in accordance with the entity's objectives. In the public sector, the concept of service potential takes the place of the test of adequate profitability applied in the private sector.	IVA 3, 3.9, GN 8, 3.6
Special Purchaser	A purchaser to whom a particular asset has Special Value because of advantages arising from its ownership that would not be available to general purchasers in the market. See also Special Value.	IVS 2, 3.4

Special, Unusual, or Extraordinary Assumptions	Before completing the acquisition of a property, a prudent purchaser in the market typically exercises due diligence by making customary enquiries about the property. It is normal for a Valuer to make assumptions as to the most likely outcome of this due diligence process and to rely on actual information regarding such matters as provided by the client. Special, unusual, or extraordinary assumptions may be any additional assumptions relating to matters covered in the due diligence process, or may relate to other issues, such as the identity of the purchaser, the physical state of the property, the presence of environmental pollutants (e.g., ground water contamination), or the ability to redevelop the property.	IVS 3, 3.5
	See also Assumptions.	
Specialised Livestock Facilities	See Dairy Farms, Livestock Ranches/Stations.	
Specialised, or Special Purpose, Agricultural Properties	Agricultural properties that do not typically produce a crop but are used for the handling, processing, or storage of crops following harvest. These properties frequently have a small land base that is extensively developed with structural improvements (grain elevators) and equipment (lifting machinery). Properties may also be classified as special purpose by the nature of the	GN 10, 3.8

commodity produced. Examples are truck farms, poultry farms, farms that produce certified crop seeds or fresh cut flowers, and racehorse breeding or training stables.

Specialised Property	A property that is rarely if ever sold in the market, except by way of a sale of the business or entity of which it is part, due to uniqueness, arising from its specialised nature and design, its configuration, size, location, or otherwise.	IVA 1, 3.4; IVA 2, 3.3; GN 8, 3.7
	Examples of specialised properties include refineries, power stations, docks, specialised manufacturing facilities, public facilities, churches, museums and properties located in particular geographical locations for operational or business reasons.	
Specialised Trading Property (STP)	See Trade Related Property.	
Special Value	An amount above Market Value that reflects particular attributes of an asset that are only of value to a Special Purchaser.	IVS 2, 3.5
	See also Synergistic Value.	

Specifica-tions for the Valuation Assignment	The first step in the Valuation Process, which establishes the context and scope/extent of the assignment and resolves any ambiguity involving the valuation issue or problem. A Valuer ensures that the analyses, information and conclusions presented in the report fit the specifications for the assignment. The specifications for the value assignment include the following seven elements:	IVS 3, 3.4

1. An identification of the real, personal (plant and machinery; furniture, fixtures, and equipment), business or other property subject to the valuation and other classes of property included in the valuation besides the primary property category;

2. An identification of the property rights (sole proprietorship, partnership, or partial interest) to be valued;

3. The intended use of the valuation and any related limitation; and the identification of any subcontractors or agents and their contribution;

4. A definition of the basis or type of value sought;

5. The date as of which the value estimate applies and the date of the intended report;

6. An identification of the scope/extent of the valuation and of the report; and

7. An identification of any contingent and limiting conditions upon which the valuation is based.

Stepped Rents	See Rent Escalations.	
Sublease-hold	A leasehold position created when a tenant or lessee in a prior lease conveys to a third party, a sublessee, the interest that the tenant, or lessee, enjoys. See also Headlease or Master Lease, Headleasehold Interest.	Property Types, 2.2.3.1
Subsequent Costs	Under the recognition principle in IAS 16, 7, an entity recognises in the carrying amount of an item of property, plant and equipment the cost of replacing part of such an item when that cost is incurred if the recognition criteria are met.	IAS 16, 13
Substitution	See Principle of Substitution.	
Summation Approach	See Cost Approach.	
Syndication	Legal entity related to a partnership; often organised by a general partner with investors as limited partners, whereby funds are pooled for the acquisition and development of real estate projects or business ventures.	Property Types, 5.1.2; 5.1.2.1

Synergistic Value	An additional element of value created by the combination of two or more interests where the value of the combined interests is worth more than the sum of the original interests. Also called Marriage Value.	IVS 2, 3.6
Tangible Assets	Assets with a physical manifestation. Examples include land and buildings, plant and machinery, fixtures and fittings, tools and equipment, and assets in the course of construction and development.	
Technical Assessment in the Extractive Industries	A technical document, prepared by (a) Technical Expert(s) that supports the Extractive Industry Valuation and is appended to, or forms part of, a Valuation Report.	GN 14, 3.15
Technical Expert in the Extractive Industries.	A person, who is responsible for all or part of the Technical Assessment that supports an Extractive Industry Valuation. A Technical expert must have appropriate experience relevant to the subject matter, and in States where required by statute or regulation, must be a member or license-holder in good standing of a professional organisation that has the authority to sanction members or licensees. An accredited specialist may not take responsibility for all or part of a Technical Assessment without also being a Technical Expert.	GN 14, 3.14

Technical Obsolescence	Term used by PP&E Valuers for Functional Obsolescence.	
Technical Review	A valuation review performed by a Valuer to form an opinion as to whether the analyses, opinions, and conclusions in the report under review are appropriate, reasonable, and supportable.	GN 11, 3.3
Tenant's Interest	See Lease Interest.	
Terminal Capitalisation Rate or Reversion Yield	The capitalisation rate used to convert income into an indication of the anticipated value of the property at the end of the holding period or property resale value.	
	In North America, the terminal capitalisation rate is also called a residual capitalisation rate or a coming-out capitalisation rate. In the Commonwealth, it is known as a reversion yield.	
Timberland	See Forestry/Timberland.	
Toxic	The status of a material, whether gas, liquid, or solid, that in its form, quantity, and location at the date of valuation has capacity to cause harm to life-forms. Toxicity refers to the degree or extent of such capacity.	GN 7, 3.3

Trade Fixtures or Tenant's Fixtures	Non-realty fixtures attached to property by the tenant and used in conducting the trade or business. See also Leasehold Improvements or Tenant's Improvements, Personal Property.	Property Types, 3.2.2; GN 5, 3.19
Trade Related Property	Certain classes of real property, which are designed for a specific types of business and that are normally bought and sold in the market, having regard to their trading potential.	IVA 2, 3.4; GN 12, 3.5
Trading Potential	Future profits to be derived from the sale of goods and products, e.g., fuel, food and drink, or the provision of specialised facilities for lodging, parking, gaming, or entertainment. Trading potential is associated with a category of properties (fuel stations, restaurants, hotels, casinos, cinemas and theatres), the market value of which includes not only land, buildings, and personal property but also intangibles, such as goodwill, and the business itself.	
Transferable Goodwill	That intangible asset that arises as a result of property-specific name and reputation, customer patronage, location, products and similar factors, which generate economic benefits. It is inherent to the trade related property, and will transfer to a new owner on sale. See also Goodwill, Personal Goodwill.	GN 4, 3.12.3; GN 6, 3.20.3; GN 12, 3.3.3

Turnover Rent or Participation Rent	Any form of lease rental arrangement in which the lessor receives a form of rental that is based upon the earnings of the lessee. Percentage rent is an example of a turnover rent.	GN 2, 3.1.10.3
Unit(s) of Comparison	Typically a factor produced by two components, which reflects precise differences between properties and facilitates analysis in the three approaches to value, e.g., price per square metre or square foot, or the ratio of a property's sale price to its net income (Net Income Multiplier/ Years' Purchase).	GN 1, 3.10
Useful Life (of Property, Plant and Equipment)	Either a) the period over which an asset is expected to be available for use by an entity; or b) the number of production or similar units expected to be obtained from the asset by an entity.	IAS 16, 6; IAS 36, 6; IAS 38, 8; IPSAS 17.13; IPSAS 21.14
	In regard to leases, useful life is defined as:	IAS 17, 4
	The estimated remaining period, from the commencement of the lease term, without limitation by the lease term, over which the economic benefits embodied in the asset are expected to be consumed by the entity.	

Utility	A relative or comparative term rather than an absolute condition, that refers to the degree of usefulness of a property.	Concepts Fundamental to Generally Accepted Valuation Principles, 7.1, 7.2, 7.3, 7.6, 7.7

The utility of agricultural land is measured by its productive capacity. If the land has development potential, its productivity is measured by how well it will support a residential, commercial, industrial or mixed use.

Optimum utility is achieved for some property if operated on an individual basis. Other property has greater utility if operated as part of a group of properties, or held and managed within an aggregate or portfolio of properties.

Utility is generally measured from a long-term perspective, ordinarily over the useful life of a property or group of properties. When a property may not have a readily discernible degree of utility at the date of valuation, full disclosure of the value definition, supporting data, and extent of special assumptions or limiting conditions is required.

Vacant Possession

In real estate this refers to a right to possession of land or built-up property in respect of which there is no current occupant.

The term, vacant possession, is Commonwealth usage.

Valuation	The process of estimating value.	
Valuation Approach	In general, a way of estimating value that employs one or more specific valuation methods. Depending on the nature and purpose of the property, three valuation approaches may be applied. These are the sales comparison, income capitalisation, and cost approaches. Their application will enable the Valuer to determine Market Value or a value other than Market Value.	GN 4, 3.23; GN 5, 3.20; GN 6, 3.38
	See Asset-Based Approach, Cost Approach, Income Capitalisation Approach, Principle of Substitution, Sales Comparison Approach.	
Valuation Assignment	See Specifications for the Valuation Assignment.	
Valuation Brief	See Specifications for the Valuation Assignment.	
Valuation Date	The date as of which the Valuer's opinion of value applies.	
Valuation Method	Within valuation approaches, a specific way to estimate a value.	GN 4, 3.24; GN 5, 3.21; GN 6, 3.39
Valuation Procedure	The act, manner, and technique of performing the steps of a valuation method.	GN 4, 3.25; GN 5, 3.22; GN 6, 3.40

Valuation Ratio	A factor wherein a value or price serves as the numerator and financial, operating, or physical data serve as the denominator.	GN 4, 3.26; GN 6, 3.41
	See also Capitalisation Factor, Income Multiplier.	
Valuation Report	A document that records the instructions for the assignment, the basis and purpose of the valuation, and the results of the analysis that led to the opinion of value. A Valuation Report may also explain the analytical processes undertaken in carrying out the valuation, and present meaningful information used in the analysis. Valuation Reports can be either oral or written. The type, content and length of a report vary according to the intended user, legal requirements, the property type, and the nature and complexity of the assignment.	IVS 3, 3.5
Valuation Review	A valuation assignment that covers a range of types and purposes. The principal characteristic all valuation reviews have in common is that one Valuer exercises impartial judgment in considering the work of another Valuer. A valuation review may support the same value conclusion in the valuation under review or it may result in disagreement with that value conclusion. Valuation reviews provide a credibility check on the valuation as well as a check on the strength of the work of the Valuer who developed it, as regards	GN 11, 3.1

the Valuer's knowledge, experience, and independence.

Valuation organisations around the world distinguish between various types of reviews, e.g., administrative (compliance) reviews, technical reviews, desk reviews, field reviews, reviews to ensure that a valuation has been carried out in accordance with professional standards (where the bases of valuation used in the valuation under review are accepted), reviews that muster general market information to support or contest the value conclusion, and reviews that examine the specific data in the valuation under review with comparable data from a sample group.

Valuation Standards	The International Valuation Standards (IVSs), unless otherwise specified.	
Value	The price most likely to concluded by the buyers and sellers of a good or service that is available for purchase. Value establishes the hypothetical or notional price that buyers and sellers are most likely to conclude for the good or service. Thus, value is not a fact, but an estimate of the likely price to be paid for a good or service available for purchase at a given time.	Introduction to IVSs 1, 2 and 3, 3.3

See also Cost, Price.

Value in Exchange	i) The value as recognised by a market in which exchange of asset ownership hypothetically, or notionally, takes place. The IVSC definition of Market Value appropriate for financial reporting is based upon the principle of value in exchange, not value in use.	IVS 2, 6.1
	ii) The value, in terms of cash, of a property which is bartered for another asset or assets. Cash being the yardstick by which the comparative value of each can be assessed.	
Value in Use	i) The present value of estimated future cash flows expected to arise from the continuing use of an asset and from its disposal at the end of its useful life.	IFRS 5, Appendix A
	ii) The present value of the future cash flows expected to be derived from an asset or cash-generating unit.	IAS 16, 6
	It should be noted that the above definitions, which apply to financial reporting, consider the value of an asset at the end of its useful life. This meaning differs from the way the term is commonly used in valuation practice.	
Value in Use of a Non-Cash-Generating Asset	The present value of the asset's remaining service potential.	IPSAS 21.14

Value of Improvements	The value added to the land by improvements such as buildings, structures or modifications to the land, of a permanent nature, involving expenditures of labour and capital, and intended to enhance the value or utility of the property. Improvements have differing patterns of use and economic lives. See also Improvements.	IVA 3, 3.10
Valuer	One who possesses the necessary qualifications, ability, and experience to execute a valuation. In some States, licensing is required before one can act as a Valuer. See also Professional Property Valuer.	Code of Conduct, 3.3
Wasting Asset	An asset which in real terms will generally depreciate in value over time. Examples include leaseholds and extractive interests.	
Working Capital	The amount by which current assets exceed current liabilities.	GN 6, 3.42
Worth	See Investment Value.	

Written Report	The results of a valuation communicated to a client in writing, which includes electronic communication. Written reports may be detailed narrative documents containing all pertinent materials examined and analyses performed to arrive at a value conclusion, or abbreviated narrative documents, including periodic updates of value, forms used by governmental and other agencies, or letters to clients.	IVS 3, 3.6

See also Oral Report.

Index

International Valuation Standards Committee

Index